100th Congress Committees

100th Congress Committees

Congressional Quarterly Inc.
1414 22nd St. N.W.
Washington, D.C. 20037

Congressional Quarterly Inc.

Congressional Quarterly Inc., an editorial research service and publishing company, serves clients in the fields of news, education, business and government. It combines specific coverage of Congress, government and politics by Congressional Quarterly with the more general subject range of an affiliated service, Editorial Research Reports.

Congressional Quarterly publishes the *Congressional Quarterly Weekly Report* and a variety of books, including college political science textbooks under the CQ Press imprint and public affairs paperbacks on developing issues and events. CQ also publishes information directories and reference books on the federal government, national elections and politics, including the *Guide to Congress,* the *Guide to the U.S. Supreme Court,* the *Guide to U.S. Elections* and *Politics in America.* The *CQ Almanac,* a compendium of legislation for one session of Congress, is published each year. *Congress and the Nation,* a record of government for a presidential term, is published every four years.

CQ publishes *The Congressional Monitor,* a daily report on current and future activities of congressional committees, and several newsletters including *Congressional Insight,* a weekly analysis of congressional action, and *Campaign Practices Reports,* a semimonthly update on campaign laws.

An electronic online information system, the Washington Alert Service, provides immediate access to CQ's databases of legislative action, votes, schedules, profiles and analyses.

Printed in the United States of America

Library of Congress Cataloging-in-Publication Data

100th Congress committees.

    1. United States. Congress — Committees — Handbooks, manuals, etc. I. Congressional Quarterly, inc. II. Title: One hundredth Congress committees.

JK1029.A155   1987   328.73′0765′0202   87-15574

ISBN-0-87187-421-0

Editor: Neal Santelmann
Production Editor and Designer: William Bonn
Editorial Coordinators: Jane Gilligan, Macon Morehouse
Contributors: Jacqueline Calmes, Janet Hook, Steven Pressman and Charles Potter
Research: Bena Fein, Douglas Sery and Amy Truesdale

Contents

The Committee System

The most distinguishing characteristic of the legislative branch is the predominant role played by the committee system. The bulk of congressional work is done in committees, not on the floor of the House or Senate. Modern law-making requires an understanding of many complex subjects, and the committee system provides a means by which members can attain a high degree of specialization in certain areas.

A committee that has subjected a bill to expert scrutiny traditionally has expected its decisions to be upheld on the floor. Committees, according to *Cannon's Procedure in the House of Representatives*, "are not infallible, but they have had long familiarity with the subject under discussion, and have made an intimate study of the particular bill before the House and after mature deliberation have made formal recommendations and, other considerations being equal, are entitled to support on the floor." [1]

However, in the Congress of the 1980s many lawmakers no longer defer to committees on the details of legislation. There are more floor challenges to more committees as members gain the expertise and staff needed to make independent judgments.

Nevertheless, it is difficult — at times virtually impossible — to circumvent a committee that is determined not to act. A bill that has been approved by a committee may be amended when it reaches the House or Senate, but extensive changes generally are much more difficult to achieve at that stage. The actions of the committees more often than not give Congress its record of legislative achievement and failure.

"On Capitol Hill, the center stage of policy making is held by the committees and subcommittees," says political scientist Roger H. Davidson. "They are the political nerve ends, the gatherers of information, the sifters of alternatives, the refiners of legislative detail." [2]

So overriding has been the influence of committees in the legislative process that scholars have called them "little legislatures" [3] and their chairmen, "petty barons." [4] Though the appellation "baron" may no longer apply in the more open and democratic Congress of today, committee chairmen — and increasingly subcommittee chairmen — wield great influence over the fate of legislation, and thus over government programs and operations.

Davidson and Walter J. Oleszek, both specialists on Congress with the Congressional Research Service of the

Library of Congress, point out that the chairmen still are crucial to the legislative process: They "call meetings and establish agendas, hire and fire committee staff, arrange hearings, designate conferees, act as floor managers, control committee funds and rooms, develop legislative strategies, chair hearings and markups [bill-drafting sessions], and regulate the internal affairs and organization of the committee.... The chairman has many procedural powers. Simply refusing to schedule a bill for a hearing may be sufficient to kill it. Or a chairman may convene meetings when proponents or opponents of the legislation are unavoidably absent. The chairman's authority derives from the support of a committee majority and a variety of formal and many became subcommittee chairmen. With more activist subcommittees came more legislation, thus adding to the workload and the need for more staff.

While the diffusion of committee power ended the era of the autocratic chairmen and made committee proceedings more accountable, the cost of those reforms was a marked slowdown in lawmaking. Younger and less experienced members began to demand a voice in policy making, and many became subcommittee chairmen. With more activist subcommittees came legislation, thus adding to the workload and the need for more staff.

The institutional changes of the 1970s pleased most members, many more of whom could now expect to become at least subcommittee chairmen of a committee during their congressional careers. But the underlying committee structure was left basically the same as it had been since enactment of the Legislative Reorganization Act of 1946. With Congress and the country facing new and more complex issues in the late 1970s and 1980s, that system was found wanting.

Nowhere were the obstacles to a coherent, smoothly run legislative program more apparent than in the energy field. When Congress was asked to respond to proposals to meet the 1970s energy crisis, the House leadership was confronted with the fact that there were more than 80 committees and subcommittees that asserted some jurisdiction over energy issues.

Less dramatic, but just as serious, overlapping of jurisdictions and committee rivalries were apparent in health, welfare, the economy, foreign policy and various other areas of legislative activity.

Though the problem was more acute in the House,

efforts there to rationalize the committee structure were less successful than in the Senate. Ambitious committee reorganization plans foundered in 1974, 1977 and 1980. Despite general dissatisfaction with the outmoded structure, members were unwilling to give up their newly won powers. The energy jurisdictional tangle, for example, which was a target of the 1974 proposals, remained unsolved in 1980 after another attempt to consolidate related committee jurisdictions met with little success. The House's answer that year was to paper over the problem by renaming the Interstate and Foreign Commerce Committee the Energy and Commerce Committee. Committee jurisdictions essentially stayed the same as before.

A 1977 Senate committee reorganization overhaul met with more success; six committees actually were abolished and a new Energy Committee, consolidating most energy-related jurisdictions except taxes, was established. That reorganization, said Sen. Adlai E. Stevenson III, D-Ill. (1970-81), who headed a study of the committee system, "democratizes the Senate, rationalizes jurisdictions and cuts far back on the multiple committee assignments which pull and haul senators into time conflicts every day." [6] Nevertheless, the final plan fell short of its sponsors' hopes, as committees with the most powerful special interests behind them emerged unscathed.

Erosion of the Chairman's Power

The innate power of the committee system often was exercised arbitrarily by committee chairmen. Until the changes of the 1970s took effect, committees usually were powers unto themselves. Strong party leadership in Congress might influence committee actions, but most committees — and their chairmen — had sufficient independence to operate pretty much as they wished. The chairmen's power was equaled only by a few party leaders who had great influence, such as Speaker Sam Rayburn, D-Texas (1913-61), or Senate Majority Leader Lyndon B. Johnson, D-Texas (1949-61).

A chairman's power resulted from the rigid operation of the seniority system, under which a person rose to a chairmanship simply through longevity in Congress. The unwritten seniority rule conferred a committee chairmanship on the member of the majority party with the longest continuous service on the committee. As long as his party retained control of Congress, he normally kept this position; if control passed to the other party, he changed places with the ranking member of the other party.

However, there were limits to the benefits of seniority, even in the period before the 1970s reforms. It was an unwritten rule in both houses that a senator or representative could not be a chairman of more than one standing committee, regardless of seniority. In 1969 Richard B. Russell, D-Ga. (1933-71), became the senior senator on the Appropriations Committee upon the retirement of Carl Hayden, D-Ariz. (1927-69). Russell already was chairman of the Armed Services Committee. He decided to take the Appropriations chairmanship, but to do so he was forced to relinquish his control of Armed Services, which he had chaired since 1951.

Rule by seniority reigned supreme until the early 1970s. Then, changing circumstances caught up with it. The principal change was the election to Congress of dozens of new members — persons who had less patience with the admonition to newcomers, credited to Speaker Rayburn, that "to get along, go along." New members, who did

not have much influence in the Senate or House, joined with disgruntled incumbents, who had chafed under the often heavy-handed rule of arbitrary chairmen. Thus, in the late 1960s and early 1970s began the revolt that was to undermine the seniority system and lead to numerous other procedural changes that redefined the role and power of committee chairmen.

Though the dramatic changes did not come until the 1970s, a portent of things to come occurred after the 1966 election defeat of Howard W. Smith, D-Va. (1931-67), the powerful chairman of the House Rules Committee. For the first time in its history, the committee adopted a set of rules governing its procedures. The new regulations denied the chairman the right to set meeting dates, required the consent of a committee majority to table (kill) a bill and set limits on proxy voting. *(Details, box, p. 15)*

The 1970s revolt began in the House as membership turnover accelerated and the proportion of younger, first- and second-term members increased. These lawmakers demanded fundamental changes in the way Congress — and particularly the committees — operated. Major changes in Democratic Party caucus rules and, to a lesser extent, in the standing rules of the House and the Senate, diluted the authority enjoyed by committee chairmen and other senior members and redistributed the power among the junior members.

The single most important factor that undermined the chairmen's authority was the decision by Democrats in both chambers to require chairmen to be elected by the party's caucus. The change came gradually, beginning in 1971. By 1975 Democrats in both chambers had adopted rules requiring a secret-ballot election of the top Democrat on each committee at the beginning of every Congress. And in that year three House chairmen were ousted in caucus elections.

The election requirement made chairmen accountable to their colleagues for their conduct. Caucus election of committee chairmen was only one of a number of changes that restricted the chairmen's power. Committees were required under the 1970 Legislative Reorganization Act to have written rules. In 1973 House Democrats adopted a "bill of rights" that reinforced subcommittee autonomy.

In subsequent years, House Democrats gave members of each committee the power to determine the number of subcommittees their committee would have. And committees with more than 20 members were required to have at least four subcommittees.

Staffing prerogatives were extended to members other than the chairman. In the House subcommittee, chairmen and ranking minority members were allowed to hire one staff person each to work on their subcommittees. In the Senate, junior members were allowed to hire up to three personal aides to work solely on a senator's committees. These changes made committee members less subservient to the chairman by giving them professional staff help on legislative issues.

Democrats in both chambers also limited the influence of chairmen and other senior members by restricting the number of chairmanships and committee slots that a member could hold. *(Details, box, pp. 8-9)*

As the decade of the 1970s closed, the committee structure was still firmly entrenched in Congress, but much of the power and prestige that had been held by the full committees had been transferred to the subcommittees and a new, larger corps of chairmen. Subcommittees took on the institutional characteristics and vested interests of their parent committees. This led to a decentralization of power and to heavier legislative workloads for members of both houses.

So great was the proliferation of subcommittees that in 1979-81 House Democrats and the Senate moved to limit the number of units a committee was allowed to establish.

The Committee Structure

There are three principal classes of committees in Congress: standing committees, those with permanently authorized staff and broad legislative mandates; select or special committees, those that are supposed to be temporary in that they are authorized to operate for a specific period of time or until the project for which they are created has been completed (the role of these committees usually is investigative rather than legislative); and joint committees, which have a membership drawn from both houses of Congress and usually are investigative or housekeeping in nature. Conference committees, a special variety of joint committee, serve only on an ad hoc basis to resolve differences in Senate and House versions of the same legislation. *(Box, p. 5)*

Below the committee level are a plethora of subcommittees, which are functional subdivisions of the committees. Like the full committees, they are composed of members of the majority and minority parties in roughly the same proportion as the party ratios on the full committees.

At the beginning of the 100th Congress in 1987 there were 277 committees (standing, special and select) and subcommittees:

- 21 Senate committees with 85 subcommittees.
- 28 House committees with 139 subcommittees (the subcommittee total did not include task forces).
- four joint committees.

Standing Committees

The standing committees are at the center of the legislative process. Legislation usually must be considered and approved in some form at the committee level before it can be sent to the House or Senate for further action.

The Legislative Reorganization Act of 1946 organized the Senate and House committees along roughly parallel lines. One of the act's purposes was to eliminate confusing and overlapping jurisdictions by grouping together related areas. The legislative committees (as distinct from the Appropriations committees) generally were regrouped to follow the major organizational divisions of the executive branch.

Responsibility for overseeing the federal bureaucracy was divided roughly as follows: Appropriations committees were to review the budget requests of the federal departments; the expenditures committees (now House Government Operations and Senate Governmental Affairs) were to oversee the general economy and efficiency of government in administering federal policy and programs; and the legislative committees, along with their other responsibilities, were to oversee the administration of federal programs in their respective fields.

Committee Size. The size of the standing committees is fixed by the standing rules of the Senate and in the House by negotiations between the majority and minority parties and formal ratification by the full membership (except that the rules specify the size of the Budget and Select Intelligence committees). In the 100th Congress, House committees ranged in size from 12 (District of Columbia and Standards of Official Conduct) to 57 (Appropriations), Senate committees from 11 (Veterans' Affairs) to 29 (Appropriations).

Party Ratios. The Constitution and the standing rules of each chamber are silent on the matter of party ratios on committees. The Senate traditionally has more or less followed the practice of filling standing committees

Senate and House committee sessions often attract not only the attention of members but of the press and public as well. Such is the case, opposite, during a confirmation hearing.

according to the strength of each party in the chamber.

The House, on the other hand, has been less inclined to allocate minority party representation on committees on the basis of the relative strength of the two parties. The majority party has felt little need to accommodate its political opposition, especially on important House committees.

In 1981 House Republicans tried to change the party ratios on four key committees — Appropriations, Budget, Rules and Ways and Means — to reflect the gains made by the party in the November 1980 congressional elections. The Democratic leadership refused, and the GOP then sought to get the ratios changed by amending the usually routine resolutions approving the standing rules, drawn up by the Democratic Caucus, and ratifying committee assignments. (Committee ratios traditionally have been established by the majority party and are not included in House rules.)

At the beginning of the 97th Congress the ratio of Democrats to Republicans in the House was about five to four; but the Democratic leadership had insisted on retaining a three-to-two ratio on the Appropriations and Budget committees, a more than two-to-one ratio on Rules and a ratio of slightly less than two-to-one on Ways and Means. Both Republican attempts were defeated on straight party-line votes, except for one Democratic defection.

Republicans then filed a lawsuit against the House leadership, charging the Democrats with unconstitutionally discriminating against GOP members and their constituents when they set the committee ratios.

The case was dismissed by the U.S. District Court for the District of Columbia on Oct. 8, 1981. The decision was appealed immediately to the U.S. Court of Appeals in Washington, D.C., which dismissed the case.

But the issue flared up again after the 1984 elections. Some House Republicans in 1985 called for a boycott of committees unless they were given more seats. The leadership of the two parties worked out a deal to give Republicans 30 more seats on standing committees than they had had in the 98th Congress, even though the GOP had gained only 14 seats in the 1984 elections. Democrats gave up 21 seats on standing committees.

Several Republicans said they were happy with the change, adding that there was still room for improvement. "We were starving to death, and we've now gotten some mush. But we're not quite at steak yet," said Lynn Martin, R-Ill., vice chairman of the Republican Conference.

Even with the extra seats, partisan skirmishing over ratios broke out on two committees. Unhappy with the way they were treated on subcommittee ratios, Republicans walked out of meetings of both the Judiciary Committee and of Energy and Commerce. Eventually, Democrats gave them more subcommittee seats and the Republicans returned.

Select and Special Committees

Select and special committees are established from time to time in both chambers to study special problems or concerns. Their size and life span usually are fixed by the resolutions that create them. Ordinarily they are not permitted to report legislation. Some of these committees, such as the permanent Select Aging Committee in the House and the Special Aging Committee in the Senate, have gone on from year to year. But in most cases, they remain in existence for only one or two Congresses.

Unlike most select committees, the Intelligence committees in both chambers consider and report legislation. But this is a special case, as the committees are permanent in everything but name. Because the panels' subject matter is narrower than that of most standing committees, they were designated as "select" rather than "standing" committees.

Joint Committees

Joint committees are created by statute or by resolution, which also fix their size. Of the four functioning in 1987, none had the authority to report legislation. One of the four, the Joint Economic Committee, was directed to examine national economic problems and review the execution of fiscal and budgetary programs, but it depended on the standing committees to frame legislative proposals. It was the only joint committee with subcommittees.

The Joint Committee on Taxation, made up of senior members of both parties from the House Ways and Means and Senate Finance committees, could make policy recommendations to those committees, but it served chiefly to provide a professional staff on tax issues.

Chairmanships of joint committees offer a special situation. Although historically the chairmen of these panels tended to be drawn from the Senate, in recent years they have rotated from one chamber to another at the beginning of each Congress. When a senator serves as chairman, the vice chairman usually is a representative, and vice versa.

The last joint committee having legislative responsibilities was Joint Atomic Energy.

Subcommittees

Subcommittees provide the ultimate division of labor within the committee system. Although they enable members of Congress to develop expertise in specialized fields, they often are criticized on grounds that they fragment responsibility, increase the difficulty of policy review and slow down the authorization and appropriation process.[7]

Subcommittees vary in importance from committee to committee. Some, especially the Appropriations subcommittees in both chambers, have well-defined jurisdictions and function with great autonomy. Much of their work — both on the House and Senate side — is routinely endorsed by the full committee without further review. Their importance was one reason that House Democrats in 1974 voted to make all Appropriations subcommittee chairmen subject to confirmation by the party caucus.

A few committees — such as the House Ways and Means and Senate Finance committees — resisted the creation of subcommittees, although there were logical subdivisions into which their work could be divided. Subcommittees were established by the Finance Committee in 1970 and by Ways and Means only in 1974 — after the Democratic Caucus voted to require them. The subcommittee requirement was established in part because of dissatisfaction with the power and performance of Ways and Means Chairman Wilbur D. Mills, D-Ark. (1939-77). (Box, pp. 18-19)

The House and Senate Budget committees were among the few panels that had no subcommittees in the 97th Congress (both committees were exempted from the subcommittee requirement). The House panel, however, did have task forces.

Conference Committees: The Final Arbiters of Legislation

The conference committee is an ad hoc joint committee appointed to reconcile differences between Senate and House versions of pending legislation. Before a bill can be sent to the president, it must be passed in identical form by both chambers. Whenever different versions of the same bill are passed and neither chamber is willing to yield to the other, a conference becomes necessary to determine the final shape of the legislation. It is unusual for the Senate or House to reject the work of a conference committee, but this can be expected to occur on the average of once or twice a session.

As a rule, conference committees are composed of the senior members of the committees that handled the bill. They are appointed by the Speaker of the House and the presiding officer of the Senate upon the recommendations of the committee chairmen. There are no rules instructing which members must be appointed conferees. However, the residual power of appointment lies with the chamber as a whole. Although the chairmen, by tradition, pick the conferees in the House, under the rules of that chamber the Speaker retains the latent power to make the appointments, subject only to the restriction that he "shall appoint no less than a majority of Members who generally supported the House position as determined by the Speaker." Most chairmen today include members who are knowledgeable about the bill in question, whether or not they are considered senior members of the committee.

There need not be an equal number of conferees (or "managers" as they are called) from each house,

because a majority vote determines the position of each house's delegation on all decisions made in the conference. Therefore, a majority of both the Senate and House delegations must agree before a provision emerges from conference as part of the final bill.

Both parties are represented on conference committees, with the majority party having a larger number, and a majority of conferees from each house must sign the conference report. In the past, conference committees met on the Senate side of the Capitol, with the most senior senator presiding, but this custom is no longer followed.

Until 1975 most conference committees met in secret. In November of that year both chambers amended their rules to require open meetings unless a majority of either chamber's conferees vote in open session to close the meeting for that day. In 1977 the House amended the rule to require open conference meetings unless the full House voted to close them. That rule was never adopted by the Senate, but in practice Senate conferees have always gone along with the representatives on those occasions — which have been limited to defense and intelligence agency bills — when the House has voted to close a conference committee.

After conferees reach agreement and their report is approved by one of the two houses, the conference committee automatically is dissolved. (If the second chamber were to disapprove the conference report, a new conference committee would have to be picked, although normally the same team of conferees would be appointed.)

Committee Rivalries

The standing committees of Congress, wrote Stephen K. Bailey in 1966, "exist to speed the work load; to facilitate meaningful deliberations on important measures and issues; to develop a degree of expertise among committee members and committee staff; and to serve as a convenient graveyard for inept proposals. They constitute the great baronies of congressional power. Many of them look outward in jealous competition with the president, with their opposite committee in the other house, and with the whole house of which they are a part." [8]

Jurisdictional Clashes. Jurisdictional disputes between and among committees have been evident since the inception of the standing committee system.[9] The Legislative Reorganization Act of 1946 attempted to eliminate the problem by defining each committee's jurisdiction in detail. But the 1946 act was not able to eliminate the problem.

As early as 1947 a fight broke out in the Senate over

referral of the controversial armed forces unification bill. In the House the measure had been handled by the Committee on Executive Expenditures (now the Government Operations Committee), which had jurisdiction over all proposals for government reorganization. But in a Senate floor vote that chamber's Armed Services Committee successfully challenged the claim of the Expenditures Committee (now the Governmental Affairs Committee) to jurisdiction over the bill.

Such problems have continued to arise because the complexities of modern legislative proposals make it impossible to define jurisdictional boundaries precisely.

In the House the problem has been aggravated by a failure to restructure the committee system to meet changing developments and national problems. The need to consolidate jurisdictions became particularly acute in the energy field, an area that has become prominent only since the mid-1970s. As noted, many committees had inherited jurisdiction over some aspect of energy policy; when President Jimmy Carter in 1977 submitted his comprehensive national energy program, the impending jurisdictional tangle forced Speaker Thomas P. O'Neill Jr., D-Mass., to establish an ad hoc energy committee to guide it through the House.

O'Neill appointed 40 loyal Democrats, with a majority favorably disposed toward the Carter plan. Five House committees reviewed portions of the bill, but O'Neill set strict deadlines for them to conduct hearings and complete action on their sections. The ad hoc committee then reviewed the separate committees' work, proposed numerous strengthening amendments and sent the bill to the Rules Committee. That panel, an arm of the leadership, obeyed O'Neill's directions to protect the bill from crippling floor amendments. (The bill was passed by the House but ran into opposition in the Senate.)

Occasionally, when the opportunity arises, a bill is drafted in such a way that it will be referred to a committee favorable to it. Oleszek cites the classic example of the 1963 civil rights bill, which was worded somewhat differently in each chamber so that it would be referred to the Judiciary Committee in the House and the Commerce Committee in the Senate. Both panels were chaired by strong proponents of the legislation, while the chairmen of the House Interstate and Foreign Commerce Committee and Senate Judiciary Committee were opposed to the legislation. "Careful drafting, therefore, coupled with favorable referral decisions in the House and Senate, prevented the bill from being bogged down in hostile committees." [10]

In the existing House committee setup, however, legislation usually is not so lucky as in the two examples cited above. Most bills are subject to strict jurisdictional interpretation and are not open to the legerdemain given the 1963 civil rights bill or the special handling the Speaker was able to give the 1977 energy bill. Oleszek observes that "committees guard their jurisdictional turfs closely, and the parliamentarians know and follow the precedents. Only instances of genuine jurisdictional ambiguity provide opportunities for the legislative draftsman and referral options for the Speaker and the presiding officer of the Senate to bypass one committee in favor of another." [11]

The desire to maintain existing committee jurisdictions figured prominently in the debate over establishment of a Senate Intelligence Committee in 1976. The committee was given exclusive legislative authority over the Central Intelligence Agency (CIA), but jurisdiction over the intelligence arms of the Federal Bureau of Investigation (FBI) and the Defense Department was shared with other committees — the Judiciary and Armed Services committees respectively. Those two committees vigorously resisted the transfer of intelligence jurisdiction from their purviews. In creating the panel, Congress required that two of its members be chosen from each of four committees that formerly held some jurisdiction over intelligence operations: Appropriations, Armed Services, Judiciary and Foreign Relations.

Multiple Referral. The more common solution to jurisdictional conflicts is to refer a bill to two or more committees, a practice called multiple referral. There are three types of multiple referrals: joint, when several committees consider a bill at the same time; sequential, when a bill is referred first to one committee, then to another and so on; and split, when parts of a bill are referred to different committees — this was the method O'Neill used for the Carter energy bill.

The House did not permit the practice of multiple referral, long in use in the Senate, until 1975. According to Davidson and Oleszek, about 200 measures in each Congress are referred to more than one committee in the Senate. On the House side, 1,241 measures (out of 10,397 introduced) were given multiple referral in the 96th Congress. [12]

Appropriations and Authorizations. The relationships between the Appropriations committees and the legislative committees frequently provide striking illustrations of inter-committee rivalries. Legislative committees handle bills authorizing funds, but only the Appropriations committees are permitted to consider the actual funding for federal agencies and programs. This distinction is strictly observed by the legislative committees. The Appropriations committees, in turn, theoretically are barred by the standing rules from inserting legislative provisions in their appropriations bills, but they habitually do so and, despite grumbling from the legislative committees, are seldom overruled on the floor.

In the Senate, almost all senators on the 29-member Appropriations Committee also are members of various legislative committees and thus can participate in deliberations on authorization bills and oversight in their fields of interest. This reduces one area of conflict as far as the Senate is concerned. But in the House, the Appropriations Committee is defined as an "exclusive" committee by the Democratic Caucus, meaning that party members, as a rule, cannot also be on other standing and select committees.

The creation of the Budget committees in 1974 added yet another dimension to the potential for committee rivalries, especially on spending decisions.

Competition Between Chambers. Committees often are in competition with their counterparts in the other chamber as well. In 1962 the decorum of Congress was shattered when the House and Senate Appropriations committees, each headed by an octogenarian chairman, brought their long-smoldering differences into public view. At issue were questions about the Senate's right to initiate its own appropriations bills, whether the Senate could add funds to House-passed bills, who would chair the conference negotiations between the two chambers and where the conference meetings would be held. The dispute blocked conferences on appropriations bills for three months and temporarily bankrupted several government agencies. Although the deadlock finally was broken, the two committees never reached full agreement on their respective roles in the appropriations process.

Proposals to create new committees illustrate another problem in trying to rationalize the committee system in Congress. For years after the House had created a separate Veterans' Affairs Committee, the Senate Finance Committee refused to relinquish its jurisdiction over veterans' legislation. A Senate Committee on Veterans' Affairs finally was created in 1970. Similarly, a proposal to split the House Education and Labor Committee into two separate committees was one of the stumbling blocks to House action on the 1970 legislative reorganization.

It is very difficult to abolish a committee, once established, even though it no longer serves any purpose. Congress in 1952 created a Joint Committee on Immigration and Nationality Policy. The committee never met and never performed any function, yet it was not abolished until 1970.

Rules and Procedures

Neither house operates under a comprehensive code of committee procedure; general guidelines and restrictions are contained in Senate and House rules, which incorporate many of the provisions in the Legislative Reorganization Acts of 1946 and 1970 and other measures. Democratic Party Caucus rules have had an even greater impact on the committee structure.

One of the basic goals of the 1946 act was to standardize committee procedures in regard to holding regular meeting days, keeping committee records and votes, reporting legislation, requiring a majority of committee members to be in attendance as a condition of transacting committee business and following set procedures during hearings.

The 1946 rules were not uniformly observed by all committees, and continuing dissatisfaction with committee operations led, in the 1970 Reorganization Act, to further efforts to reform committee procedures, particularly to make them more democratic and accountable to the membership and the public.

Each Senate and House committee is required to establish and publish rules of procedure. These rules have stipulated that each chamber's standing committees must fix regular meeting days, though the rules authorize the chairman to call additional meetings. The rules also must contain procedures under which a committee majority may call a meeting if the chairman fails to do so.

Committees were required by the 1970 act to keep transcripts of their meetings and to make public all roll-call votes. In the House the rules require that information about committee votes be made available to the public at the committees' offices; the committees are directed to provide a description of each amendment, motion, order or "other proposition" voted on and the name of each committee member voting for or against the issue as well as those present but not voting. The rules also require that the results of all votes to report legislation be published in the committee reports (but the positions of each member do not have to be included).

In the Senate, the rules are less specific. They require that a committee's report on a bill include the results of roll-call votes on "any measure or any amendment thereto" unless the results have been announced previously by the committee. Senate rules require that in reporting roll-call votes the position of each voting member is to be disclosed.

The rules stipulate that it is the chairman's "duty" to see to it that legislation approved by his committee is reported. And there are procedures by which a committee majority may force a bill out of committee if the chairman fails to do so. The rules prohibit a committee from reporting any measure unless a majority of its members are actually present, and they place certain limits on proxy voting. Members are allowed time to file supplemental and minority views for inclusion in committee reports.

Although the regulations often are set aside, committees are supposed to announce hearings at least one week in advance, in most circumstances to hold meetings in open session, and to require witnesses to file written statements in advance. The rules allow minority party members to call witnesses during at least one day of hearings on a subject.

Committee Assignments

The rules of the House and Senate state that the membership of each house shall elect its members to com-

House Budget Committee meets with chairman William H. Gray III, D, presiding. Republican Delbert L. Latta, ranking minority member, sits to Gray's left.

Rules Governing Composition . . .

The following guidelines regulate the composition of congressional committees. In the House, they are determined by the Democratic Caucus and Republican Conference. In the Senate, they are set forth in the standing rules.

House

As the ruling party in 1987, the Democrats, through their caucus, divide the various House committees into three categories: exclusive, major and nonmajor. Exclusive committees are Appropriations; Ways and Means; and Rules. Major committees are Agriculture; Armed Services; Banking, Finance and Urban Affairs; Education and Labor; Foreign Affairs; Energy and Commerce; Judiciary; and Public Works and Transportation. Nonmajor committees are Budget; District of Columbia; Government Operations; House Administration; Interior and Insular Affairs; Merchant Marine and Fisheries; Post Office and Civil Service; Science, Space and Technology; Small Business; and Veterans' Affairs. House select and joint committees remain within the purview of the House leadership, with the Speaker appointing the Democratic members and the minority leaders the Republicans.

Democrats serving on an exclusive committee may not serve on any other standing committee; the only exception is that members of the Ways and Means and Appropriations committees may sit on the Budget Committee.

The party's caucus rules guarantee all Democrats a seat on one major or exclusive committee. No Democrat may serve on more than one major and one nonmajor, or on more than two nonmajor, committees. Democrats are permitted a maximum of five subcommittee assignments. Another exception to the caucus rules allows Democrats to be assigned to either the District of Columbia or Judiciary committees regardless of other committee assignments.

Generally, Democrats are limited to one chairmanship — they may not simultaneously chair another full, select, permanent select, special, ad hoc or joint committee without the approval of the caucus. The only exceptions are that the Ways and Means Committee chairman may also serve as chairman of the Joint Committee on Taxation, and the House Administration Committee chairman may chair the Joint Printing Committee or the Joint Committee on the Library.

Committee chairmen may chair only one subcommittee and may not chair any subcommittee of another committee. No Democrat may chair more than one subcommittee of a committee with legislative jurisdiction, though Budget Committee members are exempt from this rule. The House Administration and Standards of Official Conduct committees as well as the joint committees are exempt from all caucus provisions regulating subcommittee chairmanships.

The Republican Conference dictates committee regulations for the minority party. The party's conference rules limit members of the party leadership to service on only one standing committee and prohibit them from serving as ranking minority member of any committee.

House Republicans tend to be less stringent than the Democrats in their committee regulations. The GOP defines major and minor committees essentially the same way as the Democrats, though the rules governing numbers and types of committee assign-

mittees. In practice, representatives of the two parties agree on committee assignments in advance and then submit their choices to the chambers, which simply ratify the parties' lists.

With some exceptions, the method currently in general use was adopted by the Senate in 1846 and by the House in 1911. The major difference involves the Democratic Party. Today the list of Democratic committee nominees is subject to prior approval by the party caucuses of the House and Senate.

The committee assignment procedure applies to all members and takes place at the beginning of every Congress. Barring a change in party control, however, the biannual practice usually affects only new members, who receive committee positions for the first time. Committee assignments also must be made from time to time during a session to fill vacancies caused by a member's death, resignation or voluntary transfer to another committee.[13]

At the beginning of a new Congress, resolutions are adopted by both houses containing the membership roster of the committees; the roster lists the names of the members submitted by the caucuses of the two parties. In the House, the majority party, usually after negotiations with the minority, sets the size of each committee in drawing up the membership roster that is presented to the House. (In the Senate, the size of the committees is established by the standing rules.) *(See also Party Ratios, p. 3)*

Although the procedural reforms of the 1970s established new methods for selecting committee chairmen, seniority still is rigidly adhered to in positioning members on committees and in filling vacancies, with new members being ranked at the bottom of his or her committees.

...Of Congressional Committees

ments are less precise. The Republicans' "blue ribbon" committees correspond to the Democrats exclusive committees, and it is rare for a Republican on a blue ribbon committee to sit on another committee.

Republicans may serve on one major committee and one minor committee, or on at least two minor committees. Except for certain rules for ranking committee members, the Republicans have no specific limitations on subcommittee assignments. No Republican may serve as the ranking member of more than one standing, select or ad hoc committee and of more than one subcommittee of any standing, select or ad hoc committee without the approval of the GOP Committee on Committees. No member may serve as ranking Republican member of more than two subcommittees of the standing, select and ad hoc committees on which he serves. And Republicans cannot be the ranking member on two subcommittees of the same committee. But this rule may be waived upon recommendation of the Committee on Committees.

Senate

Senate regulations dealing with the composition of committees were formalized in the 1977 committee reorganization plan. The Senate divides its standing committees into major and minor committees. Major ones are Agriculture, Nutrition and Forestry; Appropriations; Armed Services; Banking, Housing and Urban Affairs; Commerce, Science and Transportation; Energy and Natural Resources; Environment and Public Works; Finance; Foreign Relations; Governmental Affairs; Human Resources; and Judiciary. Minor committees are Rules and Administration; Veterans' Affairs; Aging; Intelligence; Small Business; the Joint Economic Committee; and the Joint Committee on Taxation.

Senators — Democrats and Republicans — may sit on two major committees and one minor committee. Each senator is limited to membership on three subcommittees of each major committee on which he serves (the Appropriations Committee is exempt from the limit) and on two subcommittees of his minor committee. The chairman or ranking minority member of a committee may serve as an ex officio member without a vote on any subcommittee of that committee. There are numerous exceptions to these regulations that protect incumbent senators who would have been in violation of these rules at the time they took effect. By agreement of the majority and minority leaders, the limits on committee service may be ignored to maintain majority party control. Senate rules also permit a temporary addition of one or two members to committees above the official limits.

Though not part of the Senate rules, the 1977 committee reorganization suggested that no member of a committee receive a second subcommittee assignment until all members of the committee had received a first assignment.

A senator may serve as chairman of only one full committee at a time and may chair only one subcommittee of each committee on which he serves. The chairman of a major committee may serve as chairman of only one subcommittee of his major committees and one subcommittee of his minor committee. The chairman of a minor committee may not serve as chairman of any subcommittee on that committee; he may chair one subcommittee of each of his major committees

Members who stay on the same committee from one Congress to another are given the same seniority ranking they had in the previous Congress, unless a death, resignation or retirement on the committee allows them to move up a notch. But if a member, even a senior member, transfers from one committee to another, he is ranked at the bottom in seniority on his new committee.

As a rule, a member of Congress remains on his major committees throughout his career, gradually working his way up by longevity. And if he has done reasonably well, and not made a lot of enemies, he usually can expect to become the chairman or ranking minority member despite the changes in seniority since the early 1970s.

Many factors are involved in the decisions of the party leadership in assigning new members to committees, but once a member is assigned a committee, seniority remains the most important single factor in determining his advancement on that committee.

While representatives generally serve on only two panels, sometimes just one, senators often serve on four. The feeling that senators were stretched too thin by serving on too many panels led Senate leaders to seek strict enforcement in 1985 of the Senate rule that limits senators to two major committees and one minor panel.

In the 98th Congress, 31 senators served on three major committees. Despite the pleas of Senate leaders, these senators were not anxious to give up assignments that they felt were important to their constituents. Internal fighting over the issue delayed the Senate from organizing, but in the end 14 senators kept three major committees each.

The Senate was not alone in producing high-pitched

committee battles in 1985. In early January, House Democrats voted 118-121 to depose Armed Services Committee Chairman Melvin Price, D-Ill., who, at 80, was viewed as too infirm to do the job. Then Democrats bypassed several more-senior committee members to elect Les Aspin, D-Wis., as chairman.

But this was an exception to the norm. Most often, particularly in the Senate, the chairman of a committee is the member of the majority party with the most committee seniority.

In the Senate, the Democratic committee roster is drawn up by the Democratic Steering Committee, headed by the party leader, who appoints the other Steering Committee members. The roster was first made subject to caucus approval in 1971. The Senate Republican committee roster is drawn up by the Republican Committee on Committees, which is appointed by the chairman of the Republican Conference (caucus), but the Republican Conference does not vote on the committee's nominations.

Resolutions containing each party's list of Senate committee assignments then go to the Senate, where approval is automatic, thus merely formalizing the committee appointments recommended by the two parties and the party ratios previously agreed upon.

In the House the Democratic committee roster is drawn up by the party's Steering and Policy Committee, whose nominations also are subject to caucus approval. (From 1911 until 1975, Democratic committee assignments were made by the Democratic members of the Ways and Means Committee.) An exception applies to the Democratic members of the Rules Committee. In 1975 the Speaker was given the power to nominate all party members of that panel, again subject to ratification by the caucus.

Republican committee nominations in the House are determined by the party's Committee on Committees, made up of one representative from each state having at least one Republican in its House delegation. The committee is subdivided into an executive committee of about 15 members who cast as many votes as there are Republican members in their state delegations. This weighted voting permits big-state members of the executive committee to dominate assignments. The nominations first are submitted to the full Committee on Committees for approval. Unlike the Democratic Caucus, the House Republican Conference does not vote on all committee nominations. However, under a 1971 procedural change it does vote on the ranking Republican member of each committee. (Details, box, p. 23)

The committee rosters prepared by the two parties then are incorporated in a single resolution, which must be adopted by the House. As in the Senate, this usually is a formality.

Factors in Assignments

Various factors govern the appointment of members to committees, including party loyalty, regional and state considerations, party ties and past loyalty, personal preferences of the leadership and previous experience.[14]

Some committees typically have an ideological bias or special-interest cast. The Agriculture committees, for example, are manned largely by members from farm states, the Interior committee by members from the Far West and Rocky Mountain states. The Armed Services committees usually have members from California, New York and the Deep South, where defense-related industries and shipbuilding plants are concentrated.

However, Davidson and Oleszek point out that "committees . . . can be tilted one way or the other by the recruitment process. During the 1980s the House Judiciary Committee was sometimes called the congressional 'Bermuda Triangle' because many measures sailed into the committee and were never heard of again." [15] It was suggested by the authors that the committee's chairman, Peter W. Rodino Jr., D-N.J., placed members with like philosophies on the committee, making it difficult for his adversaries, including those pushing the New Right agenda, to get action on their legislation.

The Oversight Function

Congress has given the executive branch broad authority over the vast array of agencies and programs it has created. As the range of activities of the federal government has grown, so has the need for Congress to oversee how the executive branch administers the laws it has passed.

"A thoughtful, well-drafted law offers no guarantee that the policy intentions of legislators will be carried out," warns Oleszek. "The laws passed by Congress are general guidelines, and sometimes their wording is deliberately vague. The implementation of legislation involves the drafting of administrative regulations by the executive agencies, and day-to-day program management by agency officials. Agency regulations and rules are the subject of 'legislative oversight' — the continuing review by Congress of how effectively the executive branch is carrying out congressional mandates." [16]

1946 Mandate

Congress did not officially recognize its responsibility for oversight until enactment of the 1946 Legislative Reorganization Act. That law mandated that the House and Senate standing committees exercise "continuous watchfulness of the execution by the administrative agencies" of any laws under their jurisdiction.

Since that time, Congress has passed several measures affecting oversight activities.[17] In the 1970 Legislative Reorganization Act, Congress increased staff assistance to all House and Senate committees, recommended that committees ascertain whether programs within their jurisdiction should be funded annually, and required most committees to issue oversight reports every two years.

Congress acted in 1974 to improve its oversight procedures when it passed the Congressional Budget and Impoundment Control Act. That act strengthened the General Accounting Office's (GAO) role in acquiring fiscal, budgetary and program-related information from federal agencies, authorized the GAO to establish an office to develop and recommend methods by which Congress could review and .evaluate federal programs and activities and authorized committees to assess the effectiveness of such programs as well as to require government agencies to carry out their own evaluations.

Oversight Committees

Related changes in committee practices adopted by the House in 1974 required committees with more than 15 members either to set up an oversight subcommittee or to require their legislative committees to carry out oversight functions. (In 1975 the minimum committee size needed to trigger the oversight requirement was raised to 20.)

Legislative subcommittees can carry out oversight only within their limited jurisdictions. On the other hand, most subcommittees set up specifically to conduct oversight usually can operate within the full committee's jurisdiction, a much broader mandate.

The House committee changes also gave seven committees — Budget, Armed Services, Education and Labor, Foreign Affairs, Interior and Insular Affairs, Science, Space and Technology and Small Business — special oversight responsibilities that permitted them to cross jurisdictional lines in conducting investigations. In another step affecting oversight, the new procedures permitted committees to triple the size of their professional staffs.

On the Senate side, the 1977 committee reorganization granted several committees "comprehensive policy oversight" responsibilities, comparable to the special oversight mandate in the House. Committees were required to include in the reports accompanying legislation the regulatory impact of each bill or joint resolution.

Oversight Panels

In 1987 there were 11 House committees with oversight subcommittees: Armed Services; Banking, Finance and Urban Affairs; Energy and Commerce; Interior and Insular Affairs; Merchant Marine and Fisheries; Post Office and Civil Service; Public Works and Transportation; Science, Space and Technology; Select Intelligence; Veterans' Affairs; and Ways and Means. In addition to these panels, there were four committees whose function was implicitly oversight: Appropriations, Budget, District of Columbia and Government Operations.

There were four Senate committees with oversight subcommittees: Agriculture, Nutrition and Forestry; Environment and Public Works; Finance; and Governmental Affairs. As in the House, there were other Senate committees with implicit oversight functions: Appropriations and Budget.

Oversight Techniques

Oleszek has identified a variety of means by which Congress exercises its oversight functions:[18]

● Hearings and investigations, the most common and recurring form of oversight. The Justice Department's settlement of an anti-trust suit against American Telephone and Telegraph Co. (AT&T) in January 1982 prompted an oversight hearing by the Senate Commerce Committee to examine the terms of the settlement. A bill that had been passed by the Senate in 1981 was pre-empted by the settlement, and Sen. Larry Pressler, R-S.D., said the hearing was "a good forum to discuss how this agreement meets the goals of [the Senate-passed bill] and what legislative action needs to be taken at this point." Some committee members expressed doubt that the Justice Department had reflected the intentions of the Senate in drafting the settlement.

● Legislative veto of executive actions by one or both houses of Congress or by the committee with jurisdiction over the subject matter. From the time of their first use during Herbert Hoover's administration in 1932, congressional vetoes became increasingly popular and eventually found their way into more than 200 laws. Yet in a landmark

decision affecting the relative powers of the legislative and executive branches of the government, the Supreme Court June 23, 1983, in a 7-2 ruling, declared the legislative veto unconstitutional. The decision, wrote Justice Byron R. White in a dissent, "strikes down in one fell swoop provisions in more laws enacted by Congress than the court has cumulatively invalidated in its entire history." Even after the decision, however, legislative vetoes were written into laws leaving observers to speculate over the long-term implications of the Supreme Court's decision.

● Authorizations, especially annual authorizations that allow for frequent reviews of agency performance, and appropriations, which Oleszek describes as probably Congress' most effective oversight tool. With the disclosures in 1974-75 of improper activities by U.S. intelligence agencies, select committees of both the House and Senate, as well as a special presidential commission, investigated the Central Intelligence Agency and other sectors of the intelligence community. Executive restructuring of the government's foreign intelligence operations and firmer congressional oversight of federal intelligence operations was accompanied by the creation of permanent Select Intelligence committees in the Senate (1976) and the House (1977). Both committees annually review the CIA's budget requests as well as oversee its clandestine operations.

● Nonstatutory controls, such as informal contacts between executive officials and committee members and staff, and statements incorporated in committee reports and conference reports, hearings and floor debates. According to Oleszek and Davidson, "nonstatutory controls may be the most common form of congressional oversight. Administrators are well advised to consider carefully such informal instructions." [19] The authors add that the courts often rely on committee report language to interpret congressional intent.

● General Accounting Office audits of agencies and programs.

● Requirements that executive agencies submit to Congress periodic reports on program implementation.

● Informal groups within Congress and organizations outside Congress that inform members about specific problems in administering programs.

● The Senate confirmation process. The Senate's power to reject a president's nominee for a high-level administration position is a latent power that is seldom exercised either in committee or on the Senate floor. Usually the threat of its use is enough to deter presidents from nominating persons totally unacceptable to Congress. However, in the early days of the Reagan administration the Senate Foreign Relations Committee voted 13-4 to recommend that the Senate not confirm the nomination of Ernest W. Lefever as assistant secretary of state for human rights. Lefever withdrew his name from consideration before the nomination went to the Senate for a vote. Certain nominees in the past had been forced to withdraw in the face of a likely adverse committee vote, but according to committee experts the Lefever case was possibly the first in which the Foreign Relations Committee had taken the step of rejecting a presidential nominee.

● Program evaluation through the use of social science and management methodology, such as surveys, cost-benefit analyses and efficiency studies.

● Casework, the handling of constituent questions and problems regarding federal agency actions, by the staffs of individual members of Congress.

● Studies by congressional support agencies, including

the Congressional Research Service, the Office of Technology Assessment and the Congressional Budget Office.

Effectiveness of Oversight

In the 1970s Congress began to express greater interest in oversight. This was attributed to several factors, such as "... dissatisfaction with big government; the rapid growth of congressional staff; revelations of executive abuses by agencies such as the FBI, CIA and IRS; the influx of new legislators skeptical of government's ability to perform effectively; and recognition that in a time of fiscal and resource scarcity Congress must make every dollar count." [20]

But some critics charged that congressional oversight remained largely ineffective. They cited the lack of institutional or political incentives to reward those members who conduct oversight; "sweetheart" alliances between the committees that have jurisdiction over the agencies that administer the programs being investigated; statutes with vague and imprecise language regarding program objectives, which thwart proper assessment; committee limitations, including unsystematic committee review of agency activities, inadequate coordination among committees sharing jurisdiction over the same agencies and programs, and congressional staffers' lack of understanding of programs approved by Congress because of frequent staff turnover.[21]

In addition, effective oversight requires the cooperation of the executive branch, and occasionally the federal bureaucracy or the White House has been recalcitrant in providing committees with the information and materials they deem necessary to carry out their oversight responsibilities.

In 1982 the investigations and oversight subcommittees of the House Public Works and Transportation Committee and the House Energy and Commerce Committee requested certain documents from the Environmental Protection Agency during their investigation of the $1.6 billion "superfund" to clean up abandoned hazardous waste dumps. The House on Dec. 16 voted EPA's administrator, Anne Gorsuch (later Burford), in contempt of Congress for refusing to turn over the materials. Gorsuch said she acted on written orders from President Reagan, dated Nov. 30, in which he instructed her to withhold certain documents because their dissemination outside the executive branch "would impair my solemn responsibility to enforce the law." The White House contended that some of the subpoenaed documents concerned potential litigation and could have jeopardized the enforcement of the superfund law. Congress traditionally has looked askance at claims of executive privilege, charging that such immunity is an infringement of its legislative and oversight prerogatives.

A number of innovations have been recommended to make legislative oversight more effective, including the so-called "sunset" legislation considered in the late 1970s that would require Congress to re-establish various federal programs on a systematic basis, thus forcing Congress to take periodic affirmative action to keep federal programs in existence. The sunset concept, popular with many younger members of Congress and supported by President Carter, drew its most significant opposition from some committee chairmen who felt it would erode their authority, give them a heavy new workload and perhaps cause inadvertent termination of some worthwhile programs.

There also have been proposals to require congressional committees to set forth in detail the goals legislation is designed to achieve and to specify the annual results expected. These proposals were never approved.

Early Use of Committees

Congressional committees became a major factor in the legislative process by evolution, not by constitutional design. The committee concept was borrowed from the British Parliament and transmitted to the New World by way of the colonial legislatures, most notably those of Pennsylvania and Virginia. But the committee system as it developed in Congress was modified and influenced by characteristics peculiar to American life.

In the early days of the Republic, when the nation's population was small and the duties of the central government were carefully circumscribed, Congress had little need for the division of labor that today's committee system provides. A people who viewed with grave suspicion the need to delegate authority to elected representatives in Washington was served by a Congress that only grudgingly delegated any of its own powers to committees.

In the early Congresses, legislative proposals were considered first in the Senate or House chamber, after which a special or select committee was appointed to work out the details of the legislation. Once the committee submitted its report on the bill, it was dissolved. Approximately 350 such committees were created during the Third Congress alone.[22]

In the House, legislation first was considered in the Committee of the Whole House on the State of the Union — usually referred to merely as the Committee of the Whole — and then sent to an ad hoc, or select, committee. (The Committee of the Whole, another procedure borrowed from the British Parliament, is nothing more than the House operating under special rules to expedite business. During the early Congresses, when it was used to oversee the select committees, debate was unlimited.)

As legislation increased in volume and complexity, permanent (standing) committees gradually replaced select committees, and legislation was referred directly to the committees without first being considered by the parent body. This procedure gave the committees initial authority over legislation, each in its specialized jurisdiction, subject to subsequent review by the full chamber.

The First Standing Committees

The House led the way in the creation of standing committees. The Committee on Elections, created in 1789, was followed by the Claims Committee in 1794 and by Commerce and Manufactures and Revision of the Laws in 1795. The number had risen to 10 by 1810. The next substantial expansion of committees did not occur until the administration of President James Monroe (1817-25). Between the War of 1812 and the Civil War the standing committee system became the standard vehicle for consideration of legislative business by the House, but it was not yet fully exploited as a source of independent power.[23]

The Senate was even slower in establishing standing committees. In the first 25 years of its existence, only four standing committees were created, and all of them on the whole were more administrative than legislative. Most of the committee work fell to select committees, usually of three members, appointed as the occasion demanded and disbanded when their task was completed. These occasions were so frequent that during the session of 1815-16 between 90 and 100 select committees were appointed. Frequently, however, related legislation would be referred to special committees already in existence and the same senators appointed to deal with the related proposals.

In 1816 the Senate, finding inconvenient the appointment of so many ad hoc committees during each session, added 11 standing committees to the existing four. By 1863 the number had grown to 19.[24]

Committee Membership

Each chamber developed its own method of making appointments to the committees. The first rule established by the House in 1789 with respect to committee appointments reserved to the whole House the power to choose the membership of all committees composed of more than three members. That rule gave way in 1790 to a rule delegating this power to the Speaker, with the reservation that the House might direct otherwise in special cases. Eventually, however, the Speaker was given the right to appoint the members as well as the chairmen of all standing committees, a power he retained until 1911.

The principle that the committees were to be bipartisan, but weighted in favor of the majority party and its policies, was established early.[25]

In making committee appointments and promotions, there were certain principles that governed the Speaker's choices. The wishes of the minority leaders in filling vacancies going to members of their party usually were respected. Generally, seniority — length of service on the committee — and factors such as geographical distribution and party loyalty were considered. But the Speaker was not bound by such criteria, and there were cases where none of those factors outweighed the Speaker's wishes. Despite complaints and various attempts to change the rule, the system remained in force until 1911, when the House again exercised the right to select the members of standing committees.

In the Senate, until 1823, assignment to a committee was made by vote of the entire membership. Members wishing to serve on a particular committee were placed on a ballot, with the choicest committee assignments going to those receiving the most votes. The senator with the largest number of votes served as chairman.

By the 1820s, however, a number of difficulties with the ballot system had become evident. The arrangement proved tedious and time consuming and provided no guarantee that the party in control of the chamber would hold a majority of seats on the committee or retain control of the committee chairmanships in the event of a vacancy. Several times in the ensuing years the Senate amended its rules to provide for appointment to committees by a designated official, usually the vice president or president pro tempore. However, abuse of the appointment power and a transfer of power between the two parties compelled the Senate to return to use of the ballot.

In 1823 a proposal that the chairmen of the five most important committees be chosen by the full Senate, and that the chairmen then have the power to make all other committee assignments, was rejected. The Senate instead amended the standing rules to give the "presiding officer" authority to make committee assignments, unless otherwise ordered by the Senate. Since Daniel D. Tompkins, vice president during the administration of James Monroe, scarcely ever entered the chamber, committee selection was left to the president pro tempore, who in effect had been chosen by and was responsible to the Senate majority leadership. But when the next vice president, John C. Calhoun, used the assignment power with obvious bias, the Senate quickly and with little dissent returned to the election method to fill committee vacancies.[26]

This time the chairmen were picked by majority vote of the entire Senate; then ballots were taken to select the other members of each committee, with members' rank on the committee determined by the size of their plurality. The Senate in 1828 changed the rules to provide for appointment to committees by the president pro tempore, but in 1833 it reverted to selection by ballot when control of the Senate changed hands. Since 1833 the Senate technically has made its committee assignments by ballot.

To avoid the inconveniences inherent in the ballot system, it became customary between 1833 and 1846 to suspend the rule by unanimous consent and designate an officer (the vice president, the president pro tempore or the "presiding officer") to assign members to committees.

The method of selecting committee members in use in 1987 was — with some modification — developed in 1846. In that year a motion to entrust the vice president with the task was defeated, and the Senate proceeded under the regular rules to make committee assignments by ballot. But after six chairmen had been selected, a debate ensued on the method of choosing the other members of the committees. At first, several committees were filled by lists — arranged in order of a member's seniority — submitted by the majority leader. After a number of committees had been filled in this manner, the ballot rule was suspended, and the Senate approved a list for the remaining vacancies that had been agreed upon by both the majority and minority leadership.[27]

Since 1846 the choice of committees usually has amounted to routine acceptance by the Senate of lists drawn up by special committees of the two major parties (today the Committee on Committees for the Republicans and the Steering Committee for the Democrats).

Committee Proliferation

The standing committee system, firmly established in the first half of the 19th century, expanded rapidly in the second half. During this period the committees developed into powerful, autonomous institutions, increasingly independent of the House and Senate and party control. Committee chairmen assumed ever greater powers over legislation. So great was their influence that Woodrow Wilson in 1885 could write: "I know not how better to describe our form of government in a single phrase than by calling it a government by the chairmen of the standing committees of Congress."[28]

The committee chairmen became even more powerful figures following the House "revolution" of 1909-10, which curtailed the powers of the Speaker and split up the House leadership. Committee seniority, already used extensively by the Speaker as a method for selecting the chairmen, was firmly established from that time on until the reforms of the 1970s.

The number of standing committees reached a peak in 1913, when there were 61 in the House and 74 in the Senate. The Appropriations, Ways and Means, Finance and Rules committees, in particular, exercised great influence; others were created and perpetuated chiefly to provide members with offices and clerical staff.

Committee Reorganization

Initial efforts to consolidate the House committee system were undertaken in 1909, when six minor committees were dropped. Two years later, when the Democrats took control, six superfluous committees were abolished. Up to that time, according to Galloway, "the reorganizations of 1910 and 1911 [were] the most spectacular and best known of any associated with Congress." [29]

Ten years later another committee reorganization took place. As a consequence of enactment of the Budget and Accounting Act of 1921, the House restored to its Appropriations Committee exclusive jurisdiction over all appropriations bills for federal departments and programs.

Before the creation of the Appropriations committees (1865 in the House and 1867 in the Senate), a single committee in each chamber had handled both revenue raising and appropriations legislation. In 1885 the House dispersed the powers of its Appropriations Committee among nine committees. [30] The Senate later followed the House example, and by 1914 eight of 14 annual appropriations bills were referred to committees other than the Appropriations panel.

Although this method allowed committees most familiar with each federal agency and its programs to consider their funding requirements, it resulted in a division of responsibility that did not permit congressional consideration or control of financial policy to be centralized. Accordingly, the House in 1920 and the Senate in 1922 restored exclusive spending powers to the Appropriations committees.

In 1921 the Senate reduced the number of its committees from 74 to 34. In many respects this rationalization of the committee structure simply was the formal abandonment of long-defunct bodies such as the Committee on Revolutionary Claims. [31] The House in 1927 reduced the number of its committees by merging 11 expenditures committees, those dealing primarily with oversight, into a single Committee on Expenditures in the Executive Departments.

The next major overhaul of the committee structure took place in 1946 with enactment of the Legislative Reorganization Act. By dropping minor committees and merging those with related functions, the act achieved a net reduction of 18 in the number of Senate committees (from 33 to 15) and of 29 in the number of House committees (from 48 to 19). The act also defined in detail the jurisdictions of each committee and attempted to set ground rules for their operations. [32]

Between 1946 and a partial reorganization of Senate committees in 1977 only minor changes were made in the committee structure in Congress. During that period many of the achievements of the 1946 act were weakened by the gradual proliferation of subcommittees and by the creation of additional committees.

By the mid-1970s the standing committees still numbered only 21 in the House and 16 in the Senate, but by then there was a total of 268 subcommittees in both houses as well as seven joint committees and a growing number of select and special committees that had been set up to examine specific problems.

The Legislative Reorganization Act of 1970 changed some committee practices but made only minor revisions in the committee structure itself. It created a new Veterans' Affairs Committee in the Senate and made cosmetic changes such as renaming the Senate Committee on Banking and Currency the Banking, Housing and Urban Affairs Committee to reflect the committee's jurisdiction more accurately. The defunct Joint Committee on Immigration and Nationality Policy was formally abolished, and a Joint Committee on Congressional Operations was established.

The 1970 act marked the beginning of a decade of efforts in Congress to change the committee structure in the House and Senate. [33] But except for the 1977 changes in Senate committees, the modifications to the committee system had little impact. On the other hand, changes in House and Senate rules and in committee and parliamentary procedures had a significant impact on the way committees operated.

The principal changes affecting committee procedures required open committee hearings in most instances; required all roll-call votes taken in committee to be made available to the public; authorized radio and television coverage of House committee hearings; authorized minority members of each House committee to select two of a committee's six permanent professional staff and permitted them to call witnesses of their choosing during at least one day of hearings on a bill; restricted newly elected senators to membership on only two major committees (and on only one of the following: Armed Services, Appropriations, Finance or Foreign Relations) and one minor, select or joint committee (committees classified as minor were District of Columbia, Post Office and Civil Service, Rules, and Veterans' Affairs; all other standing committees were considered major); and provided that a senator could not chair more than one full committee.

House Committee Changes

An ambitious effort by the House in 1973-74 to consolidate and reorganize its committee structure met with limited success. A plan recommending broad changes in committees and committee jurisdictions was blocked by entrenched interests both in and out of Congress that benefited from the existing committee system. [34]

Subcommittee Bill of Rights

The House Democratic Caucus in January 1973 adopted a so-called subcommittee bill of rights. The new caucus rules created a party caucus for Democrats on each House committee and forced the chairmen to begin sharing authority with other committee Democrats. Each committee caucus was granted the authority to select subcommittee chairmen (with members allowed to run for chairman based on their seniority ranking on the full committee), establish subcommittee jurisdictions, set party ratios on the subcommittees to reflect the party ratio of the full committee, provide a subcommittee budget and guarantee all members a major subcommittee slot where vacancies made that possible. Each subcommittee was authorized to hold hearings and set its meeting dates and to act on matters referred to it.

Under the "bill of rights," committee chairmen were required to refer designated types of legislation to each subcommittee within two weeks. They no longer could kill measures they opposed simply by pocketing them.

The Hansen Plan. The changes eventually adopted in 1974 came from a package of compromise recommendations proposed by Rep. Julia Butler Hansen, D-Wash.

Proxy Voting in Committee: The Bane of the Minority Party

Proxy voting in congressional committees permits one committee member to authorize another member to cast his votes for him in his absence. Though on first glance it appears to be an innocuous practice, it has been the bane of the minority party in Congress and a target of reformers for years.

Opponents contend that it encourages absenteeism and irresponsibility. Before the power of committee chairmen was diminished in the 1970s, it also was argued that proxy voting contributed to the domination of committees by the chairmen because the chairmen were in an ideal position to wrest proxies from committee members in return for the favors they could bestow.

And while chairmen no longer wield the power they once did, proxy voting, according to the minority party — particularly Republicans in the House — allows the majority to abuse the committee system.

Before 1970 the use of proxies was regulated either by custom or by guidelines established by individual committees; thus the practice differed from committee to committee. In some committees they never were allowed.

Proxy voting is not permitted on the floor of the Senate or House.

House

The Legislative Reorganization Act of 1970 was the first measure to address the criticisms leveled at proxy voting. That act prohibited the practice unless a committee's written rules specifically allowed it, in which case they were limited to a specific issue (a bill or an amendment or for procedural questions, for internal committee business, etc.). They also had to be in writing, designating the person on the committee authorized to use them.[1]

In October 1974 the House voted 196-166 to ban proxy voting entirely. But the ban did not last long, primarily because Democrats, who as the majority party controlled House operations, benefited from the use of proxies.

Republicans, a minority in the House for all but two Congresses since 1931, have argued that the Democrats' use of proxies allows them to extend their control over the committee system by scheduling numerous committee and subcommittee sessions at the same time.

Without proxy votes, the Democrats could not retain control of all committee business on all the committees because of scheduling conflicts.

The Democratic Caucus modified the ban at the beginning of the 94th Congress in 1975. The revision, which was added to the standing rules, once again gave committees the authority to decide whether to permit proxy voting. If a committee allowed proxies, they were to be used only on a specific amendment or procedural question. General proxies, covering all matters before a committee for either a specific time period or for an indefinite period, were prohibited. And, as before, they had to be in writing, with a member designated to cast the proxies. The proxy vote also had to be dated and could not be used to make a quorum.

Senate

For Senate committees, the 1970 act provided little restraint on the use of proxies. The law said proxy votes could not be used to report legislation if committee rules barred their use. If proxies were not forbidden on a motion to report a bill, they nevertheless could be used only upon the formal request of a senator who planned to be absent during a session.

Senate rules leave it up to individual committees to decide whether or not to allow proxies. To prevent the use of general proxies, Senate rules bar the use of a proxy if an absent member "has not been informed of the matter on which he is being recorded and has not affirmatively requested that he be so recorded." Proxies cannot be counted toward the quorum needed for reporting legislation.

In addition to proxy voting, some Senate committees permit polling, that is, holding an informal vote of committee members instead of convening the committee. Such votes usually are taken by sending a voting sheet to committee members' offices or by taking members' votes by telephone.

Because Senate rules require a quorum to be present for a committee to report legislation, polling is supposed to be restricted to issues involving legislation still pending before the committee, to matters relating to investigations and to internal committee business.

If polling is used to report legislation, any senator can challenge the bill.[2] Such was the case in December 1980 when opponents of a Carter nominee for a federal judgeship charged that the nomination had not been properly reported because the Judiciary Committee had approved it by a written poll of members.

The issue was dropped and the nominee was approved when Judiciary Chairman Edward M. Kennedy, D-Mass., gained Republican support by agreeing not to push other Carter judicial nominations pending in the committee.[3]

1. For a discussion of proxy voting in the House, see House Select Committee on Committees, *Final Report*, 96th Cong., 2d sess., 1980, 571-581.
2. For a discussion of proxy voting and polling in the Senate, see Senate Office of Legal Counsel, *Manual of Senate Committee Procedure*, February 1981, 31-38.
3. *Congressional Quarterly 1980 Almanac* (Washington, D.C.: Congressional Quarterly, 1981), 16-A, 18-A.

(1960-74), who headed the party's Committee on Organization, Study and Review.

The Hansen plan made some jurisdictional shifts — such as giving the Public Works Committee control over most transportation matters and setting up a new Select Committee on Aging — but mainly it retained the existing committee structure dating from 1946.

Along with the minor committee adjustments came more procedural changes. Each standing committee's permanent staff, beginning in 1975, was increased from six to 18 professionals and from six to 12 clerks, with the minority party receiving one-third of each category. And in what would prove to be the most controversial provision, the plan gave the minority control of one-third of the investigative funds committees use to supplement their staffs. (The Democratic Caucus subsequently repealed the provision.)

In other changes, which also took effect in 1975, committees with more than 15 members (increased to more than 20 members by the Democratic Caucus in 1975) were required to establish at least four subcommittees. This change created an important precedent in that it institutionalized subcommittees for the first time. And committees with more than 15 members (increased to more than 20 in 1975 by the caucus) were required to set up an oversight subcommittee or to require their legislative subcommittees to carry out oversight functions.

Also affecting committees were new powers given the Speaker: he was authorized to refer bills that had been introduced to more than one committee at a time or to several committees in sequence. He also could split up bills and send the parts to different committees and set deadlines for committees to complete action and issue their report on legislation given multiple referral.

Proxy voting was banned in committee. (In 1975 proxy voting was partially restored by the Democratic Caucus: proxies were allowed on a specific issue or on procedural matters, and they had to be in writing and given to a member, among other requirements.)

Finally, the House was given a directive to organize itself for the next Congress in December of election years.

The Bolling Proposals. The Hansen plan was a substitute for a much broader bipartisan proposal, drafted by a special committee composed of five Democrats and five Republicans headed by Rep. Richard Bolling, D-Mo. The Bolling committee, which had been created in January 1973, submitted its reorganization proposals the following December.

Bolling proposed to consolidate related House committee jurisdictions within one committee. A frequent criticism of the existing committee setup was that it dispersed jurisdiction on related subjects among many panels. The plan would have reduced substantially the power and influence of the House Administration and Ways and Means committees. The latter, for example, would have lost its non-tax jurisdiction over foreign trade, unemployment compensation and health insurance. The plan also would have set up new committees on Energy and Environment, Public Works and Transportation, and Commerce and Health. Members would have been limited to membership on one of the 15 major committees in the plan.

Not surprisingly, the wholesale restructuring drew a flood of protest from chairmen and committee members who would have been adversely affected, as well as from the lobbyists who dealt with those committees. The House Democratic Caucus shunted the plan to the Hansen committee, where it was watered down.

Both plans were brought to the House late in 1974, where the Bolling proposal was decisively rejected in favor of the Hansen substitute. Independent of the Hansen plan was the decision of the House to abolish the Internal Security Committee (until 1969 the House Un-American Activities Committee).

Caucus Actions Affecting Committees. Further changes in House committee operations unrelated to the Hansen plan were made in late 1974 and early 1975 by the Democratic Caucus. The impetus for these was the pickup of 43 additional seats by House Democrats in the November 1974 election, which gave the party a 291-144 majority.

Meeting in December 1974 to organize for the 94th Congress, Democrats decided to make a secret-ballot vote on the election of all committee chairmen automatic. In the past the procedure had been cumbersome. The new procedure allowed competitive nominations for chairmen if the original Steering Committee nominee was rejected. Democrats immediately made use of their new rule by deposing three committee chairmen.

In other changes, the Democratic members of the Ways and Means Committee were stripped of their power to select the party's members of House committees; this authority was transferred to a revamped Democratic Steering and Policy Committee, whose members are appointed by the Speaker. At the same time, the caucus increased the size of the Ways and Means Committee from 25 to 37 members, a change aimed at giving the committee a more liberal outlook and thus more likely to support party-backed proposals on tax revision, health insurance and other issues. The caucus also required all committees to include a statement in their reports on a bill's impact on inflation and reports on appropriations measures to include information on changes in law made in the accompanying bill.

In actions affecting the independence of subcommittees, the caucus directed that the entire Democratic membership of each committee, rather than the chairmen alone, was to determine the number and jurisdiction of a committee's subcommittees. And the caucus specified that no member of a committee could become a member of a second subcommittee of that committee until every member of the full committee had chosen a subcommittee slot. (But a grandfather clause allowed sitting members on subcommittees to protect two subcommittee slots.) The subcommittees that always had been semiautonomous were the powerful units of the House Appropriations Committee. Thus the caucus decided that, along with full committee chairmen, all nominees for chairmen of these subcommittees would have to be approved by the Democratic Caucus. (Nominees for Appropriations subcommittee chairmen were selected by the membership of each subcommittee, with the members bidding for subcommittee chairman in the order of their seniority on the subcommittee.)

The Speaker's powers were further buttressed by allowing him to select the Democratic members of the Rules Committee, subject to caucus approval.

All standing committees were given broad subpoena authority without the necessity of going to the House on each occasion to get approval. But subpoenas had to be approved by a majority of a committee.

Finally, reflecting their 1974 electoral gains, Democrats increased the party ratio on all House committees, except Standards of Official Conduct, to two Democrats to one Republican, plus one Democrat.

1977 Reorganization Plan

Another effort to restructure the committees was unsuccessful in 1977. In October of that year new recommendations for improving committee operations went down to defeat.[35] The House seemed to have had enough reform for the time being.

The Obey Commission. The new committee reorganization plan was drafted by the House Commission on Administrative Review, headed by Rep. David R. Obey, D-Wis. Included was a proposal to establish a select committee to suggest changes in committee practices. "Members have too many assignments, and jurisdictions are too confused for the strains and conflicts members currently endure to be substantially alleviated by piecemeal and procedural reform," a task force of the Obey commission had concluded. "The need for basic reform is crystal clear, and the House should act promptly to modernize the one instrument on which its effectiveness so critically depends — its committee system." [36]

Procedural Changes. In January 1977 the House approved a series of House rules changes affecting committee operations that had been endorsed by the Democratic Caucus in December 1976. In addition, it abolished the Joint Committee on Atomic Energy and stripped the House Committee on Standards of Official Conduct of its legislative jurisdictions.

In standing rules changes, committee privileges and powers were broadened; a quorum for conducting business, including bill-drafting sessions, was set at one-third of a committee's membership (for hearings, only two members need be present), and the subpoena power was extended to include subcommittees. All House-Senate conference committee meetings were required to be open to the public except when the House specifically voted to close a session (usually for national security reasons).

In a change that had been adopted by the Democratic Caucus in December 1976, the chairmen of the Ways and Means and Appropriations committees were stripped of their power to nominate the Democratic members of the Budget Committee; that power was transferred to the Democratic Steering and Policy Committee.

1979 Procedural Changes

The House Democratic Caucus, meeting in December 1978 to organize for the 96th Congress, further modified its rules on committee assignments and procedures.

The number of terms that Democrats were allowed to serve on the House Budget Committee was increased from two to three. (Under the two-term limit, seven committee members would have had to leave the 30-member committee.) Each House Democrat was limited to five subcommittee seats on House standing committees.

In a modification of a 1974 caucus rule, committees — except Appropriations — were required to allow each member to choose one subcommittee assignment before any member, without exception, could choose a second one. (In 1974 sitting members had been allowed to reserve two subcommittee positions.)

A committee chairman was prohibited from serving as chairman of any other standing, select, special or joint committee.

1980 Reorganization Failure

The House in March 1979 set up a Select Committee on Committees to once more recommend how to improve the House's internal organization and operations. But when the panel closed its doors in April 1980, it left behind barely a trace of its 13-month-long effort to change the House committee system.[37]

The panel had submitted five proposals: 1) that members be given space in the Capitol where they could work when floor action prevented them from returning to their offices; 2) that, to avoid scheduling conflicts in the House, committees be allowed to conduct business only on specified days; 3) that House Democrats be limited to five subcommittee assignments (a rule adopted in 1978 by the Democratic Caucus had applied only to subcommittee assignments on standing committees, not on select committees) and that, on a phased-in basis, each standing committee, except Appropriations, be limited to six subcommittees; 4) that one committee be designated as having primary responsibility for bills referred to more than one committee; and 5) that a separate standing committee on energy be created to untangle the existing overlapping committee jurisdictions dealing with energy-related legislation.

Of the five recommendations, not one was adopted by the House. Only one — the plan to create an energy panel — went to the House floor, where the proposal was promptly gutted. In place of the select committee's plan, the House merely decided to rename its Commerce Committee the "Energy and Commerce" Committee and to designate that panel as its lead committee on energy matters.

"I think turf was the absolute overriding issue" in the defeat of the select committee's proposals, said committee chairman Jerry M. Patterson, D-Calif. "If you want to make changes, you run into the turf wars." The committee, in its final report, concluded that "substantial internal opposition to reform will surface regardless of the scope of the reforms proposed."[38]

Senate Committee Changes

While most of the attempts to reorganize the committee system in the 1970s were directed at the House, the Senate committee system was altered in 1977 by the first comprehensive committee consolidation in either house in 31 years. Earlier, in 1975, the Senate had adopted important procedural changes involving committees.

Senate Democrats that year voted to elect committee chairmen by secret ballot whenever one-fifth of the caucus requested it. Senate Republicans had decided in 1973 to choose their top-ranking committee members by conference votes.

Senate rules were changed to require most committee meetings, bill-drafting sessions as well as hearings to be open to the public. A related rule change required Senate-House conference committees to be open to the public unless a majority of the conferees of either chamber voted in open session to close a meeting on a bill for that day. *(Conference committees, box, p. 5; related House rule, see above)*

Also in 1975, junior senators obtained committee staff assistance for the first time. A new rule authorized them to hire up to three committee staffers — depending on the number and type of committee assignments they had — to work directly for them on their committees. In the past,

House Rules Committee Became ...

The Rules Committee long has stood as a strategic gateway between the legislative committees and the floor of the House for all but the most routine legislation.

The power of the committee lies in its role of setting the rules or guidelines for floor debate on legislation. A "special rule" sets the time limit on general debate and regulates how the bill may be amended. It may forbid all amendments or, in some cases, all amendments except those proposed by the legislative committee that handled the bill. Thus the committee is able to structure the debate and the types of amendments that will be allowed on legislation or, on occasion, even prevent a bill from coming to the floor.

There have been frequent controversies throughout the history of the House over the function of the Rules Committee in the legislative process: whether it should be merely a clearinghouse, or traffic cop, for legislative business, the agent of the majority leadership, or a super-legislative committee editing the work of the other committees.

Defenders of the Rules Committee system of routing bills maintain it is the only feasible way to regulate the legislative flow efficiently in the 435-member House. And since the mid-1970s, in fact, the committee has returned to the role it performed until 1911 as an arm of the majority leadership.[1]

Changing Role of the Committee

The Rules Committee was established in 1789. Originally it was a select committee, authorized at the beginning of each Congress, with jurisdiction over House rules. However, since the rules of one Congress usually were readopted by the next, this function was not of great importance, and for many years the committee never issued a report.

In 1858 the Speaker was made a member of the committee, and in subsequent years the panel gradually increased its influence over legislation. The panel became a standing committee in 1880, and in 1883 it began the practice of issuing rules — special orders of business — for floor debate on legislation.

Other powers acquired by the committee over the years included the right to sit while the House was in session, to have its resolutions considered immediately (called privileged resolutions), and even to initiate legislation on its own, like any other legislative committee. Before 1910 the Rules Committee worked closely with the leadership in deciding what legislation could come to the floor. But in the Progressive revolt of 1909-10 against Speaker "Uncle Joe" Cannon, the committee was made independent of the leadership. Alternative methods of bringing legislation to the floor — the Discharge Calendar, Consent Calendar and Calendar Wednesday procedures — were added to the standing rules. And in 1910 a coalition of Democrats and insurgent Republicans succeeded in enlarging the Rules Committee and excluding the Speaker from it. (The ban on the Speaker was repealed in 1946, but subsequent Speakers have never sat on the committee.)

By the late 1930s the committee had come under the domination of a coalition of conservative Democrats and Republicans. From that time until the 1970s it repeatedly blocked or delayed liberal legislation.

Opposition to the obstructive tactics of the Rules Committee led, in 1949, to adoption of the "21-day rule." The rule provided that the chairman of a legislative committee that had approved a bill and requested a rule from the Rules Committee permitting the bill to be brought to the floor, could bring up the resolution if the committee failed to grant a rule within 21 calendar days of the committee's request. The rule required the Speaker to recognize the chairman of the committee wishing to call up the bill. Two years later, after the Democrats had lost 29 seats in the mid-term elections, the House repealed the 21-day rule. Although it had been used only eight times, the threat of its use was credited with prying other bills out of the Rules Committee.

House Revolt

At the beginning of the 86th Congress in 1959, a group of liberal Democrats dropped plans to seek a change in House rules that would break the conservative grip on the committee. Speaker Sam Rayburn, D-Texas (1913-61), assured them that bills reported from their committees would reach the House floor. However, the record of the 86th Congress showed that Rayburn often could not deliver on his promise. After the Rules Committee had blocked or delayed several measures that were to become key elements in the new Kennedy administration's legislative program, Democrats decided to act.

Accordingly, in 1961 the House by a narrow margin agreed to enlarge the committee from 12 to 15 members for the 87th Congress. That gave Rayburn and the administration a delicate 8-7 majority on most issues coming before the committee. By raising the number of Democrats to 10 from 8 (Republicans to 5 from 4), it permitted the appointment to the committee of two pro-administration Democrats. This enlargement was made permanent in 1963.

Nevertheless, dissatisfaction with the Rules Committee continued, and following the Democratic sweep in the 1964 elections the 21-day rule was revived. The new version of the rule, adopted by the House at the opening of the 89th Congress in 1965, did not require the Speaker to recognize a committee

... Arm of the Leadership in 1970s

chairman wishing to call up a 21-day resolution. Under the 1965 rule the Speaker retained discretion to recognize a committee chairman, so that it became highly unlikely for a bill to come up through this procedure without the approval of the House leadership. The new rule, which also was employed successfully only eight times, was abandoned in 1967 following Republican gains in the 1966 mid-term elections.

The House retained another rule, adopted in 1965, that curbed the committee's power to block conferences on legislation. Before 1965 most bills could be sent to a conference committee only through unanimous consent or adoption of a special rule issued by the Rules Committee. The 1965 change made it possible to send any bill to conference by majority vote of the House.

Despite repeal of the 21-day rule in 1967, the committee continued generally to pursue a stance more accommodating to the leadership. Several factors contributed to the committee's less conservative posture. First, it had lost its chairman of 12 years, Howard W. Smith, D-Va. (1931-67), who was defeated in a 1966 primary election. Smith was a skilled parliamentarian and the acknowledged leader of the House's conservative coalition — a voting alliance of Republicans and Southern Democrats. He was replaced as chairman by William M. Colmer, D-Miss. (1933-73). Although he also was a conservative, Colmer was unable to exert the high degree of control over legislation that Smith had exercised.

In addition, two liberal members had been added to the committee and a set of rules had been introduced to govern committee procedures. The rules took from the chairman the right to set meeting dates, a power Smith frequently had used to postpone or thwart action on bills he opposed. The consent of a majority was needed to kill a bill, and limits were placed on proxy voting.

The committee's latent powers of obstruction were obscured so long as it did not flaunt them, but in the closing days of the 1970 session the committee reverted to its old ways by refusing to approve several bills for House action.

Ally of Leadership

Liberal Democrats predicted a new era was at hand in 1973, when Colmer retired and was succeeded as chairman by Ray J. Madden, D-Ind. (1943-77). That same year, three Democrats considered loyal to the leadership were added to the committee.

The new makeup of the committee posed a different problem for the leadership. The panel approved for action a great deal of liberal legislation without regard to its chances of passage. The House

itself, more conservative than the Rules Committee for the first time in years, began looking critically at the bills it scheduled for floor action and at the special rules under which they were to be debated.

Before 1973 the vast majority of the committee's special rules were approved with little opposition by the House. Between 1929 and 1972 rules issued by the committee were defeated on 50 occasions, but in 1973 alone the House rejected 13 rules.

In an attempt to strengthen the leadership's control over the committee, the Democratic Caucus voted in December 1974 to give the Speaker the power to nominate all Democratic members of the panel, subject to caucus approval. Using this power, Speaker Carl Albert, D-Okla. (1947-77), nominated liberals to fill two vacant positions.

But, although the committee was now allied with the leadership, the panel did not function immediately as an adjunct of the leadership. There were several reasons for this, according to political scientist Bruce I. Oppenheimer, including the fact that there was little assistance in that direction from Rules Chairman Madden or his successor, James J. Delaney, D-N.Y. (1945-47, 1949-78), who chaired the committee from 1977-78.[2]

Oppenheimer cited three new roles of the committee that began to take shape in the 94th Congress (1975-77): 1) expediting, rather than delaying, legislation for floor action; 2) providing a growing number of members having little experience in managing bills on the floor with a preview of what to expect in the House; and 3) assigning a few committee members the function of informing and advising the leadership on legislative matters.[3]

The Rules panel's gradual adjustment to its new position was manifested in several areas, according to Oppenheimer.[4] The first of these was the drafting of more complex rules, which provided greater leadership control of floor debate by resolving ahead of time some of the problems that resulted from the 1970s reforms, such as jurisdictional fights, unstructured floor debates and obstructive tactics.

A second area was the increase in legislative initiatives which expanded significantly under Richard Bolling, D-Mo., who was chairman from 1979 to 1983. Two standing subcommittees were created, and the committee's staff and budget were enlarged substantially.

The current chairman is Claude Pepper, D-Fla., who has held the position since 1983.

1. For a discussion, see Bruce I. Oppenheimer, "The Changing Relationship Between House Leadership and the Committee on Rules," in *Understanding Congressional Leadership*, ed. Frank H. Mackaman (Washington, D.C.: CQ Press, 1981), 218-224.
2. Oppenheimer, "The Changing Relationship," 218.
3. Oppenheimer, "The Changing Relationship," 216-217.
4. Oppenheimer, "The Changing Relationship," 218-224.

1977 Senate Reorganization

Major changes in responsibility within Senate committees resulted from the 1977 reorganization.

The responsibilities of the Aeronautical and Space Sciences Committee were transferred to the Commerce, Science and Transportation Committee.

Matters under the jurisdiction of the District of Columbia and Post Office and Civil Service committees were transferred to the Governmental Affairs Committee.

Beginning in 1978, the functions of the Select Nutrition Committee were taken over by the Agriculture, Nutrition and Forestry Committee.

The responsibilities of the Joint Atomic Energy Committee were transferred to the Armed Services, Energy and Natural Resources, and Environment and Public Works committees.

The jurisdictions of the Joint Committee on Congressional Operations and the Select Committee to Study the Senate Committee System were transferred to the Rules Committee.

Other changes included:

Transfer of responsibility for school lunch legislation to the Agriculture Committee from the old Labor and Public Welfare Committee, now the Labor and Human Resources Committee.

A shift of foreign commerce and veterans' housing programs to the Banking Committee from the Commerce and Veterans' Affairs committees respectively.

A shift of responsibility for the naval petroleum reserves and the oil shale reserves in Alaska and for water power to Energy and Natural Resources from the Armed Services and Public Works committees respectively.

Transfer of responsibility for fisheries and wildlife, except for marine fisheries, to the Environment and Public Works Committee from the Commerce Committee.

committee staff members had been controlled by the chairmen and other senior committee members.

1977 Committee Reorganization

The Senate in 1977 approved the first major restructuring of its committee system since the Legislative Reorganization Act of 1946. The changes were the product of a special committee that studied committee operations, chaired by Sen. Adlai E. Stevenson III.[39]

The reorganization consolidated some Senate committees, revised jurisdictions of others, limited the number of committees and subcommittees a senator can belong to or chair, increased minority members' share of committee staff and directed that committee hearings and other business be computerized to avoid scheduling conflicts.

One of the biggest organizational changes was the creation of a separate Energy Committee with authority over most aspects of energy policy except taxes.

The final result fell short of the Stevenson committee's goals for consolidating and merging committees. The original plan had called for abolition of all special, select and joint committees (except Select Intelligence) and of the District of Columbia, Post Office and Civil Service, Aeronautical and Space Sciences, and Veterans' Affairs committees.

But only six committees were abolished: District of Columbia, Post Office, and Space Sciences and the joint committees on Atomic Energy, Congressional Operations and Defense Production. (The decision to end the joint committees was a unilateral Senate action. The House continued the Congressional Operations panel as a select committee for another two years.)

Special interest groups were able to preserve the Veterans' and Select Small Business committees, nearly preserved the Post Office and Civil Service Committee and thwarted plans to consolidate transportation legislation in one committee.

The 1977 changes established a committee structure consisting of 12 major committees, five minor committees and two joint committees, and committee jurisdictions and responsibilities were altered. *(Box, this page)*

Changes also were made in Senate committee procedures. With certain exceptions, each senator was limited to membership on two major committees and one minor committee. Each senator was limited to membership on three subcommittees of each major committee on which he served (the Appropriations Committee was exempted from this restriction). And each senator was limited to membership on two subcommittees of the minor committee on which he served.

Though it was not made a requirement, the Senate adopted language similar to the House's stating it to be the sense of the Senate that no member of a committee should receive a second subcommittee assignment until all members of the committee had received their first assignment.

The Senate also prohibited a senator from serving as chairman of more than one committee at the same time; prohibited a senator from serving as chairman of more than one subcommittee on each committee of which he was a member; prohibited the chairman of a major committee from serving as chairman of more than one subcommittee on his major committees and as the chairman of more than one subcommittee on his minor committee, effective at the beginning of the 96th Congress; prohibited the chairman of a minor committee from chairing a subcommittee on that committee and prohibited him from chairing more than one of each of his major committees' subcommittees, which also took effect at the beginning of the the 96th Congress.

The Senate in addition banned any committee from establishing a subcommittee without approval of the full Senate and required the Rules Committee to establish a central computerized scheduling service to keep track of meetings of Senate committees and subcommittees and House-Senate conference committees.

In a change related to staffing, the Senate required the staff of each committee to reflect the relative size of the minority and majority membership on the committee. On the request of the minority members of a committee, at least one-third of the staff of the committee was to be placed under the control of the minority party, except that staff deemed by the chairman and ranking minority member to be working for the whole committee would not be subject to the rule.

Committee Changes in the 1980s

Few rules changes affecting the committee system were made at the outset of the 97th Congress. Party ratios on Senate committees were altered to reflect the GOP takeover of the Senate following the 1980 elections. But because of substantial Democratic electoral losses (resulting in many committee vacancies) only one surviving Democrat actually lost a committee assignment.

House Democrats, in a reversal of the 1970s trend, amended their caucus rules by voting to limit the number of subcommittees and similar committee sub-units that could be established by the House's standing committees. The change had been informally decided upon in 1979. Under the 1981 caucus change, the Rules and Ways and Means committees could have up to six subcommittees and Appropriations was allowed to retain all of its 13 panels. All other standing committees were restricted to a maximum of eight or the number it had as of 1981, whichever was fewer. The new rule affected four committees: Education and Labor, Agriculture, Budget and Banking — all of which had more than eight.

The caucus also waived a party rule limiting members of the Judiciary and District of Columbia committees to only one other legislative committee assignment.

In 1984 the Senate created a select panel, headed by Sen. Dan Quayle, R-Ind., to study the growth in committees and committee assignments. In its final report, issued Dec. 15, 1984, the panel contended that the twin problems of the proliferation of committees and their attention to unimportant details needed to be resolved.

Changing Subcommittee Role

The term "committee government" has long been used to describe the policy-making process on Capitol Hill. But as Davidson has observed, "[T]oday, the term 'subcommittee government' is nearer the mark." [40]

Subcommittees now handle most of the day-to-day legislative and oversight workload of Congress. The growth in the influence of subcommittees has been attributed to several factors: "complex problems requiring specialization; interest groups' demands for subcommittees to handle their subject area; members' desires to chair subcommittees to initiate lawmaking and oversight, augment personal prestige and influence, acquire staff and office space, and gain a national platform; and majority Democrats' desire in the early 1970s to circumscribe the power of chairmen, and to 'spread the action' to more junior members." [41]

The trend toward "subcommittee government" came earlier in the Senate than in the House. The transformation has been described by Davidson as "relatively peaceful." The process was launched by the so-called Johnson Rule in 1953 when then-majority leader Lyndon Johnson initiated a plan whereby each freshman senator was given at least one major committee assignment. The process was expanded by the "open, benign leadership" of Mike Mansfield, D-Mont. (1953-77). [42]

The changeover in the House was much more difficult and acrimonious. A move to strengthen the autonomy of House subcommittees began in 1971 and culminated in

decisions taken by the Democrats in the winter of 1974-75 that allowed subcommittee chairmen and ranking minority members to hire their own staffs and forced the Ways and Means Committee to establish subcommittees.

House Subcommittees

Until the early 1970s, House subcommittees generally did not play a dominant role in the legislative process. Major exceptions were the Appropriations subcommittees and the Banking Committee's housing subcommittee. The former were organized to parallel the executive departments and agencies, and most of the annual budget review was done at that level. The staggering size and complexity of the federal budget required each subcommittee to develop an expertise and an autonomy respected and rarely challenged by other subcommittees or by the full committee.

The housing subcommittee had a long tradition of independent operation. For many years it had control of its own budget and was able to hire and retain a widely respected staff.

Although the Legislative Reorganization Act of 1946 made drastic reductions in the number of House standing committees, it spawned an explosion at the subcommittee level. In the 80th Congress alone, the 19 standing committees that remained following the 1946 act's pruning spawned more than 100 subcommittees.

The creation of a larger network of subcommittees in the years following the 1946 act did not mean that power automatically gravitated there, however. Until the early 1970s, most House committees were run by chairmen who were able to retain much of the authority for themselves and a few trusted senior members, while giving little to junior members or subcommittees.

Those chairmen could dominate committees because they had the backing of Speaker Sam Rayburn and Speaker John W. McCormack, D-Mass. (1928-71), and the support, or at least the acquiescence, of their panels' members. They could pack subcommittees with members who would do their bidding, define the subcommittees' jurisdictions and what legislation they would consider, decide when they would meet and make the decisions on how much staff, if any, subcommittees could have.

Revival of the Democratic Caucus

The day of the dominant committee chairman began to wane with the revival of the House Democratic Caucus in 1969 and the retirement of McCormack as Speaker at the end of the 1970 session. With McCormack's departure, these chairmen lost a powerful ally at the top of the House leadership structure.

The caucus revival meant that moderate and liberal Democrats elected to the House in the 1960s, who were frustrated by the operation of a committee system that tended to freeze them out of power, at last had a vehicle to change House procedures. Their actions were directed at undercutting the power of committee chairmen and strengthening the role of the subcommittees, where the opportunity lay for them to gain a greater role and make an impact on the legislative process.

The drive had a sharp generational edge. Many middle-ranking Democrats elected in the late 1950s and 1960s were allied against the senior members and the leadership. Between 1958 and 1970, 293 Democrats entered the House.

Between 1970 and 1974, another 150 Democrats were elected. From this group, many of whom tended to be more moderate or liberal than their predecessors, sprang the pressure for reform.

By the beginning of the 94th Congress (1975), Democrats who had been elected since 1958 held 108 of the 146 subcommittee chairmanships on House standing and select committees. Many of those members would have received subcommittee chairmanships even if the reforms had not been adopted, because they had accrued enough seniority. What the reforms did, however, was to give them real power when they finally took over a subcommittee.

Between 1971 and 1975, the old committee structure underwent many changes. During those four years a series of innovations was approved by the Democratic Caucus that guaranteed junior and middle-ranking Democrats greater power on subcommittees. The thrust of the changes was twofold: the authority of committee chairmen was curbed, and that of subcommittee leaders was strengthened. By 1976 subcommittees were displaying more independence, and subcommittee chairmen were playing a more active role in House floor action.

Committee Chairmen

The powers of the committee chairmen, the principal losers in the House power struggle, were pared in several ways: through changes in House rules and, more importantly, in the decisions adopted by the Democratic Caucus. All of the caucus innovations reordering committee operations were dependent, of course, on the Democratic Party remaining the majority in the House. The following decisions had the greatest impact on the committee system:

1. No Democratic member could be chairman of more than one legislative subcommittee. That change made it possible to break the hold of the more conservative senior Democrats on key subcommittees, and it gradually made middle-level and even some junior Democrats eligible for subcommittee chairmanships. Adopted at the beginning of the 92nd Congress, that rule in its first year resulted in 16 relatively young Democrats — those elected since 1958 — getting their first subcommittee chairmanships on key committees such as Judiciary, Foreign Affairs and Banking, Currency and Housing.

2. Subcommittee members were protected by a "bill of rights" adopted by the caucus in 1973. The new rules established a Democratic caucus (the Democratic committee members) on each House committee and forced chairmen to begin sharing authority with the panel's other Democrats. That was made necessary because the committee caucus was given the authority to select subcommittee chairmen, establish subcommittee jurisdictions, set party ratios on subcommittees that reflected the ratios on the full committees and provide the budgets for running the subcommittees. Also, a caucus rule was added at this time promising more choice subcommittee assignments to younger Democrats.

Committee chairmen no longer could kill legislation by quietly pocketing it. They had to refer bills to subcommittees within two weeks, unless they were to be handled by the full committee.

3. All committees with more than 20 members were required to establish at least four subcommittees. This was directed at Ways and Means, which had operated without subcommittees during most of Wilbur Mills' 16-year chair-

manship. It also established an important House precedent by institutionalizing subcommittees for the first time.

4. Another change was in subcommittee staffing. Subcommittee chairmen and the ranking minority members were authorized to hire one staff person each to work directly for them on their subcommittees.

5. Committees were required to operate through written rules. This also helped to check the arbitrary power of committee chairmen and to institutionalize subcommittees.

6. The Democratic Caucus in January 1975 specified that no Democrat could become a member of a second subcommittee on any full committee until every member of the full committee had chosen one subcommittee position. (Members on existing subcommittees, however, could protect two subcommittee slots. But this protection was eliminated in 1979.) The caucus decision was aimed principally at the House Appropriations Committee, where senior conservative Democrats dominated important subcommittees handling the budgets for defense, agriculture, labor, health, education and welfare programs.

7. In 1975 nominees for the subcommittee chairmanships of the Appropriations Committee were required to go before the caucus for approval.

8. In 1979 a caucus rule was adopted limiting each Democrat to five subcommittee seats on House committees. In addition, the caucus decided that the bidding for subcommittee chairmanships (except Appropriations) would be based on a member's seniority rank on the full committee. The procedure worked as follows: The majority party member with the most seniority would have the first crack at bidding for an open subcommittee chairmanship. If he did not receive a majority vote of the full committee, the member next in line in seniority could bid for the post. This procedure would continue down through the majority party membership until someone was elected. (Appropriations subcommittee chairmen are nominated by the members of each subcommittee. But unlike subcommittee chairmen on other committees, they must be confirmed by the Democratic Caucus.)

Impact of Subcommittee Changes

These reforms affected House committees differently. They had little effect on some, such as Agriculture, which had a tradition of largely autonomous subcommittees and good relations between the committee chairman and the membership.

The impact was much greater on those committees that had a tradition of strong central direction. In those cases — particularly Ways and Means, Interstate and Foreign Commerce (now Energy and Commerce), Interior and Insular Affairs, Foreign Affairs, Judiciary and Public Works (now Public Works and Transportation) were prime examples — the committees tended to become fragmented, with the chairman exercising much less control over the full committee, and the subcommittees assuming more independence over the legislative agenda.

Subcommittee chairmen also gained more influence on the House floor. In many cases, they began to replace the committee chairmen in managing legislation.

Increased Workload. The proliferation of subcommittees resulted in greatly increased demands on members. Subcommittees began holding more hearings, drafting more bills and handling more legislation on the floor. To meet the problem of subcommittee proliferation and to lessen members' workloads, both chambers in the late

House GOP May Alter Assignment System

A nasty battle over committee assignments for the 100th Congress left lasting bruises among House Republicans and prompted Minority Leader Robert H. Michel, R-Ill., to set up a task force to consider changes in the assignment process.

Committee assignments for the Congress, which were made in late 1986 and early 1987, split the Republican Conference between large states and small states, and put Michel on the losing end of a power play by a coalition that included the No. 2 GOP leader, Minority Whip Trent Lott of Mississippi.

Committee assignments can have a critical effect on a lawmaker's career in the House, where most legislative work is done in committee and members' ability to influence bills on the floor is very limited.

Competition is particularly fierce among Republicans, because the minority party has proportionately fewer positions on the most desirable committees to distribute among its members.

Sandbagging the Big States

The Republicans' system for filling vacancies was mysterious even to some members. It departed in significant respects from the committee-assignment process used by House Democrats.

"It's not a system that weighs qualifications or merit," said Vin Weber, a Minnesota Republican who has been both victim and victor in the process since the last Congress. "It leaves deep and lasting divisions in the conference."

Republican assignments are ratified by the GOP Committee on Committees, which includes one representative from each state that has at least one Republican in the House. But that group, a 50-member panel in the 100th Congress, is considered unworkably large, so the real job of parceling out assignments is done by the panel's executive committee, a 20-member subgroup.

Unlike the Democratic Steering and Policy Committee, where each member casts one vote on proposed assignments, members of the GOP executive panel cast votes weighted according to the number of Republicans in the state delegations they represent. This process long has been dominated by members from states with large delegations, such as California and Illinois.

But when committee slots were doled out for the 100th Congress, representatives of small states for the first time coordinated their strategies and slates. They banded together, enlisted the support of Texas members, and put together a working coalition that outvoted the big-state delegations and won choice assignments for their own candidates.

"It was as naked a power play as you can have around here," said Tom Tauke, R-Iowa, who helped engineer the small-state coalition. But he described the ploy as simply turning the tables on the big states, which had succeeded in placing their candidates on the best committees two years earlier.

"We were just as fair as they had been before," said Tauke. "Our premise was to make everyone see the need to make changes."

When a cohesive coalition is formed, "it's become a winner-take-all process," said Weber, who lost a bid for a seat on the Appropriations Committee in the 99th Congress when big states dominated. Weber was a beneficiary of the small-state strategy this year, when he won an Appropriations seat along with Jim Kolbe of Arizona and Thomas D. DeLay of Texas.

Candidates backed by Michel and other big-state representatives consistently lost out to members from small states for the most sought-after committees. Among the losers was Michel's candidate for the Appropriations Committee, Lynn Martin of Illinois.

Lott helped put together the small-state strategy, because he believed that "the small-state people have not fared as well as they should have." Although the incident was seen as a blow to Michel and created tensions between him and Lott, both men rejected the view that it was a challenge to Michel's leadership.

Changes Coming

The task force Michel set up to look into possible changes in the system is headed by Californian Robert J. Lagomarsino, who said one possible change might be to codify rules limiting the number of sought-after committees on which a member may sit.

Michel said such restrictions were informally adopted in making assignments for the 100th Congress to "spread the wealth around and keep members from getting on two good committees."

Both Lott and Michel have suggested that it might be desirable to give the GOP leadership more clout in the committee assignment process, moving closer to the system used by House Democrats in their leadership-dominated Steering and Policy Committee.

But Lott added that the leadership should not have absolute control. "Then they would have outright blame," when members face the disappointment of not getting a desired committee slot, he said.

"It's unlikely we'll have the same system the next time around," said Tauke. "But there's no way to insulate the system from some power plays."

1970s placed limits on the number of subcommittees each committee is allowed.

With the expansion of subcommittees came a steady increase in the amount of time members had to devote to subcommittee responsibilities. In 1947 the average senator served on two or three subcommittees; by 1976 he held 14 subcommittee assignments.

"Proliferation of committee panels means proliferation in assignments held by Senators. And the burdens and frustrations of too many assignments, whatever the benefits, produce inefficient division of labor, uneven distribution of responsibility, conflicts in the scheduling of meetings, waste of Senators' and staff time, unsystematic lawmaking and oversight, inadequate anticipation of major problems, and inadequate membership participation in committee decisions," stated a report of the Select Committee to Study the Senate Committee System, the panel that recommended the 1977 reorganization.[43]

As part of the 1977 reorganization, the Senate prohibited a senator from serving as chairman of more than one subcommittee on any committee on which he served. This, in effect, placed an indirect cap on subcommittee expansion by limiting the number of subcommittees of any committee to the number of majority party members on the full committee.

Senators also were allowed on only three subcommittees of each major committee on which they served (the Appropriations Committee was exempted from the limit) and on only two subcommittees of their minor committee.

The House Select Committee on Committees (the Patterson Committee) in a 1979 report emphasized the magnitude of the problem in the House: "On no other issue concerning committee system revision has the Select Committee on Committees found greater agreement on the part of a wider spectrum of Members, staffs, and students of Congress than that there are too many subcommittees in the House and that Members have too many subcommittee assignments."[44]

The Patterson committee said the proliferation of subcommittees had decentralized and fragmented the policy process and had limited members' capacity to master their work.

The number of subcommittees of House standing committees had increased from 69 in the 82nd Congress (1951-53) to 146 in the 96th Congress (1979-81). While the average number of committee/subcommittee assignments per member in 1979 was 6.2, a total of 223 members had seven or more committee/subcommittee assignments.

The Patterson committee proposed limiting each House member to a maximum of five subcommittee assignments, and — on a phased-in basis — limiting each House standing committee, except Appropriations, to a total of six subcommittees. The plan was approved by the Republican Conference, but the Democratic Caucus insisted on reviewing the proposal and it was never acted upon. The Democratic Caucus voted in December 1978 to limit Democrats to five subcommittee assignments on standing committees.

Reacting to repeated waivers of the five-subcommittee rule by the Steering and Policy Committee, the Democratic Caucus in 1987 agreed to a new restriction. The rule would now bar waivers with two exceptions: service on more than five subcommittees was allowed for members whose three full committee assignments included the less desirable District of Columbia, House Administration and Judiciary committees, or for members who were named to a full committee temporarily for the 100th Congress.

1981 Decisions Reverse Trend. In January 1981 the caucus limited the number of subcommittees or task forces that could be established by House standing committees in the 97th Congress. Under the caucus rules change, the Rules and Ways and Means committees were allowed to have up to six subcommittees while Appropriations could retain all 13 of its subcommittees. All other standing committees were limited to no more than eight subcommittees or the number of subcommittees they had as of Jan. 1, 1981, whichever was fewer. Affected were the Education and Labor, Agriculture, Budget and Banking committees, all of which had more than eight subcommittees in the 96th Congress.

A committee with more than 35 members and fewer than six subcommittees could increase the number to six if it so desired.

Footnotes

1. Clarence Cannon, *Cannon's Procedure in the House of Representatives* (Washington, D.C.: U.S. Government Printing Office, 1963), 221.
2. Roger H. Davidson, "Subcommittee Government: New Channels for Policy Making," in *The New Congress* ed. Thomas E. Mann and Norman J. Ornstein (Washington, D.C.: American Enterprise Institute for Public Policy Research, 1981), 99.
3. See George Goodwin Jr., *The Little Legislatures* (Amherst: University of Massachusetts Press, 1970).
4. Woodrow Wilson, *Congressional Government* (Cleveland: Meridian edition, 1956), 59.
5. Roger H. Davidson and Walter J. Oleszek, *Congress and Its Members*, 2d ed. (Washington, D.C.: CQ Press, 1985), 222.
6. *Congress and the Nation*, vol. 5 (Washington, D.C.: Congressional Quarterly, 1981), 881.
7. On the role of subcommittees, see Goodwin, *The Little Legislatures*, 50-59; Davidson, "Subcommittee Government," 99-133.
8. Stephen K. Bailey, *The New Congress* (New York: St. Martin's Press, 1966), 55.
9. On jurisdictional conflicts, see William L. Morrow, *Congressional Committees* (New York: Charles Scribner's Sons, 1969), 20.
10. Walter J. Oleszek, *Congressional Procedures and the Policy Process*, 2d ed. (Washington, D.C.: CQ Press, 1984), 77.
11. Oleszek, *Congressional Procedures*, 2d ed., 78.
12. Davidson and Oleszek, *Congress and Its Members*, 1st ed., 218-219.
13. Background and discussion of assignment process, see Goodwin, *The Little Legislatures*, 69-100.
14. On selection of members, cf. Randall B. Ripley, *Congress: Process and Policy* (New York: W. W. Norton & Co., 1975), 96 ff.; Davidson and Oleszek, *Congress and Its Members*, 2d ed., 214-221.
15. Davidson and Oleszek, *Congress and Its Members*, 2d ed., 221.
16. Oleszek, *Congressional Procedures and the Policy Process*, 2d ed., 225.
17. Davidson and Oleszek, *Congress and Its Members*, 2d ed., 337-342.
18. Oleszek, *Congressional Procedures*, 2d ed., 227-235.
19. Davidson and Oleszek, *Congress and Its Members*, 2d ed., 340.
20. Davidson and Oleszek, *Congress and Its Members*, 340-341.
21. Davidson and Oleszek, *Congress and Its Members*, 340-341.
22. George B. Galloway, *Congress at the Crossroads* (New York: Thomas Y. Crowell Co., 1946), 88.
23. On the evolution of the committee system, see Galloway, *Congress at the Crossroads*, 127-131, and Goodwin, *The Little Legislatures*, 10.
24. Galloway, *Congress*, 139-144; Goodwin, *The Little Legislatures*, 11-12.
25. Galloway, *Congress*, 127, 137.

26. George H. Haynes, *The Senate of the United States* (Boston: Houghton Mifflin Co., 1938), 273 ff.
27. Haynes, *The Senate,* 277.
28. Wilson, *Congressional Government,* 82.
29. Galloway, *Congress,* 135.
30. Galloway, *Congress,* 129-130.
31. Haynes, *The Senate,* 284
32. For a concise discussion of the 1946 act, see Goodwin, *The Little Legislatures,* 18-22.
33. For details on 1970 reorganization, see *Congress and the Nation,* vol. 3 (Washington, D.C.: Congressional Quarterly, 1973), 382-396.
34. For details on 1974 House reforms, see *Congressional Quarterly Almanac 1974* (Washington, D.C.: Congressional Quarterly, 1975), 634-641.
35. For details, see *Congressional Quarterly Almanac 1977* (Washington, D.C.: Congressional Quarterly, 1978), 792-797.
36. House Commission on Administrative Review, *Administrative Reorganization and Legislative Management; Vol. 2: Work Management,* 95th Cong., 1st sess., (Washington, D.C.: U.S. Government Printing Office, 1977), 38.
37. For details, see *Congressional Quarterly Almanac 1979* (Washington, D.C.: Congressional Quarterly, 1980), 595-597, and *Congressional Quarterly Almanac 1980,* (Washington, D.C.: Congressional Quarterly, 1981), 562-563.
38. House Select Committee on Committees, *Final Report of the Select Committee on Committees,* H Rept 96-866, 96th Cong., 2d sess., 1980, 2.
39. For details, see *Congressional Quarterly Almanac 1977,* 781-790.
40. Davidson, "Subcommittee Government," 99.
41. Davidson and Oleszek, *Congress and Its Members,* 2d ed., 212.
42. Davidson, "Subcommittee Government," 107.
43. Senate Temporary Select Committee to Study the Senate Committee System, *Structure of the Senate Committee System: Jurisdictions, Numbers and Sizes, and Limitations on Memberships and Chairmanships, Referral Procedures, and Scheduling,* 94th Cong., 2d sess. (Washington, D.C.: U.S. Government Printing Office, 1976), 6.
44. House Select Committee on Committees, *Limitations on the Number of Subcommittees and Subcommittee Assignments,* Committee print, 96th Cong., 2d sess., 1980, 1.

Selected Bibliography

Books

Cooper, Joseph. *The Origin of the Standing Committees and the Development of the Modern House.* Houston, Texas: William Marsh Rice University, 1971.
Davidson, Roger H. "Subcommittee Government: New Channels for Policy Making." In *The New Congress,* edited by Thomas E. Mann and Norman J. Ornstein. Washington, D. C.: American Enterprise Institute for Public Policy Research, 1981.
———. "Two Avenues of Change: House and Senate Committee Reorganization." In *Congress Reconsidered,* 2d ed., edited by Lawrence C. Dodd and Bruce I. Oppenheimer. Washington, D.C.: CQ Press, 1981.
Davidson, Roger H., and Walter J. Oleszek. *Congress and Its Members,* 2d ed. Washington, D.C.: CQ Press, 1985.
Deering, Christopher J., and Steven S. Smith. "Subcommittees in Congress." In *Congress Reconsidered,* 3d ed., edited by Lawrence C. Dodd and Bruce I. Oppenheimer. Washington, D.C.: CQ Press, 1985.
Dodd, Lawrence C., and Richard L. Schott. *Congress and the Administrative State.* New York: John Wiley and Sons, 1979.

Fenno, Richard F., Jr. *Congressmen in Committees.* Boston: Little, Brown and Co., 1973.
Goodwin, George. *The Little Legislatures: Committees of Congress.* Amherst: University of Massachusetts Press, 1970.
Gross, Bertram M. *The Legislative Struggle.* New York: McGraw-Hill, 1953.
Haynes, George H. *The Senate of the United States.* 2 vols. Boston: Houghton Mifflin Co., 1938.
McConachie, Lauros. *Congressional Committees.* New York: Thomas Y. Crowell Co., 1898.
McGown, Ada C. *The Congressional Conference Committee.* New York: Columbia University Press, 1927.
Morrow, William L. *Congressional Committees.* New York: Charles Scribner's Sons, 1969.
Ogul, Morris S. "Congressional Oversight: Structures and Incentives." In *Congress Reconsidered,* 2d ed., edited by Lawrence C. Dodd and Bruce I. Oppenheimer. Washington, D.C.: CQ Press, 1981.
———. *Congress Oversees the Bureaucracy.* Pittsburgh: University of Pittsburgh Press, 1976.
Oleszek, Walter J. *Congressional Procedures and the Policy Process,* 2d ed. Washington, D.C.: CQ Press, 1984.
Oppenheimer, Bruce I. "The Changing Relationship Between House Leadership and the Committee on Rules." In *Understanding Congressional Leadership,* edited by Frank H. Mackaman. Washington, D.C.: CQ Press, 1981.
Price, David E. "Congressional Committees in the Policy Process." In *Congress Reconsidered,* 3d ed., edited by Lawrence C. Dodd and Bruce I. Oppenheimer. Washington, D.C.: CQ Press, 1985.
Ripley, Randall B. *Power in the Senate.* New York: St. Martin's Press, 1969.
Robinson, James A. *The House Rules Committee.* Indianapolis: Bobbs-Merrill Co., 1963.
Shepsle, Kenneth A. *The Giant Jigsaw Puzzle: Democratic Committee Assignments in the Modern House.* Chicago: University of Chicago Press, 1978.
Smith, Steven S., and Christopher J. Deering. *Committees in Congress.* Washington, D.C.: CQ Press, 1984.
Volger, David. *The Third House: Conference Committees in the United States Congress.* Evanston, Ill.: Northwestern University Press, 1971.

Articles

Asher, Herbert B. "Committees and the Norm of Specialization." *Annals of the American Academy of Political and Social Science* (January 1974): 63-74.
Davidson, Roger H. "Representation and Congressional Committees." *Annals of the American Academy of Political and Social Science* (January 1974): 48-52.
Eckhardt, Bob. "The Presumption of Committee Openness Under House Rules." *Harvard Journal on Legislation* (February 1974): 279-302.
Haeberle, Steven H. "The Institutionalization of the Subcommittee in the United States House of Representatives." *Journal of Politics* (November 1978): 1054-1065.
Masters, Nicholas A. "Committee Assignments in the House of Representatives." *American Political Science Review* 55 (1961): 345-357.
Ornstein, Norman J. "Towards Restructuring the Congressional Committee System." *Annals of the American Academy of Political and Social Science* (January

1974): 133-146.

Parris, Judith H. "The Senate Reorganizes Its Committees: 1977." *Political Science Quarterly* (Summer 1979): 319-337.

Peabody, Robert L. "Committees from the Leadership Perspective: Party Leadership in the House." *Annals of the American Academy of Political and Social Science* (January 1974): 133-146.

Rohde, David W. "Committee Reform in the House of Representatives and the Subcommittee Bill of Rights." *Annals of the American Academy of Political and Social Science* (January 1974): 39-47.

Wolanin, Thomas R. "Committee Seniority and the Choice of House Subcommittee Chairmen." *Journal of Politics* (August 1974): 687-702.

Government Publications

U.S. Congress. House. Commission on Administrative Review. *Administrative Reorganization and Legislative Management.* 95th Cong., 1st sess., 1977. H Doc 95-232.

U.S. Congress. House. Commission on Administrative Review. *Final Report.* 95th Cong., 1st sess., 1977. H Doc 95-272.

U.S. Congress. House. Committee on Government Operations. *Oversight Plans of the Committees of the U.S. House of Representatives.* 94th Cong., 1st sess., 1975. H Rept 94-61.

U.S. Congress. House. Select Committee on Committees. *Committee Reform Amendments of 1974.* 93d Cong., 2d sess., 1974. H Rept 93-916.

U.S. Congress. House. Select Committee on Committees. *Hearings on Committee Organization in the House.* 93d Cong., 1st sess., 1973. Reissued 94th Cong., 1st sess., 1975. H Doc 94-187. 3 vols.

U.S. Congress. House. Select Committee on Committees. *Final Report of Select Committee on Committees.* 96th Cong., 2d sess., 1980. H Rept 96-866.

U.S. Congress. House. *Workshop on Congressional Oversight and Investigations, Dec. 1, 6, 7, 1978.* 96th Cong., 1st sess., 1979. H Doc 96-217.

U.S. Congress. Senate. Commission on the Operation of the Senate. *Toward a Modern Senate.* 94th Cong., 2d sess., 1976. S Doc 94-278.

U.S. Congress. Senate. Office of Senate Legal Counsel. *Manual on Senate Committee Rules and Procedures.* February 1981.

U.S. Congress. Senate. Temporary Select Committee to Study the Senate Committee System. *First Report, With Recommendations; Structure of the Senate Committee System: Jurisdictions, Numbers and Sizes, and Limitations on Memberships and Chairmanships, Referral, Procedures, and Scheduling.* 94th Cong., 2d sess., 1976. S Rept 94-1395.

The Influential Committees

When Sen.-elect Thomas A. Daschle got his committee assignments for the 100th Congress, it was a freshman's dream come true. The South Dakota Democrat won places on three of the four committees he applied for, including a prize rarely awarded to newcomers: a seat on the Finance Committee, one of the most prestigious panels in Congress.

That was a far cry from the experience of an ambitious freshman senator at the turn of the century. When Robert M. La Follette, R (1906-25), sought a seat on the Interstate Commerce Committee, the Wisconsin progressive wound up on seven minor committees, including one investigating the condition of the Potomac River front.

La Follette was elected at a time when the Senate had some 55 standing committees, but even in that plethora of panels he could see where the real power lay. "Of first importance is the great Finance Committee, which has charge of all bills affecting the tariff, currency and banking," he wrote.

Three-quarters of a century later, when the 100th Congress convened Jan. 6, 1987, Finance remained one of a handful of committees at the center of power.

Some panels wax and wane, but Finance, Appropriations and Ways and Means are never wholly eclipsed because they control the flow of money into and out of federal coffers. Their institutional clout may pale in comparison to what they once had: Until 1975, Ways and Means made all committee assignments for Democratic members. And the Appropriations Committee before 1974 had fewer institutional constraints in determining federal spending.

But legislatively, other forces were at work in the 100th Congress that would enhance the power of that charmed circle of committees. Their members were the dominant voices in debate on the leading issues of the day: deficit reduction and trade.

And these taxing and spending committees were thrust to the center of action more than ever before by Congress' increasing tendency to pile most of its legislative work onto a handful of essential fiscal measures. Those on panels that draft omnibus bills — such as continuing appropriations resolutions and debt limit legislation — enjoy privileged access to the bulk of Congress' work.

"Life outside those committees can be pretty dreary," said Rep. Thomas J. Downey, D-N.Y., a Ways and Means member who also served on Budget in the 99th Congress. "It's like a coal mine — only the people in the car have access to the coal."

Issues of the Moment

While the importance of money committees is as enduring as death and taxes, other committees' influence rises and falls as the national agenda shifts. For example, the now-quiescent House Education and Labor Committee had its days in the sun in the 1960s, when Congress was enacting landmark school aid laws; the Senate Energy Committee shone in the 1970s when energy policy was a major economic issue.

In the 100th Congress, trade was shaping up as an ascendant issue. Democratic leaders in both the House and Senate identified it as a top priority. A sign of its political sex appeal was the scramble among committee leaders for jurisdiction over trade legislation.

House Energy and Commerce Committee Chairman John D. Dingell, D-Mich., an aggressive chairman known for his skill at grabbing new jurisdictional territory, was expected to move to expand his panel's authority over trade. And while the Finance Committee has primary jurisdiction over trade in the Senate, Commerce Committee Chairman Ernest F. Hollings, D-S.C., also wanted to get into the act.

The attraction of the panels involved in trade and fiscal matters was reflected in the committee preferences filed with the Democratic Steering Committee by the 1987 freshman class of Senate Democrats: They overwhelmingly requested assignments to the Finance, Appropriations and Commerce committees.

"There might as well be only three committees around this place, as far as these new members are concerned," an aide to a Steering Committee member says. "You might as well take Labor, Judiciary and the others and put them off in another building."

Democrats in Charge

The balance of power among committees in the 100th Congress was thought likely to be affected by the Democrats' return to majority status in the Senate, under the leadership of Robert C. Byrd of West Virginia, and the reshuffling of the House Democratic leadership in the wake of the retirement of Speaker Thomas P. O'Neill Jr. of Massachusetts.

In the Senate, the change of party control brought in a new team of committee chairmen. Although it was not known whether the personnel change would do much to enhance or detract from the dominance of such committees as Finance or Appropriations, it could make a substantial difference on others.

For example, some observers questioned whether mild-mannered, patrician Claiborne Pell, D-R.I., would as Foreign Relations chairman be able to maintain the influence and prestige the panel regained under the 1985-86 chairmanship of Richard G. Lugar, R-Ind., after a decade of decline.

Another key question was whether the Democratic-dominated Senate committees were going to "run in all directions or whether there would be some sense of coordinated effort," said Richard F. Fenno Jr., a political scientist at the University of Rochester who has studied congressional committees.

Challenges in 1984 and 1986 to Byrd's re-election as Democratic leader were likely to increase pressure on him to assert stronger leadership and coordinate the legislative agenda. But his past performance as majority leader from 1977-80 as a guide, he was expected to give his committee chairmen wide latitude to set their own agendas and build the party consensus from them.

"The key question about these guys is always, do they want a real leader or someone to make the trains run?" said a former top Democratic staffer. "Byrd has been an adjudicator of powerful chairmen."

A different tack in the House was anticipated from the new Speaker, Jim Wright of Texas, who indicated that he intended to exercise the leadership's agenda-setting authority more aggressively than O'Neill. Some Democrats feared that approach would result in a clash with committee chairmen, but others pointed to Wright's 1986 success in engineering passage of omnibus anti-drug, trade and anti-terrorism bills that spanned several committee jurisdictions.

Wright's ascension was also likely to affect the committee most closely associated with Democratic leaders — Rules, which is considered essentially an arm of the Speaker's office. The changing of the guard could mean a tighter rein on the committee, which had a relatively free hand toward the end of O'Neill's tenure, according to Rules member David E. Bonior, D-Mich.

"Especially in the last two years, we've developed more of a sense of independence because Tip left us on our own to do whatever we wanted," said Bonior, who was named by Wright as chief deputy whip. "I expect Jim will want to put his imprimatur on us to an extent."

Sources of Power

Although Democrats' control of Congress could bring some new life to authorizing committees that were inhibited in the past six years by Republican control of the Senate, the yawning federal deficit would still keep domestic initiatives in check.

"What the budget process has done to the whole situation is devalue all the committees," said Rep. David E. Price, a freshman Democrat from North Carolina who, as a political science professor at Duke University, studied the congressional committee system. "Even Ways and Means and Appropriations are less autonomous, but they have a piece of the action in a way that authorizing committees don't."

An exception, Price said, was the House Energy and Commerce Committee, which had grown in influence and was a testament to enduring sources of committee power:

an expansive jurisdictional reach and an aggressive chairman.

As the scope of congressional activity was sharply reduced by budget constraints, a committee's ability to claim a piece of whatever action there was had grown in importance.

"Increasingly the John Dingells of this world are going to build power bases by taking a piece of everybody's jurisdiction and making sure that every bill goes through the Energy and Commerce Committee," Rep. Bob Edgar, D-Pa., said. Edgar lost his 1986 bid for a Senate seat.

Dingell had been known as the most assertive chairman in the House since he took over his post from Harley O. Staggers, D-W.Va. (1949-81), in 1981. Energy and Commerce had the largest staff and budget of any House committee in the 100th Congress.

Energy and Commerce laid claim to legislation touching major regulatory agencies, nuclear energy, toxic wastes, health research, Medicaid and Medicare, railroad retirement, telecommunications, tourism and commerce.

The committee also had one of the most active oversight subcommittees in the House.

"Everything that moves comes under the jurisdiction of Energy and Commerce," said panel member Jim Slattery, D-Kan.

The payoff for members was not just in the currency of legislative influence: The committee also seemed to be a veritable magnet for campaign contributions.

According to Common Cause, the self-styled citizens' lobby, Energy and Commerce members in the 98th Congress received, on average, more political action committee contributions than members of any other House committee.

A broad jurisdictional reach also was part of the appeal of Appropriations and Budget, which oversaw the full range of federal activity.

"Appropriations is involved in everything the government does," said House committee member Mickey Edwards, R-Okla. "Its (members have) a mandate or license to get involved in virtually anything the government spends money for."

The tax-writing committees handled not just the flow of all revenues into the federal Treasury, but also billions in federal spending for major entitlement programs, including Medicare, unemployment compensation, Social Security and welfare.

Programs under Ways and Means' jurisdiction accounted for 37.8 percent of the total federal outlays in fiscal 1985 — up from 25.3 percent in fiscal 1970. Finance's reach spread even farther because, unlike Ways and Means, the Senate panel also had control over Medicaid.

"Finance has a huge jurisdiction," said outgoing Senate Budget Committee Chairman Pete V. Domenici, R-N.M., "and jurisdiction is power."

Tax Panels: Where the Action Is

Even if the Ways and Means and Finance committees were to keep their implicit promise not to make major tax changes in the wake of the 1986 landmark overhaul of the tax code, their broad jurisdiction ensured they would continue in a leading role in the 100th Congress.

Retiring Senator Thomas F. Eagleton, D-Mo., who was a member of the Appropriations Committee for much of his Senate career, said, "The power committee now is Finance. That's where the action is now and in the future."

Recalling that Finance and Appropriations were more on a par when he first came to the Senate in 1968, Eagleton said he would choose to sit on the tax-writing panel if he had his congressional career to do over.

"The real policy decisions of the next decade are going to be centered at Ways and Means — Medicare financing, Social Security, entitlements," said Rep. Buddy MacKay, D-Fla., a Budget Committee member who lobbied unsuccessfully for more than a year for a Ways and Means seat in the 100th Congress. "Long-term health care for the elderly is the next regularly scheduled crisis."

Ways and Means' and Finance's jurisdiction over major entitlement programs meant they would continue to be central forces in deficit-reduction initiatives. These panels had been the major contributors to budget "reconciliation" packages — omnibus legislation that makes spending cuts mandated by the annual budget resolution.

In addition, these two would be the lead committees handling welfare reform and catastrophic health insurance, the only major domestic initiatives that both Congress and Reagan administration officials expressed interest in tackling.

They also had jurisdiction over legislation to raise the federal debt ceiling — one of the few "must-pass" bills that in recent years had become vehicles for scores of legislative initiatives that might not have passed on their own.

But for all its influence, even Ways and Means had seen its role fluctuate with stronger and weaker chairmen. Under the chairmanship of Wilbur D. Mills, D-Ark. (1939-77), from 1958 through 1974, Ways and Means enjoyed almost unchallenged authority over legislation under its jurisdiction — a tribute in part to Mills' long tenure and command of tax law.

His successor, Al Ullman, D-Ore. (1957-81), who was chairman from 1975-81, was a weaker leader, and the committee became more fractious. This contributed to embarrassing defeats on the floor during debate on Ways and Means bills.

In the early years of President Reagan's tenure, with Ways and Means chaired by Dan Rostenkowski, D-Ill., the initiative on tax matters came mostly from the Senate and the Reagan administration. But Rostenkowski went a long way toward restoring the committee's status with his firm handling of the 1986 tax-overhaul legislation, whose final shape he negotiated practically one-on-one with Senate Finance Chairman Bob Packwood, R-Ore.

"Rostenkowski has brought Ways and Means back to a position of prominence," Downey said. "He has the committee going along with him. We pretty much can deliver whatever we are asked to deliver."

Appropriations: Pork Power

Unlike other congressional panels, Appropriations was propelled by necessity. Tax-writing committees could or could not report major legislation in a given year, but Appropriations had to draft the bills — or one big continuing resolution as it did in 1986 — to keep the government running each year.

Increasingly, Appropriations panels were doing more than that, including in their massive bills authorizations for such pivotal policies as aid to Nicaraguan guerrillas and such controversial programs as family planning that might not have or could not have passed on their own.

"We are the only committee in the Senate that is required to perform or the government collapses," said outgoing Senate Appropriations Chairman Mark O. Hatfield, R-Ore. "These other committees can endure paralysis, but we have to perform."

However, the share of the government outlays that Appropriations controls had dwindled, as the growth of entitlement programs and interest on the national debt put more of the federal budget out of the committee's reach.

According to the Congressional Budget Office, expenditures under the jurisdiction of the Appropriations committees dropped from about two-thirds of gross federal outlays in fiscal 1970 to less than half in 1987. And while the panels' subcommittee chairmen once ran their baronies without external constraint, appropriators in 1987 had to abide by limits set by the annual budget resolution and the newer strictures of the Gramm-Rudman-Hollings anti-deficit law.

But while the Budget Committee could breathe down their necks about obeying overall spending limits, the appropriators still were the ones dealing in hard currency. The budget could say spend $10 billion less, but the Appropriations Committee says how.

As a result, Appropriations remained the choice sty for pork-barrel politics, with members retaining the ability to do favors for their constituents and colleagues. Witness the first money bill to pass under the Gramm-Rudman system: The fiscal 1986 supplemental appropriations measure included, among other things, provisions earmarking $55.6 million in defense funding for projects at universities in the home states of Appropriations members and other key lawmakers.

"Appropriations used to be able to spend whatever it wanted," a House Democratic leadership aide said. "Now it cannot spend as much as it wants but can still spend where it wants."

Especially as more and more legislation — such as the omnibus crime bill in 1984 — was built into the annual continuing resolution, members who sat on Appropriations would continue to have an important source of leverage over their colleagues.

"Appropriations is the key spot," said Edwards. "Members need you and come to you for help. If you're not on Appropriations, you are really at the mercy of other people."

Budget: Powerless Influence

Deficit reduction remains a major item of unfinished business before the 100th Congress, assuring that the House and Senate Budget committees would remain at center stage. Despite the politically thankless job facing the panels, more than a dozen Democrats applied for a seat on House Budget for the 100th Congress.

Although the Budget committees were generally counted among the inner circle of sought-after panels, the nature of their power was elusive and of a different sort from that of other panels.

The Budget committees reported no substantive legislation. The budget resolution, their principal product, would set targets that could be breached whenever the political will to meet them evaporated — such as when Congress in 1986 voted to add $1.7 billion for a politically popular anti-drug program in violation of the budget. Budget Committee members had no goodies to give out either to colleagues or their own constituents.

But the power to set broad spending priorities was a constraint on Appropriations and other committees unheard of before the budget process was set up in 1974. Until then, the Appropriations committees would write much of each year's federal budget, one bill at a time, without an overall blueprint.

Appropriations also lost a subtler form of influence because the Budget committees kicked off the annual budget process. "In the old days, Appropriations had original jurisdiction and took the first look at the president's budget," said political scientist Fenno. "The committee that gets the first crack has enormous power to set boundaries of what's going to be discussed."

Budgeteers also were armed with "reconciliation" instructions included in the annual budget resolution, which mandated that other committees make cuts to hit the budget targets. They did not tell other committees how to comply with savings instructions, but sometimes the options for meeting the targets were few. Still, getting other committees to comply was often more a matter of persuasion and negotiation than of institutional clout.

"The Budget Committee has no power, They are not a necessary hoop through which any substantive legislation must go," says Carol G. Cox, president of the Committee for a Responsible Federal Budget, a nonpartisan research group headed by former members of Congress. "Finance and Ways and Means have power; the Budget Committee has influence, and its influence derives from moral suasion."

Important differences between the chambers led many Budget Committee members to feel that the House committee was much weaker within the institution than its Senate counterpart. While there were no limits on the number of terms a senator could be a member or chairman of the Budget Committee, House rules barred members from sitting on the panel for more than three consecutive terms, or four in the case of chairmen.

"The House has a rotating committee, in my opinion, deliberately intended to keep it weak by its great adversaries in the House, the Appropriations Committee and ... the Ways and Means Committee," said Robert N. Giaimo, D-Conn. (1959-81), a former House Budget chairman.

Rules: Penniless Power

One of the most influential panels in either chamber handled not a dime of federal funding: The Rules Committee was the desk at which every major bill had to stop before going to the House floor.

With authority to draft ground rules for floor debate, the committee could block legislation, set the parameters of debate, and limit or bar amendments.

But like Appropriations and Ways and Means, Rules' influence was in many respects a pale shadow of its former self.

Because its chairman and Democratic members were appointed by the Speaker, Rules generally could do the Speaker's bidding.

But before 1974, when the Democratic Caucus gave the Speaker authority to appoint Rules members, the committee operated more as an autonomous power base than as an arm of the leadership. It often thwarted the leadership by bottling up legislation and, before 1965, legislation could not go to conference with the Senate without Rules' OK.

The Rules Committee also saw its influence diminish for a time when it got too far out of step with the House as a whole. When it was stacked with liberals in the early 1970s, it suffered a series of defeats on the floor. In 1973

alone, the House rejected 13 rules; from 1929-72, rules reported by the committee had been rejected on only 50 occasions.

But in a display of Rules' clout, the committee in 1986 thwarted the formidable chairman of the Appropriations Committee, Jamie L. Whitten, when the Mississippi Democrat tried to resuscitate the general revenue sharing program by slipping $3.4 billion into the massive continuing resolution for fiscal 1987.

Rules forced Whitten to write a new measure excluding revenue sharing, thus saving Democrats from having to make a public choice between letting the politically popular program die, busting budget limits or cutting other programs.

While Democratic leaders in the 100th Congress could call the shots on Rules for many major bills, they were not involved in every piece of legislation that went to the floor, leaving Rules members wide areas in which they could exercise their own discretion.

"I never want to get off Rules," Bonior said. "You get to dabble. . . . You're always doing favors for people."

Armed Services, Foreign Policy

Beyond those committees that handled must-pass bills, had broad jurisdiction and had a handle on important institutional controls was not simply a vast wasteland of committee impotence.

The House and Senate Armed Services committees were the central arena of debate on arms control and the defense budget, which accounted for more than 60 cents of every dollar of discretionary federal spending. The macro-decisions about the amount of money spent on the Pentagon were likely to continue to be made in the broader budget context, but Armed Services' role in deciding how that money would be spent was far more significant than it had been in the past.

"In the 1950s, we used to think of it as a real estate committee, a pork-barrel committee where members got together and got military bases for their states," Fenno said. "Now it's a weapons and policy committee."

Turf battles between the defense authorizers and appropriators had intensified after the GOP takeover of the Senate in 1981, when Sen. Ted Stevens of Alaska, eager to carve out a larger role for the Defense Appropriations Subcommittee, was installed as chairman of that panel. Some were hopeful that those jurisdictional squabbles would subside in the 100th Congress, with Appropriations Committee Chairman John C. Stennis, D-Miss., also sitting on the Armed Services Committee, and his protege, Sam Nunn of Georgia, chairing Armed Services.

The troubles afflicting the Reagan administration's foreign policy in the wake of the Iranian arms scandal were expected to turn the spotlight of public attention on the work of the Senate Foreign Relations Committee. That would add to the already high level of media attention paid to Foreign Relations members, who in the 99th Congress were influential players in the development of U.S foreign policy toward the Philippines and South Africa. Another important source of the committee's influence was its jurisdiction over treaties and the nominations of ambassadors.

But the committee sometimes had to struggle to maintain its legislative clout. The foreign aid authorization bill, the panel's chief product, was always in danger of falling victim to political problems. In 1985, Congress cleared a foreign aid bill for the first time in four years.

"Foreign aid is the least popular bill you can name," said House Foreign Affairs member Henry J. Hyde, R-Ill. "Any one who serves on Foreign Affairs does so out of sheer self-indulgence, not out of political profit back home."

The House Foreign Affairs panel was at a particular disadvantage because it was operating on turf traditionally dominated by the executive branch and the Senate. But House members could parlay membership on the panel into high visibility — as did Stephen J. Solarz, D-N.Y. Solarz, chairman of the House Foreign Affairs Subcommittee on Asian and Pacific Affairs, was a leading congressional critic of deposed Philippine President Ferdinand E. Marcos.

The Outer Circle

Other committees, hard hit in the Gramm-Rudman era, found it all but futile to create new programs.

"The authorizing committees, which should comprise the heart of (the policy-making process), are rapidly approaching irrelevance — squeezed out by the budget and appropriations processes, and caught up in jurisdictional infighting and subcommittee strangulation," House Republicans said in a proposal for procedural reforms considered at their party caucus meetings the week of Dec. 8, 1986.

Some of the inactive authorizing committees had been the cockpit for steering Great Society social programs through Congress in the 1960s. The House Education and Labor Committee had been largely reduced to a bunker for defending existing programs through the Reagan years.

The House Education panel was expected to be more active in the 100th Congress, because it would have a more receptive counterpart in a Democratic-controlled Senate Labor and Human Resources Committee. That, however, would not compensate for budgetary forces sharply limiting the turf of these panels.

But even if some of the authorizing committees were to see a modest resurgence of activity, frustration in Congress about the imbalance of power among panels was likely to remain. The 100th Congress could see increasing debate — although probably not action — on proposals to overhaul the system.

Domenici, a veteran of past panels to study the committee system, was somewhat skeptical of the prospects for structural changes in a turf-conscious institution. But he held out hope that some procedural reforms could be wrought, such as instituting a two-year cycle for budget and appropriations that would allow more time every other year for authorizing activities and oversight.

The frustration level rose in 1986, when all 13 appropriations bills were folded into one, but it was unclear where that frustration would lead in the 100th Congress.

"We're headed at some type of revamping of the whole process," said Bonior. "We've left too many people out of the process."

3

Closed Committee Meetings

Both miniskirts and "sunshine in government" reforms were fashionable in the early 1970s. Then the skirts were tossed out as inconvenient and too revealing.

Increasingly, it seemed, members of Congress were making the same complaints about sunshine rules (just as miniskirts were making a comeback). No one suggested that open meetings were about to become relics of the past; in fact, they were routine for most committees. But in drafting some of the major legislation of recent years, key panels shut their doors to the public and the press.

Most notable was the House Ways and Means Committee. Its members, pleased with the historic tax-overhaul bill that emerged from closed-door meetings in late 1985, opted again in 1987 to bar outsiders when they composed major bills on trade policy and insurance for the elderly and poor against catastrophic illnesses.

Many subcommittees of the House Appropriations Committee likewise met in private to draft each year's federal spending bills. Less often, the Senate Appropriations Committee and the Senate Finance Committee, counterpart to Ways and Means, also closed their doors.

In both chambers, defense and intelligence panels regularly met privately, while other committees did so only occasionally for work on controversial legislation.

Except for Ways and Means, it would be unclear whether committees actually met more often in private than they did a few years ago. What became clear was that they were encountering less resistance when they did close the doors from those who supported the sunshine movement in the last decade — public-interest groups and reporters.

Some former sticklers for sunshine agreed, if grudgingly, with members who said bills are better when drafted away from lobbyists' glare. Conversely, as some of these lobbyists sensed a slippage of their influence over the bill-writing process, they became the 1980s' proponents of sunshine in Congress.

Ways and Means

Given members' contention that a main reason for closed committee sessions was to bar lobbyists, it was no surprise that Ways and Means was the one panel that had unquestionably retreated from openness. With wide-ranging authority over taxes, trade, Social Security, health and welfare programs, it is perhaps the most heavily lobbied committee in the House.

"When we came to this glorious open, participatory government," said Chairman Dan Rostenkowski, an Illinois Democrat, "you know, one of my members is sitting there looking at some labor skate and thinking, 'Oh, well, how does he want me to go on this one?' Or the labor guy is running around and pulling him out to say, 'Wait a minute, you can't do this.'"

"It's just difficult to legislate. I'm not ashamed about closed doors," Rostenkowski said. "We want to get the product out. And as long as [committee aides] Rob Leonard or Ken Bowler can go into the room 20 minutes after we've adjourned, get all you people in there, and say, 'Now here's what happened,' that's all you want to know."

His question to critics of closed sessions was, "Are you disappointed in the legislation that's come out of the Ways and Means Committee?"

Many conceded they were not. "I hate to say it, but members are more willing to make tough decisions on controversial bills in closed meetings," said Democrat Don J. Pease of Ohio, a former newspaper editor who usually cast the only vote against closing Ways and Means sessions. "In a closed meeting, you can come out and say, 'I fought like a tiger for you in there, but I lost.'"

Representatives of the self-described citizens' lobby, Common Cause, which campaigned for the open-meetings rules approved by the House in 1973 and the Senate in 1975, also recognized that closed sessions, particularly in Ways and Means, at times have produced legislation less weighted with special-interest provisions. The group neither monitored committees to see which were closing meetings, as it did prior to 1985, nor protested when they did.

But, said Ann McBride, a Common Cause lobbyist, "We continue to be proponents of openness. . . . It's an extraordinarily sad commentary on the power of special interests that members of Congress are now saying, 'We have to operate in secret to hide from the special interests because they are so powerful.'"

"Members ought to have the courage to look the lobbyists right in the eyes and go against them," Pease agreed. "But as a practical matter, that's hard to do."

So he concluded that closing a tax-bill markup "is perfectly justifiable." But closing the trade bill meetings "was questionable. And catastrophic health insurance? I don't see any reason for closing that."

"I've been a little surprised that we've done it as often

as we have," said Republican Bill Frenzel of Minnesota. "With the trade bill, it was not a bad idea. But I've never figured out why we closed it on the [catastrophic] health bill."

The chairman of the health subcommittee that drafted that bill, California Democrat Fortney H. "Pete" Stark, gave several reasons, and they echoed those given by members generally to justify closed sessions.

One was to save time, Stark said, by eliminating speeches and roll-call votes that members insist on when lobbyists and reporters were present. "It's for our convenience," he said.

Another was the complexity of the issue: "If I'm going to ask a dumb question, I don't want you to know."

And a third reason was the issue's political sensitivity. "It was easy to talk about [health] benefits and look like Good Samaritans," Stark said. "But then you get to the question of financing them."

The answer to that question, and its implications for the health-care costs of workers and senior citizens, was of acute interest to lobbyists for those two groups. Pease said one reason for closing the markup was to bar representatives of the AFL-CIO and the American Association of Retired Persons (AARP).

That claim was no surprise to either group. John Rother, AARP's director of legislation, research and public policy, said, "The reason you have closed doors is to close out the people who are breathing hardest down your neck, and we were clearly in that category on catastrophic."

"The AARP position is always going to be in favor of decisions openly arrived at," he said. "I do have conflicting feelings. I guess what it comes down to, and this is really me personally speaking, is that the process should be judged by the product. The real danger with the closed-door stuff is that they'll try to sneak something by you. And I don't think that's been true."

"We would prefer to have the meetings open," said AFL-CIO lobbyist Calvin P. Johnson.

"A lot of lobbyists really complain about closed meetings," he said. "It tends to be less the men or women who are on the Hill every day working than the folks from the law firms and the accounting firms who come up here to take notes and go back and write up a newsletter and charge their clients $250 an hour. They scream and yell like crazy because they don't know what's going on. They have fewer contacts and they don't feel comfortable with grabbing a member as they go in and out and asking them what in the world is going on."

"We can find out," Johnson said. "I can find out who rolled me and let them know that we weren't pleased with that. And when they come around to us for funds or for support on something, we can let them know, 'You banged me on that one, don't look to us on this.'"

AARP's Rother said, "We usually find out within minutes" what transpired.

Other Committees

Many of the 13 House Appropriations subcommittees routinely closed their markups. Others, and the full committee, hold what jokingly had been called closed open meetings: Though open, the meetings were held in rooms too small for more than a few reporters and observers, and no documents were provided until sometimes days after a markup which made it nearly impossible to follow the action.

Mississippi Democrat Jamie L. Whitten, the full committee chairman, said markups were closed in the agriculture subcommittee that he heads because "people will give you their opinion more honestly." Written reports of subcommittees' work were withheld, he said, because often "something unexpected needs to be corrected."

Defense Subcommittee Chairman Bill Chappell Jr., a Florida Democrat, said markups often were closed because "so much of what we consider is in the national security area."

Other subcommittees could not have made that claim but nevertheless closed the doors during all or part of their markups when deciding on spending for various public-works projects and for House operations. In 1986 Kentucky Democrat William H. Natcher, chairman of the subcommittee for labor, health, human services and education programs, presided over a routine vote to close a markup and assured departing reporters and lobbyists, "Don't worry. We'll give you a good bill."

Both House and Senate rules require a majority vote in open session before a committee can close a meeting. The Senate's rule says that only certain subjects can be considered in private, including national security matters, personnel issues, criminal charges and trade or police secrets.

Senate committees generally closed less often than House panels. "I think most of us have found we can do business in the open just as well as we used to do the other way," said Florida Democrat Lawton Chiles, a leader of the 1970s' sunshine effort.

But as chairman of the Senate Budget Committee, Chiles this year resorted — like his counterparts at House Budget — to holding private meetings of committee Democrats to negotiate a budget proposal.

Members said such caucuses by definition were parties' private policy and strategy sessions. But sometimes, as at House Budget, the majority party's position became the committee bill and then the House's — often without substantive debate.

Few Objections From Press

Reporters rarely objected to closed committee meetings. That surprised Chiles, who served in the Florida Legislature, where reporters used to have to be forced from a room.

"They could care less," he said of Capitol Hill reporters. "A lot of them just work through their sources and feel like open meetings just open it up so everybody's got the same shot at the information."

"I am not an advocate of closed meetings," said Albert R. Hunt, Washington bureau chief for *The Wall Street Journal*. But, he added, "Just speaking very, very selfishly, we did better when meetings were closed because we knew the Hill, we worked it hard.... We got more stories."

"It gets very frustrating," said Jim Luther of the Associated Press, who did object when Ways and Means closed its tax markup in 1985. "The tax bill went through Ways and Means, the Finance Committee and conference in closed session."

"I can't recall any editorial response to this at all," Luther added. "In the past, newspapers screamed to high heaven. You had the biggest tax bill in at least a generation, with so many provisions to it, and so many people affected, and nobody seemed to care that it was all being done basically in secret."

4

Iran-Contra Investigations Committees

When Congress turned its attention to the Reagan administration's widening Iranian arms scandal, it also took steps to sort out how to investigate without tripping over itself.

The Dec. 4, 1986, announcement by House and Senate leaders that each chamber would create its own select investigating committee when Congress reconvened in January was aimed at avoiding the confusion of at least a half-dozen panels poking into the secret arms program in which cash was funneled to Nicaragua's "contras."

House Speaker Jim Wright, D-Texas, said that a 15-member "blue-ribbon panel" would take charge of the House's inquiry. He said the committee would "see to it that there is no needless duplication of effort" among other House panels that had already begun, or planned, arms probes. Minority Leader Robert H. Michel, R-Ill., said the special panel would help to avoid a "circus atmosphere."

Lee H. Hamilton, D-Ind., was chosen by Wright to head the House committee. He had chaired the Foreign Affairs Subcommittee on Europe and the Middle East for a decade and the Select Intelligence Committee in the 99th Congress.

Five of the nine Democrats were guaranteed a seat on the panel by virtue of chairing committees with jurisdiction over various aspects of the Iran arms deal: Foreign Affairs, Judiciary, Government Operations, Armed Services and Intelligence.

Minority Leader Michel decided against naming all the senior Republicans who sat on those five committees. He appointed the senior Republican on Foreign Affairs, and the ranking member on Intelligence. Besides designating Dick Cheney of Wyoming as the senior Republican on the panel, Michel dipped into the ranks of more junior House members for the remaining slots. *(For list of House committee members, see p. 97)*

In the Senate, an 11-member select committee was picked by Majority Leader Robert C. Byrd. He appointed as chairman Daniel K. Inouye, D-Hawaii, a former Intelligence Committee chairman and member of the Senate Watergate panel that in 1973-74 investigated the activities of the Nixon White House. Republican Leader Robert Dole, R-Kan., appointed Warren B. Rudman, R-N.H., vice chairman along with four other members of that party, giving the Democrats a six-to-five majority on the panel. *(For list of Senate committee members, see p. 59)*

On March 18, 1987, the House and Senate select com-

mittees agreed to merge most of their activities, including public hearings, which began May 5.

The creation of separate committees to investigate the Iran-contra affair came about because leaders in both chambers were reluctant to establish a joint panel. Since those committees were formed, however, they have cooperated closely, coordinating all major actions, such as seeking immunity for witnesses.

During the early stages of their work, committee leaders talked about conducting some joint hearings and holding all others on alternating days or weeks. As inevitable delays cropped up, committee members promoted the idea of holding most or all hearings jointly.

Eventually, the committees agreed to merge their operations in all but name. All hearings would be held in joint session and the staffs would be "melded," announced Rep. Hamilton. He also stressed that the joint sessions would enable the committees to finish their work earlier than if each panel held separate hearings.

Overshadowing Other Panels

The establishment of the two select committees would overshadow other congressional panels looking into the Iranian arms deal, although the others could proceed, for a while, with their own inquiries.

The Senate Intelligence Committee already had a closed-door probe under way and released its report on Jan. 29, 1987. The document did not draw conclusions. Instead, it recited the history of U.S. dealings with Iran and aid to the contras based on the testimony of 36 witnesses and thousands of pages of documents. Also listed were 14 unresolved issues that the select panel might want to investigate.

Its House counterpart called administration witnesses to testify about their role in the arms dealings. In addition, the House Foreign Affairs Committee heard testimony from Secretary of State George P. Shultz and Reagan's former national security adviser, Robert C. McFarlane.

The House Banking Committee wanted to know whether any U.S. banks or their overseas branches had a role in cash transactions generated by the Iran arms sale. Chairman Fernand J. St Germain, D-R.I., asked Attorney General Edwin Meese III for information Nov. 26, 1986.

Members of the House Judiciary Committee kept a close eye on the actions of an independent counsel who will

A Selected Chronology of Past Investigations

	Panel	Topic
1792	House Select Committee	Defense of troops in the Northwest Territory against Indian attack
1861-65	Joint Committee on the Conduct of the War	Conduct of the Civil War
1869-77	Two House and one Senate select committees	Corruption in Grant administration, Congress
1922-24	Senate Committee on Public Lands and Surveys	Teapot Dome scandal in Harding administration
1924	Senate Select Committee to Investigate the Justice Department	Failure to prosecute those involved in Teapot Dome
1934-36	Senate Special Committee Investigating the Munitions Industry	World War I arms profits
1941-48	Senate Special Committee to Investigate the National Defense Program	Wasteful war preparations
1950	Senate Special Committee to Investigate Organized Crime in Interstate Commerce	Organized crime and government corruption
1973-74	Senate Select Committee on Presidential Campaign Activities	Watergate break-in and cover-up
1975	Senate Select Committee to Study Government Operations with Respect to Intelligence Activities House Select Committee on Intelligence	CIA covert actions and FBI domestic surveillance
1982	Senate Select Committee to Study Law Enforcement Undercover Activities of Components of the Department of Justice	Propriety of Abscam investigations, arrests

investigate possible criminal violations by White House officials in the Iranian arms and contra dealings.

Congress' Objectives

Congress also was looking into possible violations of non-criminal laws, such as bans on arms exports to countries that support terrorism or prohibitions against U.S. aid to the contras that were in effect when money from Iranian arms sales were diverted to the Nicaraguan rebels.

In addition, Congress was trying to determine whether new laws were needed to guard against such dealings in the future. And much of Congress' hearings were held in open session, allowing the public to follow on television or in newspapers and magazines.

There was considerable support for merging Congress' activity into one or two select panels. "It seems to me that if people are to testify, and again and again in both houses, we really would do better to have one [panel] that the American people would focus on and the investigation would focus on," said Sen. Richard G. Lugar, R-Ind., outgoing chairman of the Foreign Relations Committee.

"The advantage of a select committee is that you don't have a duplication of effort," noted James Hamilton, a Washington lawyer who was assistant chief counsel to the Senate Watergate Committee. Once that panel "got going, basically the investigation was left to it," he said.

Some House members of the Democratic Study Group (DSG) favored a special House committee. "It was the consensus that individual committees are not prepared to carry on an investigation on their own," said Richard P. Conlon, DSG's executive director. He questioned whether existing committees would have sufficient staff and financial resources.

A House select committee also was viewed by some as a way for House members — particularly those in the Democratic majority — to share the limelight with the Senate. Said a House source: "The House has been carrying the ball quite adequately for Democrats for the past six years, and we're not about to retire from the field simply because there is now a [Democratic] majority in the Senate."

Overlapping probes would serve a useful purpose, according to Thomas E. Mann, executive director of the American Political Science Association. "If the objective is to try to produce a lot of information, to follow up a lot of leads, to uncover everything that ought to be uncovered, there is some value to redundancy and duplication," said Mann. "Of course, it's frustrating as hell to the people being investigated."

Members of the House and Senate Select Iran-Contra Committees question witness, retired Air Force major general Richard V. Secord.

During Reagan's first term, the Environmental Protection Agency (EPA) was the subject of a congressional investigation into charges that officials had failed to enforce hazardous-waste laws. At its height, in early 1983, five House subcommittees and one Senate committee had EPA probes under way. House Speaker Thomas P. O'Neill Jr., D-Mass., suggested that the House panels coordinate. But the chairmen resisted. The EPA probes subsided after Anne M. Burford resigned as head of the agency.

An Old Tradition

Congressional investigations are virtually as old as the nation itself. In 1792, the House formed a select committee to look into the defeat of American troops on the Ohio frontier by Indian tribes.

The first joint panel was created in 1861 in the aftermath of Union defeats in the Civil War battles of Bull Run and Balls Bluff. Controlled by radical Republicans opposed to President Abraham Lincoln, the panel conducted a highly critical probe of his military strategy.

The anti-communist investigations of the 1940s and 1950s, primarily associated with Sen. Joseph R. McCarthy, R-Wis., are often considered the low-water mark in congressional probes because of their power to ruin reputations based on flimsy evidence.

Senate Committees

Key to Listings, Abbreviations

ORDER OF LISTS — In the committee sections, Democrats are listed on the left in roman type. Republicans are on the right *in italics.*

Members of legislative committees and subcommittees are listed in order of their seniority on those panels.

Members of party committees are listed alphabetically.

ROOM AND TELEPHONE NUMBERS — Phone and room numbers are listed for each committee and subcommittee, and for the key staffers of committees. In addition, a list of committees on pages 80-81 includes phone and room numbers for both the majority and minority staffs of all full committees. All mail should be addressed to the main committee rooms.

Phone and room numbers for all members of Congress may be found on pages 121-126.

To reach the U.S. Capitol switchboard, call (202) 224-3121.

BUILDINGS, ADDRESSES, ZIP CODES — The following abbreviations are used for congressional office buildings:

- SD — Dirksen Senate Office Building
- SH — Hart Senate Office Building
- SR — Russell Senate Office Building
- CHOB — Cannon House Office Building
- LHOB — Longworth House Office Building
- RHOB — Rayburn House Office Building
- HOB Annex #1 — House Office Building Annex #1
- HOB Annex #2 — House Office Building Annex #2

A listing of all office buildings and their addresses appears on page 81 and a map of Capitol Hill showing the location of each building appears on page 91.

The ZIP code for all mail addressed to offices of the Senate is 20510; for the House, 20515.

Senate Party Committees, 100th Congress

DEMOCRATS

John C. Stennis
President Pro Tempore

Robert C. Byrd
Majority Leader

Alan Cranston
Majority Whip

Daniel K. Inouye
Conference Secretary

Party Leadership

President Pro Tempore — John C. Stennis, Miss. 224-5556
Deputy President Pro Tempore — George J. Mitchell, Maine 224-5556
Majority Leader — Robert C. Byrd, W.Va. 224-5556
Majority Whip — Alan Cranston, Calif. 224-2158
Chairman of the Conference — Robert C. Byrd, W.Va. 224-5551
Secretary of the Conference — Daniel K. Inouye, Hawaii........................ 224-5551
Chief Deputy Whip — Spark M. Matsunaga, Hawaii 224-6361

Deputy Whips (listed by region, each with an assistant deputy whip):

East — Patrick J. Leahy, Vt.
John D. Rockefeller IV, W.Va.
South — Jim Sasser, Tenn.
Wyche Fowler Jr., Ga.

Midwest — Alan J. Dixon, Ill.
J. James Exon, Neb.
West — Timothy E. Wirth, Colo.
Brock Adams, Wash.

Policy Committee

■ Phone: 224-5551   ■ Room: S-118 Capitol

Scheduling of legislation.

Robert C. Byrd, W.Va., chairman

Quentin N. Burdick, N.D.
Alan Cranston, Calif. †
John Glenn, Ohio

Ernest F. Hollings, S.C.
Daniel K. Inouye, Hawaii †
Claiborne Pell, R.I.

† Member ex officio from the leadership.

Legislative Review Committee

■ Phone: 224-3735   ■ Room: S-118 Capitol

Reviews legislative proposals, provides recommendations.

Dale Bumpers, Ark., chairman

Jeff Bingaman, N.M.
Howell Heflin, Ala.
Frank R. Lautenberg, N.J.

William Proxmire, Wis.
Paul S. Sarbanes, Md.
Paul Simon, Ill.

Steering Committee

■ Phone: 224-3735   ■ Room: S-309 Capitol

Makes Democratic committee assignments.

Robert C. Byrd, W.Va., chairman

Lloyd Bentsen, Texas
Joseph R. Biden Jr., Del.
David L. Boren, Okla.
Lawton Chiles, Fla.
Alan Cranston, Calif.
Dennis DeConcini, Ariz.
Christopher J. Dodd,
   Conn.
J. James Exon, Neb.
Wendell H. Ford, Ky.
Tom Harkin, Iowa
Daniel K. Inouye, Hawaii †
Edward M. Kennedy,
   Mass.

Patrick J. Leahy, Vt.
John Melcher, Mont.
Howard M. Metzenbaum,
   Ohio
George J. Mitchell, Maine
Daniel Patrick Moynihan, N.Y.
Sam Nunn, Ga.
David Pryor, Ark.
Donald W. Riegle Jr., Mich.
Jim Sasser, Tenn.
John C. Stennis, Miss.

† Member ex officio from the leadership.

Democratic Senatorial Campaign Committee

■ Phone: 224-2447   ■ 430 S. Capitol St. S.E. 20003

Campaign support committee for Democratic senatorial candidates.

John Kerry, Mass., chairman
Alan Cranston, Calif., co-chairman

Max Baucus, Mont.
Lloyd Bensten, Texas
Bill Bradley, N.J.
Robert C. Byrd, W.Va. †
Lawton Chiles, Fla.
Thomas A. Daschle, S.D.
Christopher J. Dodd, Conn.
Albert Gore Jr., Tenn.
Bob Graham, Fla.

Daniel K. Inouye, Hawaii †
J. Bennett Johnston, La.
Frank R. Lautenberg, N.J.
Carl Levin, Mich.
Barbara A. Mikulski, Md.
John D. Rockefeller IV, W.Va.
Jim Sasser, Tenn.
Paul Simon, Ill.

† Member ex officio from the leadership.

REPUBLICANS

Robert Dole
Minority Leader

Alan K. Simpson
Assistant Minority Leader

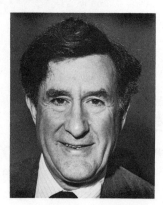

John H. Chafee
Conference Chairman

Thad Cochran
Conference Secretary

Party Leadership

Minority Leader — Robert Dole, Kan. 224-3135
Assistant Minority Leader — Alan K. Simpson, Wyo. 224-2708
Chairman of the Conference — John H. Chafee, R.I. 224-2764
Secretary of the Conference — Thad Cochran, Miss. 224-1326

Policy Committee

■ Phone: 224-2946   ■ Room: SR-347

Advises on party action and policy.

William L. Armstrong, Colo., chairman

Rudy Boschwitz, Minn.	James A. McClure, Idaho
John H. Chafee, R.I.	Frank H. Murkowski,
Thad Cochran, Miss.	Alaska
William S. Cohen, Maine	Bob Packwood, Ore.
John C. Danforth, Mo.	William V. Roth Jr., Del.
Robert Dole, Kan. †	Alan K. Simpson, Wyo.
Pete V. Domenici, N.M.	Robert T. Stafford, Vt.
Jake Garn, Utah	Strom Thurmond, S.C.
Orrin G. Hatch, Utah	John W. Warner, Va.
Mark O. Hatfield, Ore.	
John Heinz, Pa.	
Jesse Helms, N.C.	
Richard G. Lugar, Ind.	

† Member ex officio *from the leadership.*

National Republican Senatorial Committee

■ Phone: 224-2351   ■ 440 First St. N.W. 20001

Campaign support committee for Republican senatorial candidates.

Rudy Boschwitz, Minn., chairman

Christopher S. "Kit" Bond, Mo.	Bob Kasten, Wis.
Alfonse M. D'Amato, N.Y.	John McCain, Ariz.
Robert Dole, Kan. †	Mitch McConnell, Ky.
Pete V. Domenici, N.M.	Frank H. Murkowski, Alaska
Phil Gramm, Texas	Don Nickles, Okla.
Charles E. Grassley, Iowa	Bob Packwood, Ore.
Gordon J. Humphrey, N.H.	Larry Pressler, S.D.
Nancy Landon Kassebaum, Kan.	Dan Quayle, Ind.
	Arlen Specter, Pa.
	Ted Stevens, Alaska
	Steve Symms, Idaho

† Member ex officio *from the leadership.*

Committee on Committees

■ Phone: 224-4024   ■ Room: SH-517

Makes Republican committee assignments.

Paul S. Trible Jr., Va., chairman

Robert Dole, Kan. †	Warren B. Rudman, N.H.
Dave Durenberger, Minn.	Malcolm Wallop, Wyo.
Daniel J. Evans, Wash.	Lowell P. Weicker Jr., Conn.
Chic Hecht, Nev.	Pete Wilson, Calif.

† Member ex officio *from the leadership.*

Senate Committee Assignments, 100th Congress

Agriculture, Nutrition and Forestry

■ Phone: 224-2035 ■ Room: SR-328A

Agriculture in general; animal industry and diseases; crop insurance and soil conservation; farm credit and farm security; food from fresh waters; food stamp programs; forestry in general; home economics; human nutrition; inspection of livestock, meat and agricultural products; pests and pesticides; plant industry, soils and agricultural engineering; rural development, rural electrification and watersheds; school nutrition programs; matters relating to food, nutrition, hunger and rural affairs. Chairman and ranking minority member are members *ex officio* of all subcommittees of which they are not regular members.

Party Ratio: D 10 - R 9

Patrick J. Leahy
Chairman

Richard G. Lugar
Ranking Member

Patrick J. Leahy, Vt.
John Melcher, Mont.
David Pryor, Ark.
David L. Boren, Okla.
Howell Heflin, Ala.
Tom Harkin, Iowa
Kent Conrad, N.D.
Wyche Fowler Jr. Ga.
Thomas A. Daschle, S.D.
John B. Breaux, La.

Richard G. Lugar, Ind.
Robert Dole, Kan.
Jesse Helms, N.C.
Thad Cochran, Miss.
Rudy Boschwitz, Minn.
Mitch McConnell, Ky.
Christopher S. Kit Bond, Mo.
Pete Wilson, Calif.
David Karnes, Neb.

Majority Chief of Staff: Charles Riemenschneider 224-2035 Rm SR-328A
Minority Staff Director: Chuck Conner 224-6901 Rm SR-328

Subcommittees

Agricultural Credit

■ Phone: 224-2035 ■ Room: SR-328A

Boren — chairman

Harkin	*Boschwitz*
Daschle	*Cochran*
Breaux	*McConnell*
Melcher	*Karnes*

Agricultural Production and Stabilization of Prices

■ Phone: 224-2035 ■ Room: SR-328A

Melcher — chairman

Conrad	*Helms*
Heflin	*Dole*
Boren	*Cochran*
Fowler	*McConnell*
Pryor	*Bond*
Daschle	*Wilson*

Agricultural Research and General Legislation

■ Phone: 224-7240 ■ Room: 328A

Conrad — chairman

Boren	*Wilson*
	Karnes

Conservation and Forestry

■ Phone: 224-2035 ■ Room 328A

Fowler-chairman

Heflin	*Bond*

Domestic and Foreign Marketing and Product Promotion

■ Phone: 224-2035 ■ Room: SR-328A

Pryor — chairman

Daschle	*Cochran*
Melcher	*Helms*
Conrad	*Bond*
Harkin	*Wilson*
Breaux	*Boschwitz*
	Karnes

45

Nutrition and Investigations

■ Phone: 224-2035   ■ Room: SR-328A

Harkin — chairman

Melcher   *Dole*
Pryor   *Boschwitz*
Breaux   *Helms*

Rural Development and Rural Electrification

■ Phone: 224-2035   ■ Room: SR-328A

Heflin — chairman

Fowler   *McConnell*

Appropriations

■ Phone: 224-3471   ■ Room: SD-118

Appropriation of revenue for support of the government; rescission of appropriations; new spending authority under the Congressional Budget Act. Chairman and ranking minority member are members *ex officio* of all subcommittees of which they are not regular members.

Party Ratio: D 16 - R 13

John C. Stennis
Chairman

Mark O. Hatfield
Ranking Member

John C. Stennis, Miss.   *Mark O. Hatfield, Ore.*
Robert C. Byrd, W.Va.   *Ted Stevens, Alaska*
William Proxmire, Wis.   *Lowell P. Weicker Jr., Conn.*
Daniel K. Inouye, Hawaii   *James A. McClure, Idaho*
Ernest F. Hollings, S.C.   *Jake Garn, Utah*
Lawton Chiles, Fla.   *Thad Cochran, Miss.*
J. Bennett Johnston, La.   *Bob Kasten, Wis.*

Quentin N. Burdick, N.D.   *Alfonse M. D'Amato, N.Y.*
Patrick J. Leahy, Vt.   *Warren B. Rudman, N.H.*
Jim Sasser, Tenn.   *Arlen Specter, Pa.*
Dennis DeConcini, Ariz.   *Pete V. Domenici, N.M.*
Dale Bumpers, Ark.   *Charles E. Grassley, Iowa*
Frank R. Lautenberg, N.J.   *Don Nickles, Okla.*
Tom Harkin, Iowa
Barbara A. Mikulski, Md.
Harry Reid, Nev.

Majority Staff Director: Francis J. Sullivan 224-7254 Rm SD-133
Minority Staff Director: Keith Kennedy 224-7335 Rm SD-119

Subcommittees

Agriculture, Rural Development and Related Agencies

■ Phone: 224-7240   ■ Room: SD-140

Burdick — chairman

Stennis   *Cochran*
Chiles   *McClure*
Sasser   *Kasten*
Bumpers   *Specter*
Harkin   *Grassley*

Commerce, Justice, State, the Judiciary and Related Agencies

■ Phone: 224-7277   ■ Room: S-146A Capitol

Hollings — chairman

Inouye   *Rudman*
Bumpers   *Stevens*
Chiles   *Weicker*
Lautenberg   *Hatfield*
Sasser   *Kasten*

Defense

■ Phone: 224-7286   ■ Room: SD-129

Stennis — chairman

Proxmire   *Stevens*
Inouye   *Weicker*
Hollings   *Garn*
Chiles   *McClure*
Johnston   *Kasten*
Byrd   *D'Amato*
Leahy   *Rudman*
Sasser   *Cochran*
DeConcini

District of Columbia

■ Phone: 224-2727   ■ Room: S-128 Capitol

Harkin — chairman

Lautenberg	*Nickles*
Reid	*Grassley*

Energy and Water Development

■ Phone: 224-0335   ■ Room: SD-131

Johnston — chairman

Stennis	*Hatfield*
Byrd	*McClure*
Hollings	*Garn*
Burdick	*Cochran*
Sasser	*Domenici*
DeConcini	*Specter*

Foreign Operations

■ Phone: 224-7205   ■ Room: S-128 Capitol

Inouye — chairman

Johnston	*Kasten*
Leahy	*Hatfield*
DeConcini	*D'Amato*
Lautenberg	*Rudman*
Harkin	*Specter*
Mikulski	*Nickles*

HUD - Independent Agencies

■ Phone: 224-7231   ■ Room: SD-142

Proxmire — chairman

Stennis	*Garn*
Leahy	*D'Amato*
Johnston	*Domenici*
Lautenberg	*Grassley*
Mikulski	*Nickles*

Interior and Related Agencies

■ Phone: 224-7210   ■ Room: SD-122

Byrd — chairman

Johnston	*McClure*
Leahy	*Stevens*
DeConcini	*Garn*
Burdick	*Cochran*
Bumpers	*Rudman*
Hollings	*Weicker*
Reid	*Nickles*

Labor, Health and Human Services, Education and Related Agencies

■ Phone: 224-7288   ■ Room: SD-186

Chiles — chairman

Byrd	*Weicker*
Proxmire	*Hatfield*
Hollings	*Stevens*
Burdick	*Rudman*
Inouye	*Specter*
Harkin	*McClure*
Bumpers	*Domenici*

Legislative Branch

■ Phone: 224-7280   ■ Room: S-128 Capitol

Bumpers — chairman

Mikulski	*Grassley*
Reid	*Hatfield*

Military Construction

■ Phone: 224-7276   ■ Room: SD-129

Sasser — chairman

Inouye	*Specter*
Proxmire	*Garn*
Reid	*Stevens*

Transportation and Related Agencies

■ Phone: 224-7245   ■ Room: SD-156

Lautenberg — chairman

Stennis	*D'Amato*
Byrd	*Cochran*
Chiles	*Kasten*
Harkin	*Weicker*

Treasury, Postal Service and General Government

■ Phone: 224-6280   ■ Room: SD-190

DeConcini — chairman

Proxmire	*Domenici*
Mikulski	*D'Amato*

Armed Services

■ Phone: 224-3871   ■ Room: SR-222

Defense and defense policy generally; aeronautical and space activities peculiar to or primarily associated with the development of weapons systems or military operations; maintenance and operation of the Panama Canal, including the Canal Zone; military research and development; national security aspects of nuclear energy; naval petroleum reserves (except Alaska); armed forces generally; Selective Service System; strategic and critical materials. Chairman and ranking minority member are non-voting members *ex officio* of all subcommittees of which they are not regular members.

Party Ratio: D 11 - R 9

Sam Nunn
Chairman

John W. Warner
Ranking Member

Sam Nunn, Ga.	*John W. Warner, Va.*
John C. Stennis, Miss.	*Strom Thurmond, S.C.*
J. James Exon, Neb.	*Gordon J. Humphrey, N.H.*
Carl Levin, Mich.	*William S. Cohen, Maine*
Edward M. Kennedy, Mass.	*Dan Quayle, Ind.*
Jeff Bingaman, N.M.	*Pete Wilson, Calif.*
Alan J. Dixon, Ill.	*Phil Gramm, Texas*
John Glenn, Ohio	*Steve Symms, Idaho*
Albert Gore Jr., Tenn.	*John McCain, Ariz.*
Timothy E. Wirth, Colo.	
Richard C. Shelby, Ala.	

Majority Staff Director and Chief Counsel: Arnold L. Punaro
  224-3871 Rm SR-222
Minority Staff Director: Carl M. Smith 224-3871 Rm SR-222

Subcommittees

Conventional Forces and Alliance Defense

■ Phone: 224-3871   ■ Room: SR-222

Levin — chairman

Dixon	*Quayle*
Glenn	*Thurmond*
Gore	*Cohen*
Wirth	*Wilson*
Shelby	*Gramm*

Defense Industry and Technology

■ Phone: 224-3871   ■ Room: SR-222

Bingaman — chairman

Gore	*Gramm*
Dixon	*Quayle*
Wirth	*Symms*

Manpower and Personnel

■ Phone: 224-3128   ■ Room: SR-222

Glenn — chairman

Exon	*Wilson*
Kennedy	*Symms*
Shelby	*McCain*

Projection Forces and Regional Defense

■ Phone: 224-3871   ■ Room: SR-222

Kennedy — chairman

Stennis	*Cohen*
Exon	*Humphrey*
Gore	*Symms*
Shelby	*McCain*

Readiness, Sustainability and Support

■ Phone: 224-9344   ■ Room: SR-222

Dixon — chairman

Stennis	*Humphrey*
Levin	*Thurmond*
Bingaman	*Gramm*
Wirth	*McCain*

Strategic Forces and Nuclear Deterrence

■ Phone: 224-3871   ■ Room: SR-222

Exon — chairman

Stennis	*Thurmond*
Levin	*Humphrey*
Kennedy	*Cohen*
Bingaman	*Quayle*
Glenn	*Wilson*

Banking, Housing and Urban Affairs

■ Phone: 224-7391   ■ Room: SD-534

Banks, banking and financial institutions; price controls; deposit insurance; economic stabilization and growth; defense production; export and foreign trade promotion; export controls; federal monetary policy, including Federal Reserve System; financial aid to commerce and industry; issuance and redemption of notes; money and credit, including currency and coinage; nursing home construction; public and private housing, including veterans' housing; renegotiation of government contracts; urban development and mass transit; international economic policy. Chairman and ranking minority member are members *ex officio* of all subcommittees of which they are not regular members.

Party Ratio: D 11 - R 9

William Proxmire
Chairman

Jake Garn
Ranking Member

William Proxmire, Wis.	*Jake Garn, Utah*
Alan Cranston, Calif.	*John Heinz, Pa.*
Donald W. Riegle Jr., Mich.	*William L. Armstrong, Colo.*
Paul S. Sarbanes, Md.	*Alfonse M. D'Amato, N.Y.*

Christopher J. Dodd, Conn.	*Chic Hecht, Nev.*
Alan J. Dixon, Ill.	*Phil Gramm, Texas*
Jim Sasser, Tenn.	*Christopher S. "Kit" Bond,*
Terry Sanford, N.C.	*Mo.*
Richard C. Shelby, Ala.	*John H. Chafee, R.I.*
Bob Graham, Fla.	*David Karnes, Neb.*
Timothy E. Wirth, Colo.	

Majority Staff Director: Kenneth A. McLean 224-1573 Rm SD-542
Minority Staff Director: M. Danny Wall 224-1575 Rm SD-545

Subcommittees

Consumer Affairs

■ Phone: 224-1565   ■ Room: SD-541

Dodd — chairman

Proxmire	*Gramm*
Graham	*Chafee*
Wirth	*Karnes*

Housing and Urban Affairs

■ Phone: 224-6348   ■ Room: SD-535

Cranston — chairman

Riegle	*D'Amato*
Sarbanes	*Garn*
Dodd	*Hecht*
Dixon	*Chafee*
Sasser	*Heinz*

International Finance and Monetary Policy

■ Phone: 224-1564   ■ Room: SD-534

Sarbanes — chairman

Proxmire	*Heinz*
Dixon	*Garn*
Sanford	*Armstrong*
Shelby	*Gramm*
Graham	*Bond*

Securities

■ Phone: 224-5786   ■ Room: SD-546

Riegle — chairman

Cranston	*Armstrong*
Sasser	*Bond*
Sanford	*D'Amato*
Shelby	*Hecht*
Wirth	*Karnes*

Budget

■ Phone: 224-0642   ■ Room: SD-621

Federal budget generally; concurrent budget resolutions; Congressional Budget Office.

Party Ratio: D 13 - R 11

Lawton Chiles
Chairman

Pete V. Domenici
Ranking Member

Lawton Chiles, Fla.
Ernest F. Hollings, S.C.
J. Bennett Johnston, La.
Jim Sasser, Tenn.
Donald W. Riegle Jr., Mich.
J. James Exon, Neb.
Frank R. Lautenberg, N.J.
Paul Simon, Ill.
Terry Sanford, N.C.
Timothy E. Wirth, Colo.
Wyche Fowler Jr., Ga.
Kent Conrad, N.D.
Christopher J. Dodd, Conn.

Pete V. Domenici, N.M.
William L. Armstrong, Colo.
Nancy Landon Kassebaum,
Kan.
Rudy Boschwitz, Minn.
Steve Symms, Idaho
Charles E. Grassley, Iowa
Bob Kasten, Wis.
Dan Quayle, Ind.
John C. Danforth, Mo.
Don Nickles, Okla.
Warren B. Rudman, N.H.

Majority Staff Director: Richard N. Brandon 224-0642 Rm SD-621
Minority Staff Director: G. William Hoagland 224-0536 Rm SD-634

(No standing subcommittees.)

Commerce, Science and Transportation

■ Phone: 224-5115   ■ Room: SD-508

Interstate commerce and transportation generally; Coast Guard; coastal zone management; communications; highway safety; inland waterways, except construction; marine fisheries; Merchant Marine and navigation; non-military aeronautical and space sciences; oceans, weather and atmospheric activities; interoceanic canals generally; regulation of consumer products

and services; science, engineering and technology research, development and policy; sports; standards and measurement; transportation and commerce aspects of Outer Continental Shelf lands. Chairman and ranking minority member are non-voting members *ex officio* of all subcommittees of which they are not regular members.

Party Ratio: D 11 - R 9

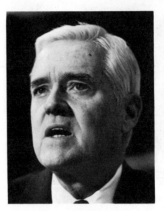

Ernest F. Hollings
Chairman

John C. Danforth
Ranking Member

Ernest F. Hollings, S.C.
Daniel K. Inouye, Hawaii
Wendell H. Ford, Ky.
Donald W. Riegle Jr., Mich.
J. James Exon, Neb.
Albert Gore Jr., Tenn.
John D. Rockefeller IV,
  W.Va.
Lloyd Bentsen, Texas
John Kerry, Mass.
John B. Breaux, La.
Brock Adams, Wash.

John C. Danforth, Mo.
Bob Packwood, Ore.
Nancy Landon Kassebaum,
* Kan.*
Larry Pressler, S.D.
Ted Stevens, Alaska
Bob Kasten, Wis.
Paul S. Trible Jr., Va.
Pete Wilson, Calif.
John McCain, Ariz.

Majority Chief Counsel and Staff Director: Ralph B. Everett 224-0427
* Rm SR-254*
Minority Chief of Staff: W. Allen Moore 224-1251 Rm SD-554

Subcommittees

Aviation

■ Phone: 224-9350   ■ Room: SH-428

Ford — chairman

Exon
Inouye
Kerry
Breaux

Kassebaum
Stevens
Kasten
McCain

Communications

■ Phone: 224-9340   ■ Room: SH-227

Inouye — chairman

Hollings	*Packwood*
Ford	*Pressler*
Gore	*Stevens*
Exon	*Wilson*
Kerry	*McCain*

Consumer

■ Phone: 224-0415   ■ Room: SH-227

Gore — chairman

Ford	*McCain*
Breaux	*Kasten*

Foreign Commerce and Tourism

■ Phone: 224-9325   ■ Room: SH-428

Rockefeller — chairman

Hollings	*Trible*
Riegle	*Packwood*
Bentsen	*Wilson*

Merchant Marine

■ Phone: 224-4914   ■ Room: SH-425

Breaux — chairman

Inouye	*Stevens*
Bentsen	*Trible*
Adams	

Science, Technology and Space

■ Phone: 224-9360   ■ Room: SH-427

Riegle — chairman

Gore	*Pressler*
Rockefeller	*Kassebaum*
Bentsen	*Trible*
Kerry	*Wilson*
Adams	

Surface Transportation

■ Phone: 224-9350   ■ Room: SH-428

Exon — chairman

Riegle	*Kasten*
Rockefeller	*Packwood*
Hollings	*Pressler*
Adams	*Kassebaum*

National Ocean Policy Study

■ Phone: 224-4912   ■ Room: SH-425

The National Ocean Policy Study is technically not a subcommittee of the Commerce, Science and Transportation Committee; no legislation is referred to it. Numerous *ex officio* members from other Senate committees and from the Senate at large serve on it.

Hollings — chairman

Kerry	*Danforth*
Inouye	*Stevens*
Ford	*Packwood*
Gore	*Kasten*
Bentsen	*Trible*
Breaux	*Wilson*
Adams	*Pressler*

Energy and Natural Resources

■ Phone: 224-4971   ■ Room: SD-364

Energy policy, regulation, conservation, research and development; coal; energy-related aspects of deep-water ports; hydroelectric power, irrigation and reclamation; mines, mining and minerals generally; national parks, recreation areas, wilderness areas, wild and scenic rivers, historic sites, military parks and battlefields; naval petroleum reserves in Alaska; non-military development of nuclear energy; oil and gas production and distribution; public lands and forests; solar energy systems; territorial possessions of the United States. Chairman and ranking minority member are members *ex officio* of all subcommittees of which they are not regular members.

Party: D 10 - R 9

J. Bennett Johnston
Chairman

James A. McClure
Ranking Member

J. Bennett Johnston, La.	*James A. McClure, Idaho*
Dale Bumpers, Ark.	*Mark O. Hatfield, Ore.*
Wendell H. Ford, Ky.	*Lowell P. Weicker Jr., Conn.*

Howard M. Metzenbaum, Ohio
John Melcher, Mont.
Bill Bradley, N.J.
Jeff Bingaman, N.M.
Timothy E. Wirth, Colo.
Wyche Fowler Jr., Ga.
Kent Conrad, N.D.

Pete V. Domenici, N.M.
Malcolm Wallop, Wyo.
Frank H. Murkowski, Alaska
Don Nickles, Okla.
Chic Hecht, Nev.
Daniel J. Evans, Wash.

Majority Staff Director: Daryl H. Owen 224-7561 Rm SD-360
Minority Staff Director: Frank M. Cushing 224-1004 Rm SD-310

Subcommittees

Energy Regulation and Conservation

■ Phone: 224-4756   ■ Room: SH-212

Metzenbaum — chairman

Bradley
Bingaman
Fowler

Nickles
Weicker
Evans

Energy Research and Development

■ Phone: 224-7569   ■ Room: SH-312

Ford — chairman

Fowler
Bumpers
Metzenbaum
Melcher

Domenici
Evans
Weicker
Hecht

Mineral Resources Development and Production

■ Phone: 224-7556   ■ Room: SD-362

Melcher — chairman

Wirth
Ford
Bingaman
Conrad

Hecht
Nickles
Wallop
Murkowski

Public Lands, National Parks and Forests

■ Phone: 224-7934   ■ Room: SD-308

Bumpers — chairman

Bingaman
Melcher
Bradley
Wirth
Fowler
Conrad

Wallop
Weicker
Hatfield
Domenici
Murkowski
Hecht

Water and Power

■ Phone: 224-6836   ■ Room: SD-306

Bradley — chairman

Conrad
Bumpers
Ford
Metzenbaum
Wirth

Evans
Hatfield
Murkowski
Wallop
Nickles

Environment and Public Works

■ Phone: 224-6176   ■ Room: SD-458

Environmental policy, research and development; air, water and noise pollution; construction and maintenance of highways; environmental aspects of Outer Continental Shelf lands; environmental effects of toxic substances, other than pesticides; fisheries and wildlife; flood control and improvements of rivers and harbors; non-military environmental regulation and control of nuclear energy; ocean dumping; public buildings and grounds; public works, bridges and dams; regional economic development; solid waste disposal and recycling; water resources.

Party Ratio: D 9 - R 7

Quentin N. Burdick
Chairman

Robert T. Stafford
Ranking Member

Quentin N. Burdick, N.D.
Daniel Patrick Moynihan, N.Y.
George J. Mitchell, Maine
Max Baucus, Mont.
Frank R. Lautenberg, N.J.
John B. Breaux, La.
Barbara A. Mikulski, Md.
Harry Reid, Nev.
Bob Graham, Fla.

Robert T. Stafford, Vt.
John H. Chafee, R.I.
Alan K. Simpson, Wyo.
Steve Symms, Idaho
Dave Durenberger, Minn.
John W. Warner, Va.
Larry Pressler, S.D.

Majority Staff Director: Peter Prowitt 224-7845 Rm SD-458
Minority Staff Director: Bailey Guard 224-7854 Rm SD-410

Subcommittees

Environmental Protection

■ Phone: 224-6691   ■ Room: SH-408

Mitchell — chairman

Moynihan	*Chafee*
Baucus	*Stafford*
Lautenberg	*Simpson*
Breaux	*Durenberger*
Graham	*Pressler*

Hazardous Wastes and Toxic Substances

■ Phone: 224-6176   ■ Room: SD-458

Baucus — chairman

Lautenberg	*Durenberger*
Mikulski	*Chafee*
Reid	*Simpson*
Graham	*Symms*

Nuclear Regulation

■ Phone: 224-6176   ■ Room: SD-458

Breaux — chairman

Moynihan	*Simpson*
Mitchell	*Symms*
Reid	*Warner*

Superfund and Environmental Oversight

■ Phone: 224-6176   ■ Room: SD-458

Lautenberg — chairman

Baucus	*Warner*
Mikulski	*Pressler*

Water Resources, Transportation and Infrastructure

■ Phone: 224-3597   ■ Room: SH-505

Moynihan — chairman

Burdick	*Symms*
Mitchell	*Stafford*
Breaux	*Chafee*
Mikulski	*Durenberger*
Reid	*Warner*
Graham	*Pressler*

Finance

■ Phone: 224-4515   ■ Room: SD-205

Revenue measures generally; taxes; tariffs and import quotas; foreign trade agreements; customs; revenue sharing; federal debt limit; Social Security; health programs financed by taxes or trust funds. Chairman and ranking minority member are members *ex officio* of all subcommittees of which they are not regular members.

Party Ratio: D 11 - R 9

Lloyd Bentsen **Chairman**	**Bob Packwood** **Ranking Member**

Lloyd Bentsen, Texas	*Bob Packwood, Ore.*
Spark M. Matsunaga, Hawaii	*Robert Dole, Kan.*
	William V. Roth Jr., Del.
Daniel Patrick Moynihan, N.Y.	*John C. Danforth, Mo.*
	John H. Chafee, R.I.
Max Baucus, Mont.	*John Heinz, Pa.*
David L. Boren, Okla.	*Malcolm Wallop, Wyo.*
Bill Bradley, N.J.	*Dave Durenberger, Minn.*
George J. Mitchell, Maine	*William L. Armstrong, Colo.*
David Pryor, Ark.	
Donald W. Riegle Jr., Mich.	
John D. Rockefeller IV, W.Va.	
Tom Daschle, S.D.	

Majority Staff Director and Chief Counsel: William J. Wilkins 224-4515 Rm SD-205
Minority Chief of Staff: Mary McAuliffe 224-5315 Rm SD-G08

Subcommittees

Energy and Agricultural Taxation

■ Phone: 224-4515   ■ Room: SD-205

Boren — chairman

Matsunaga	*Wallop*
Daschle	*Armstrong*

Health

■ Phone: 224-4515   ■ Room: SD-205

Mitchell — chairman

Bentsen	*Durenberger*
Baucus	*Packwood*
Bradley	*Dole*
Pryor	*Chafee*
Riegle	*Heinz*
Rockefeller	

International Debt

■ Phone: 224-4515   ■ Room: SD-205

Bradley — chairman

Riegle	*Roth*
Rockefeller	*Dole*
	Danforth

International Trade

■ Phone: 224-4515   ■ Room: SD-205

Matsunaga — chairman

Bentsen	*Danforth*
Moynihan	*Packwood*
Baucus	*Roth*
Boren	*Chafee*
Bradley	*Heinz*
Mitchell	*Wallop*
Riegle	*Armstrong*
Rockefeller	*Durenberger*
Daschle	

Private Retirement Plans and Oversight of the Internal Revenue Service

■ Phone: 224-4515   ■ Room: SD-205

Pryor — chairman

Bentsen	*Heinz*

Social Security and Family Policy

■ Phone: 224-4515   ■ Room: SD-205

Moynihan — chairman

Boren	*Dole*
Mitchell	*Durenberger*
Daschle	*Armstrong*

Taxation and Debt Management

■ Phone: 224-4515   ■ Room: SD-205

Baucus — chairman

Matsunaga	*Chafee*
Moynihan	*Roth*
Pryor	*Danforth*
	Wallop

Foreign Relations

■ Phone: 224-4651   ■ Room: SD-446

Relations of the United States with foreign nations generally; treaties; foreign economic, military, technical and humanitarian assistance; foreign loans; diplomatic service; International Red Cross; international aspects of nuclear energy; International Monetary Fund; intervention abroad and declarations of war; foreign trade; national security; oceans and international environmental and scientific affairs; protection of U.S. citizens abroad; United Nations; World Bank and other development assistance organizations. Chairman and ranking minority member are members *ex officio* of all subcommittees of which they are not regular members.

Party Radio: D 10 - R 9

Claiborne Pell Chairman	Jesse Helms Ranking Member

Claiborne Pell, R.I.	*Jesse Helms, N.C.*
Joseph R. Biden Jr., Del.	*Richard G. Lugar, Ind.*
Paul S. Sarbanes, Md.	*Nancy Landon Kassebaum,*
Alan Cranston, Calif.	*Kan.*
Christopher J. Dodd, Conn.	*Rudy Boschwitz, Minn.*
John Kerry, Mass.	*Larry Pressler, S.D.*
Paul Simon, Ill.	*Frank H. Murkowski, Alaska*
Terry Sanford, N.C.	*Paul S. Trible Jr., Va.*
Brock Adams, Wash.	*Daniel J. Evans, Wash.*
Daniel P. Moynihan, N.Y.	*Mitch McConnell, Ky.*

Majority Staff Director: Geryld B. Christianson 224-4651 Rm SD-439
Minority Staff Director: James Lucier 224-7391 Rm SD-447

Subcommittees

African Affairs

■ Phone: 224-4651   ■ Room: SD-423

Simon — chairman

Sanford	*Kassebaum*
Moynihan	*Helms*

East Asian and Pacific Affairs

■ Phone: 224-4651   ■ Room: SD-423

Cranston — chairman

Dodd	*Murkowski*
Kerry	*Evans*
Adams	*Lugar*
Vacancy	*McConnell*

European Affairs

■ Phone: 224-4651   ■ Room: SD-423

Biden — chairman

Sarbanes	*Pressler*
Simon	*Trible*
Vacancy	*Boschwitz*

International Economic Policy, Trade, Oceans and Environment

■ Phone: 224-4651   ■ Room: SD-423

Sanford — chairman

Sarbanes	*Evans*
Dodd	*Murkowski*
Adams	*Lugar*

Near Eastern and South Asian Affairs

■ Phone: 224-4651   ■ Room: SD-423

Sarbanes — chairman

Cranston	*Boschwitz*
Sanford	*McConnell*
Moynihan	*Pressler*

Terrorism, Narcotics and International Communications

■ Phone: 224-4651   ■ Room: SD-423

Kerry — chairman

Adams	*McConnell*
Moynihan	*Murkowski*

Western Hemisphere and Peace Corps Affairs

■ Phone: 224-4651   ■ Room: SD-423

Dodd — chairman

Cranston	*Lugar*
Kerry	*Kassebaum*
Sanford	*Trible*
Pell	*Evans*

Governmental Affairs

■ Phone: 224-4751   ■ Room: SD-340

Budget and accounting measures; census and statistics; federal civil service; congressional organization; intergovernmental relations; government information; District of Columbia; organization and management of nuclear export policy; executive branch reorganization; Postal Service; efficiency, economy and effectiveness of government. Chairman and ranking minority member are non-voting members *ex officio* of all subcommittees of which they are not regular members.

Party Ratio: D 8 - R 6

John Glenn
Chairman

William V. Roth Jr.
Ranking Member

John Glenn, Oh.	*William V. Roth Jr., Del.*
Lawton Chiles, Fla.	*Ted Stevens, Alaska*
Sam Nunn, Ga.	*William S. Cohen, Maine*
Carl Levin, Mich.	*Warren B. Rudman, N.H.*

Jim Sasser, Tenn.
David Pryor, Ark.
George J. Mitchell, Maine
Jeff Bingaman, N.M.

John Heinz, Pa.
Paul S. Trible Jr., Va.

Majority Staff Director: Len Weiss 224-4751 Rm SD-340
Minority Staff Director: Jo Anne Barnhart 224-2627 Rm SD-346

Subcommittees

Federal Services, Post Office and Civil Service

■ Phone: 224-2254   ■ Room: SH-601

Pryor — chairman

Sasser
Bingaman

Stevens
Trible

Federal Spending, Budget and Accounting

■ Phone: 224-9000   ■ Room: SD-326

Chiles — chairman

Nunn
Levin
Bingaman

Rudman
Stevens
Heinz

Government Efficiency, Federalism and the District of Columbia

■ Phone: 224-4718   ■ Room: SH-432

Sasser — chairman

Levin
Mitchell

Heinz
Cohen

Oversight of Government Management

■ Phone: 224-3682   ■ Room: SH-442

Levin — chairman

Chiles
Pryor
Mitchell
Bingaman

Cohen
Rudman
Heinz
Stevens

Permanent Subcommittee on Investigations

■ Phone: 224-3721   ■ Room: SR-100

Nunn — chairman

Glenn
Chiles
Levin
Sasser
Pryor
Mitchell

Roth
Stevens
Cohen
Rudman
Trible

Judiciary

■ Phone: 224-5225   ■ Room: SD-224

Civil and criminal judicial proceedings generally; penitentiaries; bankruptcy, mutiny, espionage and counterfeiting; civil liberties; constitutional amendments; apportionment of representatives; government information; immigration and naturalization; interstate compacts generally; claims against the United States; patents, copyrights and trademarks; monopolies and unlawful restraints of trade; holidays and celebrations.

Party Ratio: D 8 - R 6

Joseph R. Biden Jr.
Chairman

Strom Thurmond
Ranking Member

Joseph R. Biden Jr., Del.
Edward M. Kennedy, Mass.
Robert C. Byrd, W.Va.
Howard M. Metzenbaum, Ohio
Dennis DeConcini, Ariz.
Patrick J. Leahy, Vt.
Howell Heflin, Ala.
Paul Simon, Ill.

Strom Thurmond, S.C.
Alan K. Simpson, Wyo.
Charles E. Grassley, Iowa
Orrin G. Hatch, Utah
Arlen Specter, Pa.
Gordon J. Humphrey, N.H.

Majority Chief Counsel: Mark Gitenstein 224-5225 Rm SD-224
Minority Chief Counsel and Staff Director: Dennis W. Shedd 224-2891 Rm SD-148

Subcommittees

Antitrust, Monopolies and Business Rights

■ Phone: 224-5701　　　■ Room: SH-308

Metzenbaum — chairman

DeConcini	*Thurmond*
Heflin	*Specter*
Simon	*Humphrey*
Kennedy	*Hatch*

Constitution

■ Phone: 224-5573　　　■ Room: SD-519

Simon — chairman

Metzenbaum	*Specter*
DeConcini	*Hatch*
Kennedy	

Courts and Administrative Practice

■ Phone: 224-4022　　　■ Room: SH-223

Heflin — chairman

Metzenbaum	*Grassley*
DeConcini	*Thurmond*

Immigration and Refugee Affairs

■ Phone: 224-7877　　　■ Room: SD-518

Kennnedy — chairman

Simon	*Simpson*

Patents, Copyrights and Trademarks

■ Phone: 224-8178　　　■ Room: SH-327

DeConcini — chairman

Kennedy	*Hatch*
Leahy	*Simpson*
Heflin	*Grassley*

Technology and the Law

■ Phone: 224-3407　　　■ Room: SH-815

Leahy — chairman

DeConcini	*Humphrey*

Labor and Human Resources

■ Phone: 224-5375　　　■ Room: SD-428

Education, labor, health and public welfare generally; aging; arts and humanities; biomedical research and development; child labor; convict labor; American National Red Cross; equal employment opportunity; handicapped individuals; labor standards and statistics; mediation and arbitration of labor disputes; occupational safety and health; private pension plans; public health; railway labor and retirement; regulation of foreign laborers; student loans; wages and hours. Chairman and ranking minority member are members *ex officio* of all subcommittees of which they are not regular members.

Party Ratio: D 9 - R 7

Edward M. Kennedy **Chairman**	**Orrin G. Hatch** **Ranking Member**

Edward M. Kennedy, Mass.	*Orrin G. Hatch, Utah*
Claiborne Pell, R.I.	*Robert T. Stafford, Vt.*
Howard M. Metzenbaum, Ohio	*Dan Quayle, Ind.*
Spark M. Matsunaga, Hawaii	*Strom Thurmond, S.C.*
Christopher J. Dodd, Conn.	*Lowell P. Weicker Jr., Conn.*
Paul Simon, Ill.	*Thad Cochran, Miss.*
Tom Harkin, Iowa.	*Gordon J. Humphrey, N.H.*
Brock Adams, Wash.	
Barbara A. Mikulski, Md.	

*Majority Staff Director and Chief Counsel: Thomas M. Rollins
224-5375 Rm SD-428
Minority Staff Director: Hayden G. Bryan 224-1283 Rm SH-833*

Subcommittees

Aging

■ Phone: 224-3239   ■ Room: SH-404

Matsunaga — chairman

Pell	*Cochran*
Metzenbaum	*Thurmond*
Dodd	*Weicker*

Children, Family, Drugs and Alcoholism

■ Phone: 224-5630   ■ Room: SH-639

Dodd — chairman

Pell	*Thurmond*
Harkin	*Cochran*
Adams	*Hatch*

Education, Arts and Humanities

■ Phone: 224-7666   ■ Room: SD-648

Pell — chairman

Metzenbaum	*Stafford*
Matsunaga	*Hatch*
Dodd	*Quayle*
Simon	*Thurmond*
Mikulski	*Weicker*

Employment and Productivity

■ Phone: 224-5575   ■ Room: SD-644

Simon — chairman

Harkin	*Humphrey*
Adams	*Hatch*
Mikulski	*Quayle*

Handicapped

■ Phone: 224-6265   ■ Room: SH-113

Harkin — chairman

Metzenbaum	*Weicker*
Simon	*Stafford*
Adams	*Cochran*

Labor

■ Phone: 224-5546   ■ Room: SH-608

Metzenbaum — chairman

Matsunaga	*Quayle*
Harkin	*Humphrey*
Mikulski	*Stafford*

Rules and Administration

■ Phone: 224-6352   ■ Room: SR-305

Senate administration generally; corrupt practices; qualifications of senators; contested elections; federal elections generally; Government Printing Office; *Congressional Record;* meetings of Congress and attendance of members; presidential succession; the Capitol, congressional office buildings, the Library of Congress, the Smithsonian Institution and the Botanic Garden.

Party Ratio: D 9 - R 7

Wendell H. Ford
Chairman

Ted Stevens
Ranking Member

Wendell H. Ford, Ky.
Claiborne Pell, R.I.
Robert C. Byrd, W.Va.
Daniel K. Inouye, Hawaii
Dennis DeConcini, Ariz.
Albert Gore Jr., Tenn.
Daniel Patrick Moynihan, N.Y.
Christopher J. Dodd, Conn.
Brock Adams, Wash.

Ted Stevens, Alaska
Mark O. Hatfield, Ore.
James A. McClure, Idaho
Jesse Helms, N.C.
John W. Warner, Va.
Robert Dole, Kan.
Jake Garn, Utah

Majority Staff Director: James King 224-6351 Rm SR-305
Minority Staff Director: Wayne A. Schley 224-8923 Rm SR-479

(No standing subcommittees.)

Select Committee on Secret Military Assistance to Iran and the Nicaraguan Opposition

■ Phone: 224-9960   ■ Room: SH-901

Conduct an investigation and study of activities by the National Security Council and other agencies of the U.S. government with respect to the direct or indirect sale, shipment, or other provision of arms to Iran and the use of the proceeds from any such transaction to provide assistance to any faction or insurgency in Nicaragua or in any other foreign country, or to further any other purpose, and related matters.

Party Ratio: D 6 - R 5

Daniel K. Inouye
Chairman

Warren B. Rudman
Vice Chairman

Daniel K. Inouye, Hawaii
George J. Mitchell, Maine
Sam Nunn, Ga.
Paul S. Sarbanes, Md.
Howell Heflin, Ala.
David L. Boren, Okla.

Warren B. Rudman, N.H.
James A. McClure, Idaho
Orrin G. Hatch, Utah
William S. Cohen, Maine
Paul S. Trible Jr., Va.

Executive Director: Mary Jane Chicchi 224-9960 Rm SH-901
Chief Counsel: Arthur L. Liman 224-9960 Rm SH-901

(No standing subcommittees.)

Select Ethics

■ Phone: 224-2981   ■ Room: SH-220

Studies and investigates standards and conduct of Senate members and employees and may recommend remedial action.

Party Ratio: D 3 - R 3

Howell Heflin
Chairman

Warren B. Rudman
Vice Chairman

Howell Heflin, Ala.
David Pryor, Ark.
Terry Sanford, N.C.

Warren B. Rudman, N.H.
Jesse Helms, N.C.
Nancy Landon Kassebaum, Kan.

Acting Staff Director and Chief Counsel: Wilson Abney 224-2981 Rm SH-220

(No standing subcommittees.)

Select Indian Affairs

■ Phone: 224-2251   ■ Room: SH-838

Problems and opportunities of Indians, including Indian land management and trust responsibilities, education, health, special services, loan programs and Indian claims against the United States.

Party Ratio: D 5 - R 3

Daniel K. Inouye
Chairman

Daniel J. Evans
Vice Chairman

Daniel K. Inouye, Hawaii
John Melcher, Mont.
Dennis DeConcini, Ariz.
Quentin N. Burdick, N.D.
Thomas A. Daschle, S.D.

Daniel J. Evans, Wash.
Frank H. Murkowski, Alaska
John McCain, Ariz.

Majority Staff Director: Alan R. Parker 224-2251 Rm SH-838
Minority Counsel: Joe Mentor Jr. 224-2251 Rm SH-838

(No standing subcommittees.)

Select Intelligence

Phone: 224-1700   Room: SH-211

Legislative and budgetary authority over the Central Intelligence Agency, the Defense Intelligence Agency, the National Security Agency and intelligence activities of the Federal Bureau of Investigation and other components of the federal intelligence community. The majority leader and minority leader are members *ex officio* of the committee.

Party Ratio: D 8 - R 7

| **David L. Boren** **Chairman** | **William S. Cohen** **Vice Chairman** |

David L. Boren, Okla.
Lloyd Bentsen, Texas
Sam Nunn, Ga.
Ernest F. Hollings, S.C.
Bill Bradley, N.J.
Alan Cranston, Calif.
Dennis DeConcini, Ariz.
Howard M. Metzenbaum, Ohio

William S. Cohen, Maine
William V. Roth Jr., Del.
Orrin G. Hatch, Utah
Frank H. Murkowski, Alaska
Arlen Specter, Pa.
Chic Hecht, Nev.
John W. Warner, Va.

Majority Staff Director: Sven Holmes 224-1700 Rm SH-211
Minority Staff Director: Jim Dykstra 224-1700 Rm SH-211

(No standing subcommittees.)

Small Business

■ Phone: 224-5175   ■ Room: SR-428A

Problems of small business; Small Business Administration.

Party Ratio: D 10 - R 9

Dale Bumpers
Chairman

Lowell P. Weicker Jr.
Ranking Member

Dale Bumpers, Ark.
Sam Nunn, Ga.
Jim Sasser, Tenn.
Max Baucus, Mont.
Carl Levin, Mich.
Alan J. Dixon, Ill.
David L. Boren, Okla.
Tom Harkin, Iowa
John Kerry, Mass.
Barbara A. Mikulski, Md.

Lowell P. Weicker Jr., Conn.
Rudy Boschwitz, Minn.
Warren B. Rudman, N.H.
Alfonse M. D'Amato, N.Y.
Bob Kasten, Wis.
Larry Pressler, S.D.
Malcolm Wallop, Wyo.
Christopher S. "Kit" Bond, Mo.
David Karnes, Neb.

Majority Chief Counsel and Staff Director: John W. Ball 224-8497 Rm SR-428A
Minority Staff Director: Robert J. Dotchin 224-8494 Rm SH-622

Subcommittees

Competition and Antitrust Enforcement

■ Phone: 224-5175   ■ Room: SR-428A

Harkin — chairman

Bumpers   *Wallop*

Export Expansion

■ Phone: 224-5175   ■ Room: SR-428A

Sasser — chairman

Bumpers	*Boschwitz*
Nunn	*D'Amato*
Harkin	*Wallop*

Government Contracting and Paperwork Reduction

■ Phone: 224-5175   ■ Room: SR-428A

Dixon — chairman

Sasser	*Kasten*
Mikulski	*Rudman*

Innovation, Technology and Productivity

■ Phone: 224-5175   ■ Room: SR-428A

Levin — chairman

Baucus	*Rudman*
Boren	*Weicker*
Kerry	*Bond*

Rural Economy and Family Farming

■ Phone: 224-5175   ■ Room: SR-428A

Baucus — chairman

Nunn	*D'Amato*
Levin	*Boschwitz*
Dixon	*Kasten*
Boren	*Pressler*

Urban and Minority-Owned Business Development

■ Phone: 224-5175   ■ Room: SR-428A

Kerry — chairman

Mikulski	*Bond*

Special Aging

■ Phone: 224-5364   ■ Room: SH-628

Problems and opportunities of older people including health, income, employment, housing and care and assistance. Reports findings and makes recommendations to the Senate, but cannot report legislation.

Party Ratio: D 10 - R 9

John Melcher
Chairman

John Heinz
Ranking Member

John Melcher, Mont.	*John Heinz, Pa.*
John Glenn, Ohio	*William S. Cohen, Maine*
Lawton Chiles, Fla.	*Larry Pressler, S.D.*
David Pryor, Ark.	*Charles E. Grassley, Iowa*
Bill Bradley, N.J.	*Pete Wilson, Calif.*
Quentin N. Burdick, N.D.	*Pete V. Domenici, N.M.*
J. Bennett Johnston, La.	*John H. Chafee, R.I.*
John B. Breaux, La.	*David Durenberger, Minn.*
Richard C. Shelby, Ala.	*Alan K. Simpson, Wyo.*
Harry Reid, Nev.	

Majority Staff Director: Max I. Richtman 224-5364 Rm SH-628
Minority Staff Director: Stephen R. McConnell 224-1467 Rm SD-G41

(No standing subcommittees.)

Veterans' Affairs

■ Phone: 224-9126   ■ Room: SR-414

Veterans' measures generally; compensation; armed forces life insurance; national cemeteries; pensions; readjustment benefits; veterans' hospitals, medical care and treatment; vocational rehabilitation and education.

Party Ratio: D 6 - R 5

Alan Cranston
Chairman

Frank H. Murkowski
Ranking Member

Alan Cranston, Calif.
Spark M. Matsunaga, Hawaii
Dennis DeConcini, Ariz.
George J. Mitchell, Maine
John D. Rockefeller IV, W.Va.
Bob Graham, Fla.

Frank H. Murkowski, Alaska
Alan K. Simpson, Wyo.
Strom Thurmond, S.C.
Robert T. Stafford, Vt.
Arlen Specter, Pa.

Majority Chief Counsel and Staff Director: Jonathan Steinberg
224-6202 Rm SR-414
Minority Chief Counsel and Staff Director: Anthony J. Principi
224-4487 Rm SH-202

(No standing subcommittees.)

House Committees

House Party Committees, 100th Congress

DEMOCRATS

Jim Wright
Speaker of the House

Thomas S. Foley
Majority Leader

Tony Coelho
Majority Whip

Richard A. Gephardt
Caucus Chairman

Party Leadership

Speaker of the House — Jim Wright, Texas.................................... 224-8040
Majority Leader — Thomas S. Foley, Wash...................................... 224-5604
Majority Whip — Tony Coelho, Calif.. 224-3130
Chairman of the Caucus — Richard A. Gephardt, Mo............................ 226-3210
Vice Chairman of the Caucus — Mary Rose Oakar, Ohio 226-3210
Chief Deputy Whip — David E. Bonior, Mich. 225-0080
Deputy Whips — Dennis E. Eckart, Ohio; W.G. "Bill" Hefner, N.C.; Steny H. Hoyer, Md.; Daniel A. Mica, Fla.; Norman Y. Mineta, Calif.; Joe Moakley, Mass.; Charles B. Rangel, N.Y.; Marty Russo, Ill.; Patricia Schroeder, Colo.; Pat Williams, Mont.
Whip Task Force Chairmen — Martin Frost, Texas; Bart Gordon, Tenn.; David R. Obey, Wis.; Leon E. Panetta, Calif.
At-Large Whips — Les Aspin, Wis.; Les AuCoin, Ore.; Tom Bevill, Ala.; Rick Boucher, Va.; Barbara Boxer, Calif.; Joseph E. Brennan, Maine; Terry L. Bruce, Ill.; Benjamin L. Cardin, Md.; Bob Carr, Mich.; Ronald D. Coleman, Texas; Butler Derrick, S.C.; Byron L. Dorgan, N.D.; Vic Fazio, Calif.; William D. Ford, Mich.; Barney Frank, Mass.; Sam Gejdenson, Conn.; Dan Glickman, Kan.; William H. Gray III, Pa.; Ed Jenkins, Ga.; Jim Jontz, Ind.; Barbara B. Kennelly, Conn.; Dale E. Kildee, Mich.; H. Martin Lancaster, N.C.; Mickey Leland, Texas; Mike Lowry, Wash.; Bruce A. Morrison, Conn.; Robert J. Mrazek, N.Y.; John P. Murtha, Pa.; Timothy J. Penny, Minn.; Bill Richardson, N.M.; Charlie Rose, N.C.; Dan Rostenkowski, Ill.; Philip R. Sharp, Ind.; Gerry Sikorski, Minn.; Norman Sisisky, Va.; Louise M. Slaughter, N.Y.; John M. Spratt Jr., S.C.; Al Swift, Wash.; Mike Synar, Okla.; Peter J. Visclosky, Ind.; Alan Wheat, Mo.; Bob Wise, W.Va.; Howard Wolpe, Mich.; Ron Wyden, Ore.

Assistant Whips, by zone numbers:

1. Chester G. Atkins, Mass. — Connecticut, Massachusetts, Rhode Island, Maine
2. Henry J. Nowak, N.Y., and Charles E. Schumer, N.Y. — New York
3. Peter H. Kostmayer, Pa. — Pennsylvania
4. William J. Hughes, N.J. — Delaware, Maryland, New Jersey
5. Tim Valentine, N.C. — North Carolina, Virginia
6. Charles Hatcher, Ga. — Georgia, South Carolina
7. Dennis M. Hertel, Mich. — Michigan
8. Bruce F. Vento, Minn. — Minnesota, Wisconsin

9. Carroll Hubbard Jr., Ky. — Indiana, Kentucky
10. Thomas A. Luken, Ohio — Ohio, West Virginia
11. Harold E. Ford, Tenn. — Louisiana, Mississippi, Tennessee
12. Lawrence J. Smith, Fla. — Alabama, Florida
13. Harold L. Volkmer, Mo. — Iowa, Missouri
14. Sidney R. Yates, Ill. — Illinois
15. J. J. Pickle, Texas, and Henry B. Gonzalez, Texas — Texas
16. Tommy F. Robinson, Ark. — Arkansas, Kansas, Oklahoma
17. David E. Skaggs, Colo. — Arizona, Colorado, Montana, Nevada, New Mexico, North Dakota, South Dakota, Utah
18. Don Bonker, Wash. — Hawaii, Idaho, Oregon, Washington
19. Richard H. Lehman, Calif., and Mel Levine, Calif. — California

The five states not covered — Alaska, Nebraska, New Hampshire, Vermont and Wyoming — have no Democratic representatives.

Steering and Policy Committee

■ Phone: 226-3260   ■ Room: 114 HOB Annex #1

Scheduling of legislation and Democratic committee assignments.

Jim Wright, Texas, chairman
Thomas S. Foley, Wash., vice chairman
Richard A. Gephardt, Mo., 2nd vice chairman

Beryl Anthony Jr., Ark. †
David E. Bonior, Mich. †
Jack Brooks, Texas
Jim Chapman, Texas
Tony Coelho, Calif. †
Butler Derrick, S.C.
Norman D. Dicks, Wash.
John D. Dingell, Mich.
Brian J. Donnelly, Mass.
Joseph D. Early, Mass.
Ronnie G. Flippo, Ala.
Harold E. Ford, Tenn.
Dan Glickman, Kan.
William H. Gray III, Pa. †
Steny H. Hoyer, Md.

Marcy Kaptur, Ohio
Dave McCurdy, Okla.
Matthew F. McHugh, N.Y.
Daniel A. Mica, Fla.
Mary Rose Oaker, Ohio †
James L. Oberstar, Minn.
Claude Pepper, Fla. †
Dan Rostenkowski, Ill. †
Marty Russo, Ill.
Louis Stokes, Ohio
Bob Traxler, Mich.
Henry A. Waxman, Calif.
Jamie L. Whitten, Miss. †

† Member ex officio from the leadership.

Personnel Committee

■ Phone: 225-4068   ■ Room: B343 RHOB

Selects, appoints and supervises Democratic patronage positions.

Jack Brooks, Texas

Democratic Congressional Campaign Committee

■ Phone: 863-1500   ■ 430 S. Capitol St. S.E. 20003

Campaign support committee for Democratic House candidates.

Beryl Anthony Jr., Ark., chairman
Dan Rostenkowski, Ill., vice chairman

Co-Chairs: Michael A. Andrews, Texas; Richard J. Durbin, Ill.; Dennis E. Eckart, Ohio *; Mel Levine, Calif.; Lawrence J. Smith, Fla. *

Daniel K. Akaka, Hawaii
Bill Alexander, Ark.
Frank Annunzio, Ill.
Les AuCoin, Ore.
Tom Bevill, Ala.
James Bilbray, Nev.
Don Bonker, Wash.
Joseph E. Brennan, Maine
Beverly B. Byron, Md.
Thomas R. Carper, Del.
Bill Chappell Jr., Fla.
William L. Clay, Mo.
Tony Coelho, Calif. *
Ron de Lugo, Virgin
  Islands
John D. Dingell, Mich.
Byron L. Dorgan, N.D.
Wayne Dowdy, Miss.
Mervyn M. Dymally, Calif. *
Joseph D. Early, Mass.
Walter E. Fauntroy, D.C.
Vic Fazio, Calif. *
Edward F. Feighan, Ohio
James J. Florio, N.J.
Thomas S. Foley, Wash. *
Martin Frost, Texas
Jaime B. Fuster, Puerto
  Rico
Sam Gejdenson, Conn.
Richard A. Gephardt,
  Mo. *

Bart Gordon, Tenn.
Lee H. Hamilton, Ind.
W. G. "Bill" Hefner, N.C.
Ed Jenkins, Ga.
Tim Johnson, S.D.
Gerald D. Kleczka, Wis.
Richard H. Lehman, Calif.
Mike Lowry, Wash.
Alan B. Mollohan, W.Va.
John P. Murtha, Pa.
David R. Nagle, Iowa
Mary Rose Oakar, Ohio *
James L. Oberstar, Minn.
Wayne Owens, Utah
Carl C. Perkins, Ky.
Bill Richardson, N.M.
Fernand J. St Germain, R.I.
Patricia Schroeder, Colo.
Charles E. Schumer, N.Y.
Norman Sisisky, Va.
Jim Slattery, Kan.
John M. Spratt Jr., S.C.
Richard H. Stallings, Idaho
Fofō I. F. Sunia, American
  Samoa
Mike Synar, Okla.
W. J. "Billy" Tauzin, La.
Morris K. Udall, Ariz.
Pat Williams, Mont.
Jim Wright, Texas †

† Member ex officio from the leadership.
* Member appointed by the Speaker of the House.

REPUBLICANS

Robert H. Michel
Minority Leader

Trent Lott
Minority Whip

Dick Cheney
Conference Chairman

Lynn Martin
Conference Vice Chairman

Party Leadership

Minority Leader — Robert H. Michel, Ill. 225-0600
Minority Whip — Trent Lott, Miss. 225-0197
Chairman of the Conference — Dick Cheney, Wyo. 225-5107
Vice Chairman of the Conference — Lynn Martin, Ill. 225-5107
Secretary of the Conference — Robert J. Lagomarsino, Calif. 225-5107
Chief Deputy Whip — Edward R. Madigan, Ill. 225-4236
Deputy Whips — Steve Bartlett, Texas; Judd Gregg, N.H.; Carl D.
    Pursell, Mich.; Joe Skeen, Ariz.; Olympia J. Snowe, Maine
Sophomore Class Whip — Bill Schuette, Mich. 225-3561
Freshman Class Whip — Lamar Smith, Texas 225-4236

The assistant minority whips are divided into four divisions, each with an overall regional whip and assistant whips in charge of
a specific number of members as follows:

New England and Mid-Atlantic States — Dean A. Gallo,
    N.J. (10 states, 42 members):

David O'B. Martin, N.Y. (10 members)
John G. Rowland, Conn. (8 members)
Richard T. Schulze, Pa. (12 members)
Gerald B. H. Solomon, N.Y. (8 members)

Western and Plains States — Duncan Hunter,
    Calif. (16 states and 1 territory, 49 members):

Hank Brown, Colo. (11 members)
Bill Lowery, Calif. (12 members)
Manuel Lujan Jr., N.M. (10 members)
Sid Morrison, Wash. (12 members)

Midwestern States — Arlan Stangeland, Minn.
    (8 states, 45 members):

Dan Burton, Ind. (10 members)
E. Thomas Coleman, Mo. (12 members)
Vin Weber, Minn. (10 members)
Chalmers P. Wylie, Ohio (9 members)

Southern States — Don Sundquist, Tenn. (12 states,
    42 members)

Thomas J. Bliley Jr., Va. (10 members)
Thomas D. DeLay, Texas (10 members)
William L. Dickinson, Ala. (8 members)
Andy Ireland, Fla. (10 members)

The four states not covered — Delaware, North Dakota, South Dakota, West Virginia — have no Republican representatives.

Committee on Committees

■ Phone: 225-0600   ■ Room: H-230 Capitol

Makes Republican committee assignments.

Robert H. Michel, Ill., chairman

Bill Archer, Texas
Richard H. Baker, La.
Helen Delich Bentley, Md.
Ben Blaz, Guam
William S. Broomfield, Mich.
Hank Brown, Colo.
Jack Buechner, Mo.
Jim Bunning, Ky.
Rod Chandler, Wash.
Dick Cheney, Wyo.
Dan Coats, Ind.
Sylvio O. Conte, Mass.
Jim Courter, N.J.
Larry Craig, Idaho
Thomas D. DeLay, Texas
William L. Dickinson, Ala.
Mickey Edwards, Okla.
Bill Frenzel, Minn.
Judd Gregg, N.H.
John Paul Hammerschmidt, Ark.
James V. Hansen, Utah
Frank Horton, N.Y.
James M. Jeffords, Vt.

Nancy L. Johnson, Conn.
Delbert L. Latta, Ohio
Jerry Lewis, Calif.
Trent Lott, Miss.
Ron Marlenee, Mont.
J. Alex McMillan, N.C.
Joseph M. McDade, Pa.
Jan Meyers, Kan.
Stan Parris, Va.
Toby Roth, Wis.
Patricia F. Saiki, Hawaii
Claudine Schneider, R.I.
Joe Skeen, N.M.
Robert F. Smith, Ore.
Virginia Smith, Neb.
Olympia J. Snowe, Maine
Floyd Spence, S.C.
Bob Stump, Ariz.
Don Sundquist, Tenn.
Pat Swindall, Ga.
Tom Tauke, Iowa
Barbara F. Vucanovich, Nev.
C. W. Bill Young, Fla.
Don Young, Alaska

Policy Committee

■ Phone: 225-6168   ■ Room: 1620 LHOB

Advises on party action and policy.

Jerry Lewis, Calif., chairman

Doug Bereuter, Neb.
Jack Buechner, Mo.
Silvio O. Conte, Mass.
Larry Combest, Texas
Thomas D. DeLay, Texas
John J. Duncan, Tenn.
Mickey Edwards, Okla.
Hamilton Fish Jr., N.Y.
Bill Frenzel, Minn.
Bill Goodling, Pa.
Fred Grandy, Iowa
Paul B. Henry, Mich.
Jack F. Kemp, N.Y.
Ernie Konnyu, Calif.
Robert J. Lagomarsino, Calif.

Delbert L. Latta, Ohio
Trent Lott, Miss.
Lynn Martin, Ill.
Bill McCollum, Fla.
Robert H. Michel, Ill.
James H. Quillen, Tenn.
Ralph Regula, Ohio
John J. Rhodes III, Ariz.
H. James Saxton, N.J.
Bill Schuette, Mich.
Gerald B. H. Solomon, N.Y.
Floyd Spence, S.C.
Guy Vander Jagt, Mich.
Barbara F. Vucanovich, Nev.

National Republican Congressional Committee

■ Phone: 479-7000   ■ 320 First St. S.E. 20003

Campaign support committee for Republican House candidates.

Guy Vander Jagt, Mich., chairman

Michael Bilirakis, Fla.
Ben Blaz, Guam
Sonny Callahan, Ala.
Dick Cheney, Wyo. †
Howard Coble, N.C.
Silvio O. Conte, Mass.
Lawrence Coughlin, Pa.
Larry E. Craig, Idaho
Hal Daub, Neb.
John J. Duncan, Tenn.
Mickey Edwards, Okla.
Jack Fields, Texas
Newt Gingrich, Ga.
John Paul Hammerschmidt, Ark.
John Hiler, Ind.
James M. Inhofe, Okla.
James M. Jeffords, Vt.
Jack F. Kemp, N.Y. †
Jim Kolbe, Ariz.
Robert J. Lagomarsino, Calif. †
Jerry Lewis, Calif. †
Jim Lightfoot, Iowa
Bob Livingston, La.
Trent Lott, Miss. †
Manuel Lujan Jr., N.M.
Ron Marlenee, Mont.
David O'B. Martin, N.Y.

Lynn Martin, Ill. †
Robert H. Michel, Ill. †
John R. Miller, Wash.
Clarence E. Miller, Ohio
Constance A. Morella, Md.
Sid Morrison, Wash.
Howard C. Nielson, Utah
John Edward Porter, Ill.
Matthew J. Rinaldo, N.J.
Pat Roberts, Kan.
Harold Rogers, Ky.
Patricia F. Saiki, Hawaii
Dan Schaefer, Colo.
Claudine Schneider, R.I.
F. James Sensenbrenner Jr., Minn.
Denny Smith, Ore.
Robert C. Smith, N.H.
Olympia J. Snowe, Maine
Floyd Spence, S.C.
Gene Taylor, Mo.
William M. Thomas, Calif.
Barbara F. Vucanovich, Nev.
Vin Weber, Minn.
Frank R. Wolf, Va.
Don Young, Alaska
Vacancy, Conn.

† Member ex officio from the leadership.

Research Committee

■ Phone: 225-0871   ■ 1616 LHOB

At leadership's request, provides information and recommendations on specific policy issues likely to come before Congress.

Mickey Edwards, Okla., chairman

All Republican representatives are members of the committee. Task force chairmen are as follows:

Budget Reform — Ralph Regula, Ohio
Defense Reform — J. Alex McMillan, N.C.
Energy — Beau Boulter, Texas
Family Values — John R. Kasich, Ohio
High Technology — Don Ritter, Pa.
Regulatory Reform — Dick Armey, Texas
Rural Communities — Jim Lightfoot, Iowa
Trade and Competitiveness — Don Sundquist, Tenn.

House Committee Assignments, 100th Congress

Agriculture

■ Phone: 225-2171   ■ Room: 1301 LHOB

Agriculture generally; production, marketing and stabilization of agricultural prices; animal industry and diseases of animals; crop insurance and soil conservation; dairy industry; farm credit and security; forestry in general; human nutrition; home economics; inspection of livestock and meat products; plant industry, soils and agricultural engineering; rural electrification; commodities exchanges; rural development. Chairman and ranking minority member are members *ex officio* of all subcommittees of which they are not regular members.

Party Ratio: D 26 - R 17

E. "Kika" de la Garza
Chairman

Edward R. Madigan
Ranking Member

E. "Kika" de la Garza,
  Texas
Walter B. Jones, N.C.
Ed Jones, Tenn.
George E. Brown Jr., Calif.
Charlie Rose, N.C.
Glenn English, Okla.
Leon E. Panetta, Calif.
Jerry Huckaby, La.
Dan Glickman, Kan.
Tony Coelho, Calif.
Charles W. Stenholm,
  Texas
Harold L. Volkmer, Mo.
Charles Hatcher, Ga.
Robin Tallon, S.C.
Harley O. Staggers Jr.,
  W.Va.
Lane Evans, Ill.
Robert Lindsay Thomas,
  Ga.

Edward R. Madigan, Ill.
James M. Jeffords, Vt.
E. Thomas Coleman, Mo.
Ron Marlenee, Mont.
Larry J. Hopkins, Ky.
Arlan Stangeland, Minn.
Pat Roberts, Kan.
Bill Emerson, Mo.
Sid Morrison, Wash.
Steve Gunderson, Wis.
Tom Lewis, Fla.
Robert F. Smith, Ore.
Larry Combest, Texas
Bill Schuette, Mich.
Fred Grandy, Iowa
Wally Herger, Calif.
Clyde C. Holloway, La.

Jim Olin, Va.
Timothy J. Penny, Minn.
Richard H. Stallings,
  Idaho
David R. Nagle, Iowa
Jim Jontz, Ind.
Tim Johnson, S.D.
Claude Harris, Ala.
Ben Nighthorse Campbell,
  Colo.
Mike Espy, Miss.

Majority Chief of Staff: A. Mario Castillo 225-2171 Rm 1301 LHOB
Minority Counsel: John Hogan 225-2171 Rm 1301 LHOB

Subcommittees

Conservation, Credit and Rural Development

■ Phone: 225-1867   ■ Room: 1336 LHOB

Jones (Tenn.) — chairman

Tallon	*Coleman*
Evans	*Jeffords*
Thomas	*Morrison*
Stallings	*Gunderson*
English	*Combest*
Coelho	*Grandy*
Penny	
Nagle	
Jontz	

Cotton, Rice and Sugar

■ Phone: 225-1867   ■ Room: 1336 LHOB

Huckaby — chairman

Espy	*Stangeland*
Jones (Tenn.)	*Emerson*
Stallings	*Lewis*
Harris	*Combest*
Coelho	*Herger*
Stenholm	*Holloway*
Tallon	
Rose	
English	

Department Operations, Research and Foreign Agriculture

■ Phone: 225-0301   ■ Room: 1430 LHOB

Brown — chairman

Panetta	*Roberts*
Glickman	*Coleman*
Stenholm	*Morrison*
Hatcher	*Gunderson*
Staggers	*Grandy*
Espy	
Rose	

Domestic Marketing, Consumer Relations and Nutrition

■ Phone: 225-0301   ■ Room: 1430 LHOB

Panetta — chairman

Staggers	*Emerson*
Huckaby	*Lewis*
Glickman	*Schuette*
Olin	*Herger*
Coelho	
Espy	

Forests, Family Farms and Energy

■ Phone: 225-1867   ■ Room: 1336 LHOB

Volkmer — chairman

Olin	*Morrison*
Campbell	*Marlenee*
Panetta	*Smith*
Hatcher	*Schuette*
Stallings	*Herger*
Johnson	*Holloway*
Harris	
Jontz	
Vacancy	

Livestock, Dairy and Poultry

■ Phone: 225-1496   ■ Room: 1301A LHOB

Stenholm — chairman

Olin	*Jeffords*
Harris	*Hopkins*
Campbell	*Stangeland*
Rose	*Gunderson*
Coelho	*Lewis*
Volkmer	*Smith*
Johnson	
Jones (Tenn.)	
Nagle	

Tobacco and Peanuts

■ Phone: 225-8906   ■ Room: 1534 LHOB

Rose — chairman

Jones (N.C.)	*Hopkins*
Hatcher	*Roberts*
Tallon	*Combest*
Thomas	*Holloway*
English	
Stenholm	

Wheat, Soybeans and Feed Grains

■ Phone: 225-1494   ■ Room: 1301A LHOB

Glickman — chairman

Johnson	*Marlenee*
English	*Stangeland*
Huckaby	*Roberts*
Evans	*Emerson*
Penny	*Smith*
Nagle	*Schuette*
Jontz	*Grandy*
Volkmer	
Espy	
Jones (N.C.)	

Appropriations

■ Phone: 225-2771   ■ Room: H-218 Capitol

Appropriation of revenue for support of the federal government; rescissions of appropriations; transfers of unexpended balances; new spending authority under the Congressional Budget Act. Chairman and ranking minority member are members *ex officio* of all subcommittees of which they are not regular members.

Party Ratio: D 35 - R 22

Jamie L. Whitten
Chairman

Silvio O. Conte
Ranking Member

Jamie L. Whitten, Miss.

Edward P. Boland, Mass.

William H. Natcher, Ky.

Neal Smith, Iowa

Sidney R. Yates, Ill.

David R. Obey, Wis.

Edward R. Roybal, Calif.

Louis Stokes, Ohio

Tom Bevill, Ala.

Bill Chappell Jr., Fla.

Bill Alexander, Ark.

John P. Murtha, Pa.

Bob Traxler, Mich.

Joseph D. Early, Mass.

Charles Wilson, Texas

Lindy (Mrs. Hale) Boggs, La.

Norman D. Dicks, Wash.

Matthew F. McHugh, N.Y.

William Lehman, Fla.

Martin Olav Sabo, Minn.

Julian C. Dixon, Calif.

Vic Fazio, Calif.

W. G. "Bill" Hefner, N.C.

Les AuCoin, Ore.

Daniel K. Akaka, Hawaii

Wes Watkins, Okla.

William H. Gray III, Pa.

Bernard J. Dwyer, N.J.

Bill Boner, Tenn.

Steny H. Hoyer, Md.

Bob Carr, Mich.

Robert J. Mrazek, N.Y.

Richard J. Durbin, Ill.

Ronald D. Coleman, Texas

Alan B. Mollohan, W.Va.

Silvio O. Conte, Mass.

Joseph M. McDade, Pa.

John T. Myers, Ind.

Clarence E. Miller, Ohio

Lawrence Coughlin, Pa.

C. W. Bill Young, Fla.

Jack F. Kemp, N.Y.

Ralph Regula, Ohio

Virginia Smith, Neb.

Carl D. Pursell, Mich.

Mickey Edwards, Okla.

Bob Livingston, La.

Bill Green, N.Y.

Jerry Lewis, Calif.

John Edward Porter, Ill.

Harold Rogers, Ky.

Joe Skeen, N.M.

Frank R. Wolf, Va.

Bill Lowery, Calif.

Vin Weber, Minn.

Thomas D. DeLay, Texas

Jim Kolbe, Ariz.

Majority Staff Director: Frederick G. Mohrman 225-2771
Rm H-218 Capitol
Minority Staff Director: Mike F. Hugo 225-3481 Rm 1016 LHOB

Subcommittees

Commerce, Justice and State, the Judiciary and Related Agencies

■ Phone: 225-3351   ■ Room: H-309 Capitol

Smith (Iowa) — chairman

Alexander	*Rogers*
Early	*Regula*
Dwyer	*Kolbe*
Carr	
Mollohan	

Defense

■ Phone: 225-2847   ■ Room: H-144 Capitol

Chappell — chairman

Murtha	*McDade*
Dicks	*Young*
Wilson	*Miller*
Hefner	*Livingston*
AuCoin	
Sabo	

District of Columbia

■ Phone: 225-5338   ■ Room: H-302 Capitol

Dixon — chairman

Natcher	*Coughlin*
Stokes	*Green*
Sabo	*Regula*
AuCoin	
Hoyer	

Energy and Water Development

■ Phone: 225-3421   ■ Room: 2362 RHOB

Bevill — chairman

Boggs	*Myers*
Chappell	*Smith (Neb.)*
Fazio	*Pursell*
Watkins	
Boner	

Foreign Operations

■ Phone: 225-2041   ■ Room: H-307 Capitol

Obey — chairman

Yates	*Edwards*
McHugh	*Kemp*
Lehman	*Lewis*
Wilson	*Porter*
Dixon	
Gray	
Mrazek	

HUD - Independent Agencies

■ Phone: 225-3241   ■ Room: H-143 Capitol

Boland — chairman

Traxler	*Green*
Stokes	*Coughlin*
Boggs	*Lewis*
Boner	
Mollohan	

Interior and Related Agencies

■ Phone: 225-3081   ■ Room: B308 RHOB

Yates — chairman

Murtha	*Regula*
Dicks	*McDade*
Boland	*Lowery*
AuCoin	
Bevill	

Labor, Health and Human Services, Education and Related Agencies

■ Phone: 225-3508   ■ Room: 2358 RHOB

Natcher — chairman

Smith (Iowa)	*Conte*
Obey	*Pursell*
Roybal	*Porter*
Stokes	*Young*
Early	*Weber*
Dwyer	
Hoyer	

Legislative Branch

■ Phone: 225-5338   ■ Room: H-301 Capitol

Fazio — chairman

Obey	*Lewis*
Alexander	*Conte*
Murtha	*Myers*
Traxler	*Porter*
Boggs	

Military Construction

■ Phone: 225-3047   ■ Room: B300 RHOB

Hefner — chairman

Alexander	*Lowery*
Coleman	*Edwards*
Bevill	*Kolbe*
Early	*DeLay*
Wilson	
Dicks	
Fazio	

Rural Development, Agriculture and Related Agencies

■ Phone: 225-2638   ■ Room: 2362 RHOB

Whitten — chairman

Traxler	*Smith (Neb.)*
McHugh	*Myers*
Natcher	*Skeen*
Akaka	*Weber*
Watkins	
Durbin	
Smith (Iowa)	

Transportation and Related Agencies

■ Phone: 225-2141   ■ Room: 2358 RHOB

Lehman — chairman

Gray	*Coughlin*
Carr	*Conte*
Durbin	*Wolf*
Mrazek	*DeLay*
Sabo	

Treasury, Postal Service and General Government

■ Phone: 225-5834   ■ Room: H-164 Capitol

Roybal — chairman

Akaka	*Skeen*
Hoyer	*Lowery*
Coleman	*Wolf*
Boland	
Yates	

Armed Services

■ Phone: 225-4151   ■ Room: 2120 RHOB

Common defense generally; Department of Defense; ammunition depots; forts; arsenals; Army, Navy and Air Force reservations and establishments; naval petroleum and oil shale reserves; scientific research and development in support of the armed services; Selective Service System; strategic and critical materials; military applications of nuclear energy; soldiers' and sailors' homes.

Party Ratio: D 31 - R 20 †

Les Aspin
Chairman

William L. Dickinson
Ranking Member

Les Aspin, Wis.	*William L. Dickinson, Ala.*
Melvin Price, Ill.	*Floyd Spence, S.C.*
Charles E. Bennett, Fla.	*Robert E. Badham, Calif.*
Samuel S. Stratton, N.Y.	*Bob Stump, Ariz.*
Bill Nichols, Ala.	*Jim Courter, N.J.*
Dan Daniel, Va.	*Larry J. Hopkins, Ky.*
G. V. "Sonny"	*Robert W. Davis, Mich.*
Montgomery, Miss.	*Duncan Hunter, Calif.*
Ronald V. Dellums, Calif.	*David O'B. Martin, N.Y.*
Patricia Schroeder, Colo.	*John R. Kasich, Ohio*
Beverly B. Byron, Md.	*Lynn Martin, Ill.*
Nicholas Mavroules, Mass.	*Herbert H. Bateman, Va.*
Earl Hutto, Fla.	*Mac Sweeney, Texas*
Ike Skelton, Mo.	*Ben Blaz, Guam †*
Marvin Leath, Texas	*Andy Ireland, Fla.*
Dave McCurdy, Okla.	*James V. Hansen, Utah*
Thomas M. Foglietta, Pa.	*John G. Rowland, Conn.*
Roy Dyson, Md.	*Curt Weldon, Pa.*
Dennis M. Hertel, Mich.	*Jon Kyl, Ariz.*
Marilyn Lloyd, Tenn.	*Arthur Ravenel Jr., S.C.*
Norman Sisisky, Va.	*Jack Davis, Ill.*
Richard Ray, Ga.	
John M. Spratt Jr., S.C.	
Frank McCloskey, Ind.	
Solomon P. Ortiz, Texas	
George "Buddy" Darden, Ga.	
Tommy F. Robinson, Ark.	
Albert G. Bustamante, Texas	

Barbara Boxer, Calif.
George J. Hochbrueckner, N.Y.
Joseph E. Brennan, Maine
Owen B. Pickett, Va.

† Party ratios do not include delegates or resident commissioner.

Staff Director: G. Kim Wincup 225-4158 Rm 2120 RHOB

Subcommittees

Investigations

■ Phone: 225-4221   ■ Room: 2339 RHOB

Nichols — chairman

Mavroules	*Hopkins*
Sisisky	*Stump*
Spratt	*Kasich*
McCloskey	*Kyl*
Ortiz	*Sweeney*
Boxer	*Ireland*
Stratton	
Dellums	
Byron	

Military Installations and Facilities

■ Phone: 225-7120   ■ Room: 2120 RHOB

Dellums — chairman

Montgomery	*Martin (N.Y.)*
Hutto	*Dickinson*
Skelton	*Martin (Ill.)*
Leath	*Blaz*
McCurdy	*Spence*
Foglietta	*Ravenel*
Hertel	*Weldon*
Ortiz	
Robinson	

Military Personnel and Compensation

■ Phone: 225-7560   ■ Room: 2343 RHOB

Byron — chairman

Montgomery	*Bateman*
Schroeder	*Kyl*
Skelton	*Ravenel*
Dyson	*Davis (Ill.)*
Ray	*Weldon*
Bustamante	
Pickett	
Nichols	

Procurement and Military Nuclear Systems

■ Phone: 225-1240   ■ Room: 2343 RHOB

Stratton — chairman

Mavroules	*Badham*
Skelton	*Courter*
Leath	*Davis (Mich.)*
Dyson	*Hopkins*
Lloyd	*Blaz*
Sisisky	*Ireland*
Ray	*Hansen*
Spratt	*Rowland*
Bustamante	
Bennett	

Readiness

■ Phone: 225-7991   ■ Room: 2340 RHOB

Daniel — chairman

Hutto	*Kasich*
Leath	*Martin (N.Y.)*
Ray	*Davis (Ill.)*
Darden	*Hansen*
Robinson	*Rowland*
Hockbrueckner	
Nichols	

Research and Development

■ Phone: 225-3168   ■ Room: 2120 RHOB

Price — chairman

Aspin	*Dickinson*
Schroeder	*Courter*
McCurdy	*Davis (Mich.)*
Hertel	*Stump*
McCloskey	*Hunter*
Darden	*Martin (Ill.)*
Boxer	*Sweeney*
Hochbrueckner	
Brennan	
Pickett	

Seapower and Strategic and Critical Materials

■ Phone: 225-6704   ■ Room: 2343 RHOB

Bennett — chairman

Hutto	*Spence*
Foglietta	*Hunter*
Dyson	*Bateman*
Sisisky	*Badham*
Ortiz	*Weldon*
Hochbrueckner	
Brennan	
Pickett	

Banking, Finance and Urban Affairs

■ Phone: 225-4247   ■ Room: 2129 RHOB

Banks and banking including deposit insurance and federal monetary policy; money and credit; currency; issuance and redemption of notes; gold and silver; coinage; valuation and revaluation of the dollar; urban development; private and public housing; economic stabilization; defense production; renegotiation; price controls; international finance; financial aid to commerce and industry.

Party Ratio: D 30 - R 20 †

Fernand J. St Germain
Chairman

Chalmers P. Wylie
Ranking Member

Fernand J. St Germain, R.I.	*Chalmers P. Wylie, Ohio*
Henry B. Gonzalez, Texas	*Jim Leach, Iowa*
Frank Annunzio, Ill.	*Norman D. Shumway, Calif.*
Walter E. Fauntroy, D.C. †	*Stan Parris, Va.*
Stephen L. Neal, N.C.	*Bill McCollum, Fla.*
Carroll Hubbard Jr., Ky.	*George C. Wortley, N.Y.*
John J. LaFalce, N.Y.	*Marge Roukema, N.J.*
Mary Rose Oakar, Ohio	*Doug Bereuter, Neb.*
Bruce F. Vento, Minn.	*David Dreier, Calif.*
Doug Barnard Jr., Ga.	*John Hiler, Ind.*
Robert Garcia, N.Y.	*Tom Ridge, Pa.*
Charles E. Schumer, N.Y.	*Steve Bartlett, Texas*
Barney Frank, Mass.	*Toby Roth, Wis.*
Buddy Roemer, La.	*Al McCandless, Calif.*
Richard H. Lehman, Calif.	*J. Alex McMillan, N.C.*
Bruce A. Morrison, Conn.	*H. James Saxton, N.J.*
Marcy Kaptur, Ohio	*Pat Swindall, Ga.*
Ben Erdreich, Ala.	*Patricia F. Saiki, Hawaii*
Thomas R. Carper, Del.	*Jim Bunning, Ky.*
Esteban Edward Torres, Calif.	*Vacancy*
Gerald D. Kleczka, Wis.	
Bill Nelson, Fla.	
Paul E. Kanjorski, Pa.	
Thomas J. Manton, N.Y.	
Liz J. Patterson, S.C.	
Tom McMillen, Md.	

Joseph P. Kennedy II, Mass.
Floyd H. Flake, N.Y.
Kweisi Mfume, Md.
David E. Price, N.C.
Nancy Pelosi, Calif.*

† Party ratios do not include delegates or resident commissioner.

Majority Clerk and Staff Director: Paul Nelson 225-7057 Rm 2129 RHOB
Minority Staff Director: Bob Ruddy 225-7502 Rm B301-C RHOB

Subcommittees

Consumer Affairs and Coinage

■ Phone: 226-3280   ■ Room: 212 HOB Annex #1

Annunzio — chairman

St Germain	Hiler
Gonzalez	Wylie
Vacancy	Ridge
Vacancy	

Domestic Monetary Policy

■ Phone: 226-7315   ■ Room: 109 HOB Annex #2

Neal — chairman

Fauntroy	McCollum
Barnard	Leach
Hubbard	Saxton
Frank	

Economic Stabilization

■ Phone: 225-7145   ■ Room: H2-140 HOB Annex #2

Oakar — chairman

LaFalce	Shumway
Vento	Wortley
Kaptur	McCandless
Kanjorski	McMillan
Barnard	Roth
Garcia	Saxton
Patterson	Saiki
McMillen	Swindall
Flake	Vacancy
Mfume	
Price	
Vacancy	
Vacancy	

* Nancy Pelosi had not received subcommittee assignments as of June 23, 1987.

Financial Institutions Supervision, Regulation and Insurance

■ Phone: 225-2926   ■ Room: B303 RHOB

St Germain — chairman

Annunzio	Wylie
Hubbard	Leach
Barnard	Shumway
LaFalce	McCollum
Oakar	Wortley
Vento	Dreier
Schumer	Parris
Frank	Roukema
Lehman	Bereuter
Roemer	Bartlett
Kaptur	Roth
Nelson	Hiler
Kanjorski	Ridge
Manton	McCandless
Gonzalez	McMillan
Neal	Saxton
Morrison	Swindall
Erdreich	
Carper	
Torres	
Kleczka	
Patterson	
McMillen	
Price	
Kennedy	

General Oversight and Investigations

■ Phone: 225-2828   ■ Room: B304 RHOB

Hubbard — chairman

Gonzalez	Parris
Barnard	Dreier
Kanjorski	Bartlett
Roemer	McCandless
Erdreich	McMillan
Patterson	Bunning
Flake	
Vacancy	

Housing and Community Development

■ Phone: 225-7054   ■ Room: 2129 RHOB

Gonzalez — chairman

St Germain	Roukema
Fauntroy	Wylie
Oakar	Wortley
Vento	McCollum
Garcia	Bereuter
Schumer	Dreier
Frank	Hiler
	Ridge

Lehman
Morrison
Kaptur
Erdreich
Carper
Torres
Roemer
Kleczka
Kanjorski
Manton
Neal
Hubbard
Kennedy
Flake
Mfume

Bartlett
Roth
Saxton
Swindall
Saiki
Bunning
Vacancy

International Development Institutions and Finance

■ Phone: 226-7511   ■ Room: 139 HOB Annex #2

Fauntroy — chairman

LaFalce
Torres
Morrison
Schumer
Kennedy
Mfume
Vacancy
Vacancy

Bereuter
Roukema
McCandless
Saiki
Swindall
Bunning

International Finance, Trade and Monetary Policy

■ Phone: 225-1271   ■ Room: 604 HOB Annex #1

Garcia — chairman

Neal
LaFalce
Fauntroy
Kleczka
Manton
Roemer
Lehman
Carper
Vacancy
Vacancy

Leach
Shumway
Parris
McMillan
Bunning
Swindall
Saiki

Budget

■ Phone: 226-7200   ■ Room: 214 HOB Annex #1

Federal budget generally; concurrent budget resolutions; Congressional Budget Office. Chairman and ranking minority member are members *ex officio* of all task forces of which they are not regular members. The majority leader is a member *ex officio* of all task forces.

Party Ratio: D 21 - R 14

William H. Gray III
Chairman

Delbert L. Latta
Ranking Member

William H. Gray III, Pa.
Thomas S. Foley, Wash.
Mike Lowry, Wash.
Butler Derrick, S.C.
George Miller, Calif.
Pat Williams, Mont.
Howard Wolpe, Mich.
Martin Frost, Texas
Vic Fazio, Calif.
Marty Russo, Ill.
Ed Jenkins, Ga.
Marvin Leath, Texas
Charles E. Schumer, N.Y.
Barbara Boxer, Calif.
Buddy MacKay, Fla.
Jim Slattery, Kan.
Chester G. Atkins, Mass.
James L. Oberstar, Minn.
Frank J. Guarini, N.J.
Richard J. Durbin, Ill.
Mike Espy, Miss.

Delbert L. Latta, Ohio
Bill Gradison, Ohio
Connie Mack, Fla.
Bill Goodling, Pa.
Denny Smith, Ore.
Beau Boulter, Texas
Mickey Edwards, Okla.
William M. Thomas, Calif.
Harold Rogers, Ky.
Don Sundquist, Tenn.
Nancy L. Johnson, Conn.
Dick Armey, Texas
Jack Buechner, Mo.
Amo Houghton, N.Y.

Majority Executive Director: Steven Pruitt 226-7234 Rm 222 HOB Annex #1
Minority Staff Director: Martha Phillips 226-7270 Rm H2-278 HOB Annex #2

Task Forces

Budget Process
Derrick — chairman

Miller	Gradison
Frost	Smith
Fazio	Boulter
MacKay	Edwards
Atkins	Thomas
Oberstar	Rogers
	Sundquist
	Armey

Community and Natural Resources
Wolpe — chairman

Williams	Edwards
Fazio	Armey
Jenkins	
Slattery	
Atkins	
Oberstar	
Durbin	
Espy	

Defense and International Affairs
Fazio — chairman

Miller	Latta
Wolpe	Mack
Frost	Smith
Russo	Boulter
Leath	Edwards
Boxer	Rogers
MacKay	Sundquist
Slattery	Buechner
Atkins	
Oberstar	
Guarini	

Economic and Trade Policy
Lowry — chairman

Derrick	Boulter
Williams	Gradison
Russo	Edwards
Schumer	Thomas
MacKay	Rogers
Slattery	Sundquist
Guarini	Johnson
Espy	Armey
	Buechner
	Houghton

Health
Frost — chairman

Schumer	Johnson
MacKay	Gradison
	Mack
	Goodling

Human Resources
Williams — chairman

Lowry	Goodling
Durbin	Johnson
Espy	

Income Security
Russo — chairman

Miller	Mack
Fazio	Gradison
Boxer	Goodling
	Thomas
	Houghton

State and Local Government
Miller — chairman

Jenkins	Smith
Schumer	
Boxer	

District of Columbia

■ Phone: 225-4457 ■ Room: 1310 LHOB

Municipal affairs of the District of Columbia.

Party Ratio: D 7 - R 4 †

Ronald V. Dellums
Chairman

Stan Parris
Ranking Member

Ronald V. Dellums, Calif.	*Stan Parris, Va.*
Walter E. Fauntroy, D.C. †	*Thomas J. Bliley Jr., Va.*
Romano L. Mazzoli, Ky.	*Larry Combest, Texas*
Fortney H. "Pete" Stark, Calif.	*Lynn Martin, Ill.*
William H. Gray III, Pa.	
Mervyn M. Dymally, Calif.	
Alan Wheat, Mo.	
Vacancy	

† Party ratios do not include delegates or resident commissioner.

Majority Staff Director: Edward C. Sylvester Jr. 225-4457 Rm 1310 LHOB
Minority Staff Director: John Gnorski 225-7158 Rm 1307 LHOB

Subcommittees

Fiscal Affairs and Health

■ Phone: 225-4457 ■ Room: 507 HOB Annex #1

Fauntroy — chairman

Dellums	*Bliley*
Stark	*Parris*
Gray	*Combest*
Vacancy	

Government Operations and Metropolitan Affairs

■ Phone: 225-4457 ■ Room: 507 HOB Annex #1

Wheat — chairman

Gray	*Combest*
Stark	*Parris*
Fauntroy	*Martin*
Vacancy	

Judiciary and Education

■ Phone: 225-4457 ■ Room: 441 CHOB

Dymally — chairman

Mazzoli	*Martin*
Wheat	*Bliley*
Vacancy	*Parris*
Vacancy	

Education and Labor

■ Phone: 225-4527 ■ Room: 2181 RHOB

Education and labor generally; child labor; convict labor; labor standards and statistics; mediation and arbitration of labor disputes; regulation of foreign laborers; school food programs; vocational rehabilitation; wages and hours; welfare of miners; work incentive programs; Indian education; juvenile delinquency; human services programs; Gallaudet College; Howard University. Chairman and ranking minority member are members *ex officio* of all subcommittees of which they are not regular members.

Party Ratio: D 21 - R 13

Augustus F. Hawkins
Chairman

James M. Jeffords
Ranking Member

Augustus F. Hawkins, Calif.
William D. Ford, Mich.
Joseph M. Gaydos, Pa.
William L. Clay, Mo.
Mario Biaggi, N.Y.
Austin J. Murphy, Pa.
Dale E. Kildee, Mich.
Pat Williams, Mont.
Matthew G. Martinez, Calif.
Major R. Owens, N.Y.
Charles A. Hayes, Ill.
Carl C. Perkins, Ky.
Thomas C. Sawyer, Ohio
Stephen J. Solarz, N.Y. *
Bob Wise, W.Va. *
Timothy J. Penny, Minn. *
Bill Richardson, N.M. *
Tommy F. Robinson, Ark. *
Peter J. Visclosky, Ind. *
Chester G. Atkins, Mass. *
Jim Jontz, Ind. *

James M. Jeffords, Vt.
Bill Goodling, Pa.
E. Thomas Coleman, Mo.
Thomas E. Petri, Wis.
Marge Roukema, N.J.
Steve Gunderson, Wis.
Steve Bartlett, Texas
Tom Tauke, Iowa
Dick Armey, Texas
Harris W. Fawell, Ill.
Paul B. Henry, Mich.
Fred Grandy, Iowa
Cass Ballenger, N.C.

* Member appointed temporarily for the 100th Congress only.

Majority Staff Director: Susan G. McGuire 225-6913 Rm 2181 RHOB
Minority Staff Directors: Beth Buehlmann 225-1743 Rm 2100 RHOB
and Mark Powden 225-3725 Rm 2101 RHOB

Subcommittees

Elementary, Secondary and Vocational Education

■ Phone: 225-4368   ■ Room: B346-C RHOB

Hawkins — chairman

Ford	*Goodling*
Kildee	*Bartlett*
Williams	*Fawell*
Martinez	*Henry*
Perkins	*Grandy*
Biaggi	*Gunderson*
Hayes	*Petri*
Sawyer	*Roukema*
Solarz	
Wise	
Richardson	
Robinson	
Visclosky	
Atkins	

Employment Opportunities

■ Phone: 225-7594   ■ Room: 402 CHOB

Martinez — chairman

Williams	*Gunderson*
Hayes	*Henry*
Owens	*Grandy*
Richardson	
Atkins	
Jontz	

Health and Safety

■ Phone: 225-6876   ■ Room: B345-A RHOB

Gaydos — chairman

Murphy	*Henry*
Ford	*Ballenger*
Clay	

Human Resources

■ Phone: 225-1850   ■ Room: 320 CHOB

Kildee — chairman

Sawyer	*Tauke*
Biaggi	*Coleman*
Solarz	*Grandy*
Visclosky	
Vacancy	

Labor-Management Relations

■ Phone: 225-5768   ■ Room: 2451 RHOB

Clay — chairman

Ford	*Roukema*
Kildee	*Armey*
Biaggi	*Fawell*
Hayes	*Ballenger*
Owens	*Petri*
Sawyer	
Murphy	
Jontz	

Labor Standards

■ Phone: 225-1927   ■ Room: B346-A RHOB

Murphy — chairman

Williams	*Petri*
Penny	*Bartlett*
Wise	
Robinson	

Postsecondary Education

■ Phone: 226-3681   ■ Room: 617 HOB Annex #1

Williams — chairman

Ford	*Coleman*
Owens	*Goodling*
Hayes	*Roukema*
Perkins	*Tauke*
Gaydos	*Armey*
Martinez	
Robinson	
Atkins	

Select Education

■ Phone: 226-7532   ■ Room: 518 HOB Annex #1

Owens — chairman

Williams   *Bartlett*
Biaggi

Energy and Commerce

■ Phone: 225-2927   ■ Room: 2125 RHOB

Interstate and foreign commerce generally; national energy policy generally; exploration, production, storage, supply, marketing, pricing and regulation of energy resources; nuclear energy; solar energy; energy conservation; generation and marketing of power; inland waterways; railroads and railway labor and retirement; communications generally; securities and exchanges; consumer affairs; travel and tourism; public health and quarantine; health care facilities; biomedical research and development. Chairman and ranking minority member are members *ex officio* of all subcommittees of which they are not regular members.

Party Ratio: D 25 - R 17

John D. Dingell
Chairman

Norman F. Lent
Ranking Member

John D. Dingell, Mich.
James H. Scheuer, N.Y.
Henry A. Waxman, Calif.
Philip R. Sharp, Ind.
James J. Florio, N.J.
Edward J. Markey, Mass.
Thomas A. Luken, Ohio
Doug Walgren, Pa.
Al Swift, Wash.
Mickey Leland, Texas
Cardiss Collins, Ill.
Mike Synar, Okla.

Norman F. Lent, N.Y.
Edward R. Madigan, Ill.
Carlos J. Moorhead, Calif.
Matthew J. Rinaldo, N.J.
William E. Dannemeyer,
  Calif.
Bob Whittaker, Kan.
Tom Tauke, Iowa
Don Ritter, Pa.
Dan Coats, Ind.
Thomas J. Bliley Jr., Va.
Jack Fields, Texas

W. J. "Billy" Tauzin, La.
Ron Wyden, Ore.
Ralph M. Hall, Texas
Dennis E. Eckart, Ohio
Wayne Dowdy, Miss.
Bill Richardson, N.M.
Jim Slattery, Kan.
Gerry Sikorski, Minn.
John Bryant, Texas
Jim Bates, Calif.
Rick Boucher, Va.
Jim Cooper, Tenn.
Terry L. Bruce, Ill.

Michael G. Oxley, Ohio
Howard C. Nielson, Utah
Michael Bilirakis, Fla.
Dan Schaefer, Colo.
Joe L. Barton, Texas
Sonny Callahan, Ala.

Majority Staff Director: William Michael Kitzmiller 225-2927 Rm 2125 RHOB
Minority Chief Counsel and Staff Director: Paul Smith 225-3641 Rm 2322 RHOB

Subcommittees

Commerce, Consumer Protection And Competitiveness

■ Phone: 226-3160   ■ Room: 151 HOB Annex #2

Florio — chairman

Scheuer   *Dannemeyer*
Bates   *Rinaldo*
Waxman   *Ritter*
Sharp   *Nielson*
Collins   *Barton*
Eckart
Richardson

Energy and Power

■ Phone: 226-2500   ■ Room:331 HOB Annex #2

Sharp — chairman

Walgren   *Moorhead*
Swift   *Dannemeyer*
Synar   *Fields*
Tauzin   *Oxley*
Richardson   *Bilirakis*
Bryant   *Schaefer*
Bruce   *Barton*
Markey   *Callahan*
Leland
Wyden
Hall
Dowdy

Health and the Environment

■ Phone: 225-4952   ■ Room: 2415 RHOB

Waxman — chairman

Scheuer	*Madigan*
Walgren	*Dannemeyer*
Wyden	*Whittaker*
Sikorski	*Tauke*
Bates	*Coats*
Bruce	*Bliley*
Leland	*Fields*
Collins	
Hall	
Dowdy	

Oversight and Investigations

■ Phone: 225-4441   ■ Room: 2323 RHOB

Dingell — chairman

Wyden	*Lent*
Eckart	*Coats*
Slattery	*Bliley*
Sikorski	*Oxley*
Boucher	*Schaefer*
Cooper	*Bilirakis*
Luken	
Walgren	

Telecommunications And Finance

■ Phone: 226-2424   ■ Room: 316 HOB Annex #2

Markey — chairman

Swift	*Rinaldo*
Leland	*Moorhead*
Collins	*Tauke*
Synar	*Ritter*
Tauzin	*Coats*
Dowdy	*Bliley*
Slattery	*Fields*
Bryant	*Oxley*
Hall	*Nielson*
Eckart	
Richardson	
Boucher	
Cooper	

Transportation, Tourism and Hazardous Materials

■ Phone: 225-9304   ■ Room: H-324 HOB Annex #2

Luken — chairman

Florio	*Whittaker*
Tauzin	*Tauke*
Slattery	*Bilirakis*
Sikorski	*Schaefer*
Bryant	*Callahan*
Bates	
Boucher	

Foreign Affairs

■ Phone: 225-5021   ■ Room: 2170 RHOB

Relations of the United States with foreign nations generally; foreign loans; international conferences and congresses; intervention abroad and declarations of war; diplomatic service; foreign trade; neutrality; protection of Americans abroad; Red Cross; United Nations; international economic policy; export controls including non-proliferation of nuclear technology and hardware; international commodity agreements; trading with the enemy; international financial and monetary organizations.

Party Ratio: D 25 - R 17 †

Dante B. Fascell	**William S. Broomfield**
Chairman	**Ranking Member**

Dante B. Fascell, Fla.	*William S. Broomfield,*
Lee H. Hamilton, Ind.	*Mich.*
Gus Yatron, Pa.	*Benjamin A. Gilman, N.Y.*
Stephen J. Solarz, N.Y.	*Robert J. Lagomarsino,*
Don Bonker, Wash.	*Calif.*
Gerry E. Studds, Mass.	*Jim Leach, Iowa*
Daniel A. Mica, Fla.	*Toby Roth, Wis.*

Howard Wolpe, Mich.
George W. Crockett Jr.,
  Mich.
Sam Gejdenson, Conn.
Mervyn M. Dymally, Calif.
Tom Lantos, Calif.
Peter H. Kostmayer, Pa.
Robert G. Torricelli, N.J.
Lawrence J. Smith, Fla.
Howard L. Berman, Calif.
Mel Levine, Calif.
Edward F. Feighan, Ohio
Ted Weiss, N.Y.
Gary L. Ackerman, N.Y.
Morris K. Udall, Ariz.
Chester G. Atkins, Mass.
James McClure Clarke, N.C.
Jaime B. Fuster, Puerto
  Rico †
James Bilbray, Nev.
Wayne Owens, Utah
Fofó I. F. Sunia,
  American Samoa †

Olympia J. Snowe, Maine
Henry J. Hyde, Ill.
Gerald B. H. Solomon, N.Y.
Doug Bereuter, Neb.
Bob Dornan, Calif.
Christopher H. Smith, N.J.
Connie Mack, Fla.
Michael DeWine, Ohio
Dan Burton, Ind.
Jan Meyers, Kan.
John R. Miller, Wash.
Donald E. "Buz" Lukens, Ohio
Ben Blaz, Guam †

† Party ratios do not include delegates or resident commissioner.

Majority Chief of Staff: John J. Brady 225-5021 Rm 2170 RHOB
Minority Staff Director: Steve Berry 225-6735 Rm B360 RHOB

Subcommittees

Africa

■ Phone: 226-7807   ■ Room: 705 HOB Annex #1

Wolpe — chairman

Crockett	*Burton*
Clarke	*Lukens*
Bilbray	*Blaz*
Sunia	*Dornan*
Owens	

Arms Control, International Security and Science

■ Phone: 225-8926   ■ Room: 2401 RHOB

Fascell — chairman

Berman	*Broomfield*
Udall	*Leach*
Clarke	*Snowe*
Hamilton	*Hyde*
Studds	*Burton*
Lantos	
Weiss	

Asian and Pacific Affairs

■ Phone: 226-7801   ■ Room: 707 HOB Annex #1

Solarz — chairman

Dymally	*Leach*
Atkins	*Blaz*
Sunia	*Lagomarsino*
Torricelli	*Roth*
Ackerman	

Europe and the Middle East

■ Phone: 225-3345   ■ Room: B359 RHOB

Hamilton — chairman

Lantos	*Gilman*
Torricelli	*Meyers*
Smith (Fla.)	*Lukens*
Levine	*Bereuter*
Feighan	*Smith (N.J.)*
Ackerman	
Owens	

Human Rights and International Organizations

■ Phone: 226-7825   ■ Room: B358 RHOB

Yatron — chairman

Fuster	*Solomon*
Lantos	*Smith (N.J.)*
Feighan	*Meyers*
Weiss	*Miller*
Ackerman	

International Economic Policy and Trade

■ Phone: 226-7820   ■ Room: 702 HOB Annex #1

Bonker — chairman

Bilbray	*Roth*
Mica	*Bereuter*
Wolpe	*Miller*
Gejdenson	*Solomon*
Berman	*Dornan*
Levine	
Feighan	

International Operations

■ Phone: 225-3424   ■ Room: 816 HOB Annex #1

Mica — chairman

Yatron	*Snowe*
Dymally	*Gilman*
Kostmayer	*Mack*
Smith (Fla.)	*DeWine*
Atkins	

Western Hemisphere Affairs

■ Phone: 226-7812   ■ Room: 709 HOB Annex #1

Crockett — chairman

Studds	*Lagomarsino*
Gejdenson	*Hyde*
Kostmayer	*Dornan*
Weiss	*Mack*
Fuster	*DeWine*
Solarz	
Bonker	

Government Operations

■ Phone: 225-5051   ■ Room: 2157 RHOB

Budget and accounting measures; overall economy and efficiency in government, including federal procurement; executive branch reorganization; general revenue sharing; intergovernmental relations; National Archives. Chairman and ranking minority member are members *ex officio* of all subcommittees of which they are not regular members.

Party Ratio: D 24 - R 15

Jack Brooks
Chairman

Frank Horton
Ranking Member

Jack Brooks, Texas	*Frank Horton, N.Y.*
John Conyers Jr., Mich.	*Robert S. Walker, Pa.*
Cardiss Collins, Ill.	*William F. Clinger Jr., Pa.*
Glenn English, Okla.	*Al McCandless, Calif.*
Henry A. Waxman, Calif.	*Larry E. Craig, Idaho*
Ted Weiss, N.Y.	*Howard C. Nielson, Utah*
Mike Synar, Okla.	*Joseph J. DioGuardi, N.Y.*
Stephen L. Neal, N.C.	*Jim Lightfoot, Iowa*
Doug Barnard Jr., Ga.	*Beau Boulter, Texas*
Barney Frank, Mass.	*Donald E. "Buz" Lukens,*
Tom Lantos, Calif.	*Ohio*
Bob Wise, W.Va.	*Amo Houghton, N.Y.*
Major R. Owens, N.Y.	*Dennis Hastert, Ill.*
Edolphus Towns, N.Y.	*Jon Kyl, Ariz.*
John M. Spratt Jr., S.C.	*Ernie Konnyu, Calif.*
Joe Kolter, Pa.	*James M. Inhofe, Okla.*
Ben Erdreich, Ala.	
Gerald D. Kleczka, Wis.	
Albert G. Bustamante, Texas	
Matthew G. Martinez, Calif.	
Thomas C. Sawyer, Ohio	
Louise M. Slaughter, N.Y.	
Bill Grant, Fla.	
Nancy Pelosi, Calif.*	

Majority General Counsel: William M. Jones 225-5051 Rm 2157 RHOB
Minority Counsel and Staff Director: Stephen M. Daniels 225-5074 Rm 2153 RHOB

Subcommittees

Commerce, Consumer and Monetary Affairs

■ Phone: 225-4407   ■ Room: B377 RHOB

Barnard — chairman

Spratt	*Craig*
Kolter	*Konnyu*
Erdreich	*Inhofe*
Bustamante	*Houghton*
Martinez	

Employment and Housing

■ Phone: 225-6751   ■ Room: B349-A RHOB

Lantos — chairman

Slaughter	*DioGuardi*
Grant	*Kyl*
Weiss	*Konnyu*
Vacancy	

* Nancy Pelosi had not received subcommittee assignments as of June 23, 1987.

Environment, Energy and Natural Resources

■ Phone: 225-6427   ■ Room: B371-B RHOB

Synar — chairman

Towns	*Clinger*
Bustamante	*Kyl*
Waxman	*Boulter*
Martinez	
Vacancy	

Legislation and National Security

■ Phone: 225-5147   ■ Room: B373 RHOB

Brooks — chairman

Conyers	*Horton*
Neal	*Walker*
Frank	*Boulter*
Wise	*Lukens*
Erdreich	
Kleczka	

Government Activities and Transportation

■ Phone: 225-7920   ■ Room: B350-A RHOB

Collins — chairman

Owens	*Nielson*
Wise	*Hastert*
Kolter	*Lukens*
Kleczka	
Sawyer	

Government Information, Justice and Agriculture

■ Phone: 225-3741   ■ Room: B349-C RHOB

English — chairman

Slaughter	*McCandless*
Grant	*Houghton*
Towns	*Hastert*
Spratt	
Vacancy	

Human Resources And Intergovernmental Relations

■ Phone: 225-2548   ■ Room: B372 RHOB

Weiss — chairman

Sawyer	*Lightfoot*
Conyers	*Konnyu*
Waxman	*Inhofe*
Frank	

House Administration

■ Phone: 225-2061   ■ Room: H-326 Capitol

House administration generally; contested elections; federal elections generally; corrupt practices; qualifications of members of the House; *Congressional Record;* the Capitol; Library of Congress; Smithsonian Institution; Botanic Garden. Chairman and ranking minority member are non-voting members *ex officio* of all subcommittees of which they are not regular members.

Party Ratio: D 12 - R 7

Frank Annunzio
Chairman

Bill Frenzel
Ranking Member

Frank Annunzio, Ill.	*Bill Frenzel, Minn.*
Joseph M. Gaydos, Pa.	*William L. Dickinson, Ala.*
Ed Jones, Tenn.	*Robert E. Badham, Calif.*
Charlie Rose, N.C.	*Newt Gingrich, Ga.*
Leon E. Panetta, Calif.	*William M. Thomas, Calif.*
Al Swift, Wash.	*Barbara F. Vucanovich, Nev.*
Mary Rose Oakar, Ohio	*Pat Roberts, Kan.*
Tony Coelho, Calif.	
Jim Bates, Calif.	
William L. Clay, Mo.	
Sam Gejdenson, Conn.	
Vacancy	

Majority Staff Director: David C. Sharman 225-2061 Rm H-326 Capitol
Minority Staff Director: Linda Nave 225-8281 Rm H-330 Capitol

Subcommittees

Accounts

■ Phone: 226-7540   ■ Room: 611 HOB Annex #1

Gaydos — chairman

Swift	*Badham*
Oakar	*Thomas*
Coelho	*Roberts*
Clay	*Vucanovich*
Gejdenson	
Panetta	

Elections

■ Phone: 226-7616   ■ Room: 802 HOB Annex #1

Swift — chairman

Rose	*Thomas*
Panetta	*Vucanovich*
Oakar	*Roberts*
Clay	*Frenzel*
Bates	
Coelho	

Libraries and Memorials

■ Phone: 226-7641   ■ Room: 720 HOB Annex #1

Oakar — chairman

Jones	*Gingrich*
Gejdenson	*Frenzel*

Office Systems

■ Phone: 225-1608   ■ Room: 722 HOB Annex #1

Rose — chairman

Clay	*Thomas*
Gejdenson	*Dickinson*

Personnel and Police

■ Phone: 226-2307   ■ Room: 612 HOB Annex #1

Panetta — chairman

Coelho	*Roberts*
Jones	*Dickinson*

Procurement and Printing

■ Phone: 225-4568   ■ Room: 105 CHOB

Jones — chairman

Gaydos	*Gingrich*
Bates	*Badham*

Interior and Insular Affairs

■ Phone: 225-2761   ■ Room: 1324 LHOB

Public lands, parks and natural resources generally; Geological Survey; interstate water compacts; irrigation and reclamation; Indian affairs; minerals, mines and mining; petroleum conservation on public lands; regulation of domestic nuclear energy industry, including waste disposal; territorial affairs of the United States. Chairman and ranking minority member are non-voting members *ex officio* of all subcommittees of which they are not regular members.

Party Ratio: D 23 - R 14 †

Morris K. Udall
Chairman

Don Young
Ranking Member

Morris K. Udall, Ariz.	*Don Young, Alaska*
George Miller, Calif.	*Manuel Lujan Jr., N.M.*
Philip R. Sharp, Ind.	*Robert J. Lagomarsino, Calif.*
Edward J. Markey, Mass.	*Ron Marlenee, Mont.*
Austin J. Murphy, Pa.	*Dick Cheney, Wyo.*
Nick J. Rahall II, W.Va.	*Charles Pashayan Jr., Calif.*
Bruce F. Vento, Minn.	*Larry E. Craig, Idaho*
Jerry Huckaby, La.	*Denny Smith, Ore.*
Dale E. Kildee, Mich.	*James V. Hansen, Utah*
Tony Coelho, Calif.	*Bill Emerson, Mo.*
Beverly B. Byron, Md.	*Barbara F. Vucanovich, Nev.*
Ron de Lugo, Virgin Islands †	*Ben Blaz, Guam †*
Sam Gejdenson, Conn.	*John J. Rhodes III, Ariz.*

Peter H. Kostmayer, Pa.
Richard H. Lehman, Calif.
Bill Richardson, N.M.
Fofō I. F. Sunia, American
  Samoa †
George "Buddy" Darden,
  Ga.
Peter J. Visclosky, Ind.
Jaime B. Fuster, Puerto
  Rico †
Mel Levine, Calif.
James McClure Clarke, N.C.
Wayne Owens, Utah
John Lewis, Ga.
Ben Nighthorse Campbell,
  Colo.
Peter A. DeFazio, Ore.

Elton Gallegly, Calif.
Richard H. Baker, La.

† Party ratios do not include delegates or resident commissioner.

*Majority Staff Director and Counsel: Stanley Scoville 225-2761
  Rm 1324 LHOB
Chief Minority Counsel: Richard A. Agnew 225-6065 Rm 1329 LHOB*

Subcommittees

Energy and the Environment

■ Phone: 225-8331   ■ Room: 1327 LHOB

Udall — chairman

Miller	*Lujan*
Sharp	*Young*
Markey	*Marlenee*
Murphy	*Pashayan*
Rahall	*Craig*
Huckaby	*Vucanovich*
Gejdenson	*Blaz*
Darden	*Rhodes*
Fuster	*Baker*
Levine	
Clarke	
Owens	

General Oversight and Investigations

■ Phone: 226-4085   ■ Room: 815 HOB Annex #1

Gejdenson — chairman

Miller	*Smith*
DeFazio	*Hansen*
	Emerson

Insular and International Affairs

■ Phone: 225-9297   ■ Room: 1626 LHOB

de Lugo — chairman

Udall	*Lagomarsino*
Vento	*Blaz*
Sunia	*Gallegly*
Darden	*Baker*
Fuster	
Clarke	
Lewis	

Mining and Natural Resources

■ Phone: 226-7761   ■ Room: 819 HOB Annex #1

Rahall — chairman

Miller	*Craig*
Murphy	*Marlenee*
Kostmayer	*Emerson*
Owens	*Vucanovich*
Campbell	
Udall	

National Parks and Public Lands

■ Phone: 226-7736   ■ Room: 812 HOB Annex #1

Vento — chairman

Markey	*Marlenee*
Rahall	*Lagomarsino*
Huckaby	*Cheney*
Kildee	*Pashayan*
Coelho	*Craig*
Byron	*Hansen*
de Lugo	*Emerson*
Kostmayer	*Vucanovich*
Lehman	*Blaz*
Richardson	*Rhodes*
Sunia	*Gallegly*
Darden	
Visclosky	
Fuster	
Levine	
Clarke	
Lewis	
DeFazio	

Water and Power Resources

■ Phone: 225-6042   ■ Room: 1522 LHOB

Miller — chairman

Udall	*Pashayan*
Sharp	*Young*
Markey	*Lujan*
Kildee	*Cheney*
Coelho	*Smith*
Byron	*Hansen*
Kostmayer	*Rhodes*
Lehman	*Gallegly*
Richardson	*Baker*
Levine	
Owens	
Campbell	
DeFazio	

Judiciary

■ Phone: 225-3951   ■ Room: 2137 RHOB

Civil and criminal judicial proceedings generally; federal courts and judges; bankruptcy, mutiny, espionage and counterfeiting; civil liberties; constitutional amendments; immigration and naturalization; interstate compacts; claims against the United States; apportionment of representatives; meetings of Congress and attendance of members; penitentiaries; patents, copyrights and trademarks; presidential succession; monopolies and unlawful restraints of trade; internal security. Chairman and ranking member are non-voting members *ex officio* of all subcommittees of which they are not regular members.

Party Ratio: D 21 - R 14

Peter W. Rodino Jr.
Chairman

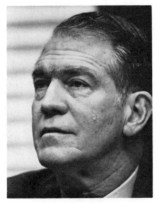

Hamilton Fish Jr.
Ranking Member

Peter W. Rodino Jr., N.J.	*Hamilton Fish Jr., N.Y.*
Jack Brooks, Texas	*Carlos J. Moorhead, Calif.*
Robert W. Kastenmeier, Wis.	*Henry J. Hyde, Ill.*
Don Edwards, Calif.	*Dan Lungren, Calif.*
John Conyers Jr., Mich.	*F. James Sensenbrenner Jr., Wis.*

Romano L. Mazzoli, Ky.	*Bill McCollum, Fla.*
William J. Hughes, N.J.	*E. Clay Shaw Jr., Fla.*
Mike Synar, Okla.	*George W. Gekas, Pa.*
Patricia Schroeder, Colo.	*Michael DeWine, Ohio*
Dan Glickman, Kan.	*William E. Dannemeyer, Calif.*
Barney Frank, Mass.	
George W. Crockett Jr., Mich.	*Pat Swindall, Ga.*
Charles E. Schumer, N.Y.	*Howard Coble, N.C.*
Bruce A. Morrison, Conn.	*D. French Slaughter Jr., Va.*
Edward F. Feighan, Ohio	*Lamar Smith, Texas*
Lawrence J. Smith, Fla.	
Howard L. Berman, Calif.	
Rick Boucher, Va.	
Harley O. Staggers Jr., W.Va.	
John Bryant, Texas	
Benjamin L. Cardin, Md.	

Majority Staff Director: Arthur P. Endres Jr. 225-7709 Rm 2137 RHOB
Minority Chief Counsel: Alan F. Coffey Jr. 225-6906 Rm B351-C RHOB

Subcommittees

Administrative Law and Governmental Relations

■ Phone: 225-5741   ■ Room: B351-A RHOB

Frank — chairman

Brooks	*Shaw*
Glickman	*Swindall*
Morrison	*Coble*
Berman	*Smith*
Cardin	

Civil and Constitutional Rights

■ Phone: 226-7680   ■ Room: 806 HOB Annex #1

Edwards — chairman

Kastenmeier	*Sensenbrenner*
Conyers	*DeWine*
Schroeder	*Dannemeyer*
Schumer	

Courts, Civil Liberties and the Administration of Justice

■ Phone: 225-3926   ■ Room: 2137 RHOB

Kastenmeier — chairman

Synar	*Moorhead*
Schroeder	*Hyde*
Crockett	*Lungren*
Morrison	*DeWine*
Berman	*Coble*
Boucher	*Slaughter*
Bryant	
Cardin	

Crime

■ Phone: 225-1695   ■ Room: 207 CHOB

Hughes — chairman

Mazzoli	*McCollum*
Crockett	*Smith*
Feighan	*Shaw*
Smith	*Gekas*
Staggers	

Criminal Justice

■ Phone: 226-2406   ■ Room: 362 HOB Annex #2

Conyers — chairman

Edwards	*Gekas*
Synar	*Fish*
Boucher	*Swindall*
Bryant	

Immigration, Refugees and International Law

■ Phone: 225-5727   ■ Room: 2137-D RHOB

Mazzoli — chairman

Frank	*Swindall*
Schumer	*Fish*
Morrison	*McCollum*
Berman	*Slaughter*
Bryant	

Monopolies and Commercial Law

■ Phone: 225-2825   ■ Room: B353 RHOB

Rodino — chairman

Brooks	*Fish*
Edwards	*Dannemeyer*
Mazzoli	*Moorhead*
Hughes	*Hyde*
Glickman	*Lungren*
Feighan	*Sensenbrenner*
Smith	
Staggers	

Merchant Marine and Fisheries

■ Phone: 225-4047   ■ Room: 1334 LHOB

Merchant marine generally; oceanography and marine affairs including coastal zone management; Coast Guard; fisheries and wildlife; regulation of common carriers by water and inspection of merchant marine vessels, lights and signals, lifesaving equipment and fire protection; navigation; Panama Canal, Canal Zone and interoceanic canals generally; registration and licensing of vessels; rules and international arrangements to prevent collisions at sea; international fishing agreements; Coast Guard and Merchant Marine academies and state maritime academies. Chairman and ranking minority member are members *ex officio* of all subcommittees of which they are not regular members.

Party Ratio: D 25 - R 17

Walter B. Jones
Chairman

Robert W. Davis
Ranking Member

Walter B. Jones, N.C.	*Robert W. Davis, Mich.*
Mario Biaggi, N.Y.	*Don Young, Alaska*
Glenn M. Anderson, Calif.	*Norman F. Lent, N.Y.*
Gerry E. Studds, Mass.	*Norman D. Shumway, Calif.*
Carroll Hubbard Jr., Ky.	*Jack Fields, Texas*
Don Bonker, Wash.	*Claudine Schneider, R.I.*
William J. Hughes, N.J.	*Herbert H. Bateman, Va.*

Mike Lowry, Wash.
Earl Hutto, Fla.
W. J. "Billy" Tauzin, La.
Thomas M. Foglietta, Pa.
Dennis M. Hertel, Mich.
Roy Dyson, Md.
William O. Lipinski, Ill.
Robert A. Borski, Pa.
Thomas R. Carper, Del.
Douglas H. Bosco, Calif.
Robin Tallon, S.C.
Robert Lindsay Thomas, Ga.
Solomon P. Ortiz, Texas
Charles E. Bennett, Fla.
Thomas J. Manton, N.Y.
Owen B. Pickett, Va.
Joseph E. Brennan, Maine
George J. Hochbrueckner, N.Y.

H. James Saxton, N.J.
John R. Miller, Wash.
Helen Delich Bentley, Md.
Howard Coble, N.C.
Mac Sweeney, Texas
Joseph J. DioGuardi, N.Y.
Curt Weldon, Pa.
Patricia F. Saiki, Hawaii
Wally Herger, Calif.
Jim Bunning, Ky.

Majority Chief Counsel: Edmund B. Welch 225-4047 Rm 1334 LHOB
Minority Staff Director: George D. Pence 225-2650 Rm 1337 LHOB

Subcommittees

Coast Guard and Navigation

■ Phone: 226-3587   ■ Room: 547 HOB Annex #2

Hutto — chairman

Hughes	*Davis †*
Studds	*Young*
Lipinski	*Bateman*
Carper	*Coble*
Thomas	*Sweeney*
Pickett	*DioGuardi*
Brennan	*Weldon*
Hochbrueckner	*Saiki*
Hertel	*Bunning*
Bennett	
Lowry	

† Due to restructuring by the Democrats, the Republicans will drop one member to maintain proper party ratios.

Fisheries and Wildlife Conservation and the Environment

■ Phone: 226-3533   ■ Room: 543 HOB Annex #2

Studds — chairman

Bonker	*Young*
Dyson	*Schneider*
Carper	*Bateman*
Bosco	*Saxton*
Thomas	*Miller*

Ortiz	*Sweeney*
Manton	*DioGuardi*
Anderson	*Weldon*
Hughes	*Saiki*
Lowry	*Herger*
Hutto	*Bunning*
Tauzin	
Hertel	

Merchant Marine

■ Phone: 226-3500   ■ Room: 531 HOB Annex #2

Anderson — acting chairman †

Biaggi	*Lent*
Hubbard	*Young*
Foglietta	*Shumway*
Hertel	*Fields*
Lipinski	*Bateman*
Borski	*Saxton*
Tallon	*Miller*
Bennett	*Bentley*
Pickett	*Coble*
Brennan	*Sweeney*
Hochbrueckner	
Bonker	
Dyson	
Thomas	

† Rep. Anderson was named acting chairman after Rep. Biaggi was forced to relinquish his chairmanship following his indictment on charges of bribery, fraud, conspiracy and obstruction of justice on March 16. House Democratic Caucus rules require that an indicted member step down from his chairmanship for the duration of the session or until charges are dismissed.

Oceanography

■ Phone: 226-3508   ■ Room: 542 HOB Annex #2

Lowry — chairman

Foglietta	*Shumway*
Borski	*Schneider*
Tallon	*Saxton*
Studds	*DioGuardi*
Hughes	*Saiki*
Bonker	*Herger*

Oversight and Investigations

■ Phone: 225-4047   ■ Room: 1334 LHOB

Jones — chairman

Lowry	*Schneider*
	Bentley

Panama Canal/
Outer Continental Shelf

■ Phone: 226-3514   ■ Room: 544 HOB Annex #2

Tauzin — chairman

Ortiz	*Fields*
Manton	*Shumway*
Lowry	*Bentley*
Foglietta	*Coble*
Bosco	*Weldon*
Brennan	*Herger*

Gerry Sikorski, Minn.
Frank McCloskey, Ind.
Gary L. Ackerman, N.Y.
Mervyn M. Dymally, Calif.
Morris K. Udall, Ariz.
Ron de Lugo, Virgin Islands †

† Party ratios do not include delegates or resident commissioner.

Majority Staff Director: Thomas R. DeYulia 225-4054 Rm 309 CHOB
Minority Staff Director: Joseph A. Fisher 225-0073 Rm 300 CHOB

Subcommittees

Census and Population

■ Phone: 226-7523   ■ Room: 608 HOB Annex #1

Dymally — chairman

Garcia	*Morella*
Sikorski	*Burton*

Civil Service

■ Phone: 225-4025   ■ Room: 122 CHOB

Schroeder — chairman

Solarz	*Pashayan*
Clay	*Horton*

Compensation and Employee Benefits

■ Phone: 226-7546   ■ Room: 511 HOB Annex #1

Ackerman — chairman

Oakar	*Myers*
Leland	*Morella*

Human Resources

■ Phone: 225-2821   ■ Room: 406 CHOB

Sikorski — chairman

Yatron	*Burton*
McCloskey	*Gilman*

Investigations

■ Phone: 225-6295   ■ Room: 219 CHOB

Ford — chairman

Yatron	*Taylor*
Oakar	*Gilman*

Post Office and Civil Service

■ Phone: 225-4054   ■ Room: 309 CHOB

Postal and federal civil services; census and the collection of statistics generally; Hatch Act; holidays and celebrations.

Party Ratio: D 13 - R 8 †

William D. Ford
Chairman

Gene Taylor
Ranking Member

William D. Ford, Mich.	*Gene Taylor, Mo.*
William L. Clay, Mo.	*Benjamin A. Gilman, N.Y.*
Patricia Schroeder, Colo.	*Charles Pashayan Jr., Calif.*
Stephen J. Solarz, N.Y.	*Frank Horton, N.Y.*
Robert Garcia, N.Y.	*John T. Myers, Ind.*
Mickey Leland, Texas	*Don Young, Alaska*
Gus Yatron, Pa.	*Dan Burton, Ind.*
Mary Rose Oakar, Ohio	*Constance A. Morella, Md.*

Postal Operations and Services

■ Phone: 225-9124   ■ Room: 209 CHOB

Leland — chairman

Clay
Garcia
de Lugo

Horton
Pashayan
Young

Postal Personnel and Modernization

■ Phone: 226-7520   ■ Room: 603 HOB Annex #1

McCloskey — chairman

Dymally
Ackerman

Young
Myers

Public Works and Transportation

■ Phone: 225-4472   ■ Room: 2165 RHOB

Flood control and improvement of rivers and harbors; construction and maintenance of roads; oil and other pollution of navigable waters; public buildings and grounds; public works for the benefit of navigation including bridges and dams; water power; transportation, except railroads; Botanic Garden; Library of Congress; Smithsonian Institution. Chairman and ranking minority member are members *ex officio* of all subcommittees of which they are not regular members.

Party Ratio: D 30 - R 20 †

James J. Howard
Chairman

John Paul Hammerschmidt
Ranking Member

James J. Howard, N.J.
Glenn M. Anderson, Calif.
Robert A. Roe, N.J.

John Paul Hammerschmidt,
Ark.
Bud Shuster, Pa.

Norman Y. Mineta, Calif.
James L. Oberstar, Minn.
Henry J. Nowak, N.Y.
Nick J. Rahall II, W.Va.
Douglas Applegate, Ohio
Ron de Lugo, Virgin
 Islands †
Gus Savage, Ill.
Fofō I. F. Sunia, American
 Somoa †
Douglas H. Bosco, Calif.
Robert A. Borski, Pa.
Joe Kolter, Pa.
Tim Valentine, N.C.
Edolphus Towns, N.Y.
William O. Lipinski, Ill.
J. Roy Rowland, Ga.
Bob Wise, W.Va.
Kenneth J. Gray, Ill.
Peter J. Visclosky, Ind.
James A. Traficant Jr., Ohio
Jim Chapman, Texas
H. Martin Lancaster, N.C.
Louise M. Slaughter, N.Y.
John Lewis, Ga.
Peter A. DeFazio, Ore.
Benjamin L. Cardin, Md.
Bill Grant, Fla.
David E. Skaggs, Colo.
Jimmy Hayes, La.
Carl C. Perkins, Ky.

Arlan Stangeland, Minn.
Newt Gingrich, Ga.
William F. Clinger Jr., Pa.
Guy V. Molinari, N.Y.
E. Clay Shaw Jr., Fla.
Bob McEwen, Ohio
Thomas E. Petri, Wis.
Don Sundquist, Tenn.
Nancy L. Johnson, Conn.
Ron Packard, Calif.
Sherwood Boehlert, N.Y.
Dean A. Gallo, N.J.
Helen Delich Bentley, Md.
Jim Lightfoot, Iowa
Dennis Hastert, Ill.
James M. Inhofe, Okla.
Cass Ballenger, N.C.
Fred Upton, Mich.

† Party ratios do not include delegates or resident commissioner.

Special Counsel to the Chairman/Majority Staff Director: Salvatore J.
 D'Amico 225-4472 Rm 2165 RHOB
Minority Staff Director: Michael J. Toohey 225-9446 Rm 2163 RHOB

Subcommittees

Aviation

■ Phone: 225-9161   ■ Room: 2251 RHOB

Mineta — chairman

de Lugo
Valentine
Visclosky
Chapman
DeFazio
Skaggs
Anderson
Savage
Sunia
Kolter
Towns
Lipinski
Rowland
Cardin
Bosco
Perkins

Gingrich
Shuster
Stangeland
Petri
Sundquist
Packard
Boehlert
Lightfoot
Inhofe
Ballenger

Economic Development

■ Phone: 225-6151   ■ Room: B376 RHOB

Savage — chairman

Lewis	*Shaw*
Oberstar	*Clinger*
Rahall	*McEwen*
Applegate	*Johnson*
Gray	*Boehlert*
Hayes	*Bentley*
Towns	*Ballenger*
Lipinski	
Traficant	
Vacancy	

Investigations and Oversight

■ Phone: 225-3274   ■ Room: B376 RHOB

Oberstar — chairman

Roe	*Clinger*
Mineta	*Shuster*
Nowak	*Gingrich*
Borski	*Molinari*
Kolter	*McEwen*
Rowland	*Johnson (Conn.)*
Gray	*Bentley*
Lancaster	
Slaughter	
Towns	

Public Buildings and Grounds

■ Phone: 225-9161   ■ Room: 2251 RHOB

Sunia — chairman

Lancaster	*Molinari*
Savage	*Stangeland*
Lewis	*Sundquist*
Cardin	*Gallo*
Grant	
Skaggs	
Anderson	

Surface Transportation

■ Phone: 225-4472   ■ Room: 2165 RHOB

Anderson — chairman

Rahall	*Shuster*
Applegate	*Gingrich*
Bosco	*Clinger*
Borski	*Shaw*
Kolter	*McEwen*
Towns	*Petri*
Lipinski	*Packard*
Rowland	*Boehlert*
Wise	*Gallo*
Gray	*Lightfoot*
Traficant	*Hastert*
Lancaster	*Upton*
Slaughter	
Grant	
Roe	
Mineta	
Nowak	
de Lugo	

Water Resources

■ Phone: 225-0060   ■ Room: B370A RHOB

Nowak — chairman

Roe	*Stangeland*
Cardin	*Molinari*
Hayes	*Shaw*
de Lugo	*Petri*
Borski	*Sundquist*
Valentine	*Johnson*
Wise	*Packard*
Visclosky	*Gallo*
Traficant	*Bentley*
Chapman	*Lightfoot*
Slaughter	*Hastert*
Lewis	*Inhofe*
DeFazio	*Upton*
Grant	
Skaggs	
Anderson	
Oberstar	
Applegate	
Bosco	
Savage	

Rules

■ Phone: 225-9486   ■ Room: H-312 Capitol

Rules and order of business of the House; emergency waivers under the Congressional Budget Act of required reporting date for bills and resolutions authorizing new budget authority; recesses and final adjournments of Congress.

Party Ratio: D 9 - R 4

Claude Pepper
Chairman

James H. Quillen
Ranking Member

Claude Pepper, Fla.
Joe Moakley, Mass.
Butler Derrick, S.C.
Anthony C. Beilenson, Calif.
Martin Frost, Texas
David E. Bonior, Mich.
Tony P. Hall, Ohio
Alan Wheat, Mo.
Bart Gordon, Tenn.

James H. Quillen, Tenn.
Delbert L. Latta, Ohio
Trent Lott, Miss.
Gene Taylor, Mo.

Majority Staff Director/General Counsel: Thomas Spulak 225-9486
Rm H-312 Capitol
Minority Counsel: William D. Crosby Jr. 225-6991 Rm H-305 Capitol

Subcommittees

Legislative Process

■ Phone: 225-1037   ■ Room: 1629 LHOB

Derrick — chairman

Frost	*Lott*
Wheat	*Taylor*
Gordon	
Pepper	

Rules of the House

■ Phone: 225-9091   ■ Room: H-152 Capitol

Moakley — chairman

Beilenson	*Taylor*
Bonior	*Lott*
Hall	
Pepper	

Science, Space and Technology

■ Phone: 225-6371   ■ Room: 2321 RHOB

Astronautical research and development, including resources, personnel, equipment and facilities; Bureau of Standards, standardization of weights and measures and the metric system; National Aeronautics and Space Administration; National Aeronautics and Space Council; National Science Foundation; outer space, including exploration and control; science scholarships; scientific research, development and demonstration; federally owned or operated non-military energy laboratories; civil aviation research and development; environmental research and development; energy research, development and demonstration; National Weather Service. Chairman and ranking minority member are members *ex officio* of all subcommittees of which they are not regular members.

Party Ratio: D 27 - R 18

Robert A. Roe
Chairman

Manuel Lujan Jr.
Ranking Member

Robert A. Roe, N.J.
George E. Brown Jr., Calif.
James H. Scheuer, N.Y.
Marilyn Lloyd, Tenn.
Doug Walgren, Pa.
Dan Glickman, Kan.
Harold L. Volkmer, Mo.
Bill Nelson, Fla.
Ralph M. Hall, Texas

Manuel Lujan Jr., N.M.
Robert S. Walker, Pa.
F. James Sensenbrenner
Jr., Wis.
Claudine Schneider, R.I.
Sherwood Boehlert, N.Y.
Tom Lewis, Fla.
Don Ritter, Pa.
Sid Morrison, Wash.

Dave McCurdy, Okla.
Norman Y. Mineta, Calif.
Buddy MacKay, Fla.
Tim Valentine, N.C.
Robert G. Torricelli, N.J.
Rick Boucher, Va.
Terry L. Bruce, Ill.
Richard H. Stallings, Idaho
James A. Traficant Jr., Ohio
Jim Chapman, Texas
Lee H. Hamilton, Ind.
Henry J. Nowak, N.Y
Carl C. Perkins, Ky.
Tom McMillen, Md.
David E. Price, N.C.
David R. Nagle, Iowa
Jimmy Hayes, La.
David E. Skaggs, Colo.

Ron Packard, Calif.
Robert C. Smith, N.H.
Paul B. Henry, Mich.
Harris W. Fawell, Ill.
D. French Slaughter Jr., Va.
Lamar Smith, Texas
Ernie Konnyu, Calif.
Jack Buechner, Mo.
Joel Hefley, Colo.
Constance A. Morella, Md.

Majority Executive Director: Harold P. Hanson 225-6375
  Rm 2321 RHOB
Minority Staff Director: R. Thomas Weimer 225-8772 Rm 2320 RHOB

Subcommittees

Energy Research and Development

■ Phone: 225-8056   ■ Room: B374 RHOB

Lloyd — chairman

Boucher
Bruce
Stallings
Walgren
Valentine
Traficant
Chapman

Morrison
Fawell
Smith (Texas)
Konnyu
Morella

International Scientific Cooperation

■ Phone: 225-3636   ■ Room: 822 HOB Annex #1

Hall — chairman

Lloyd
MacKay
Torricelli
Stallings
Scheuer
Vacancy

Sensenbrenner
Boehlert
Packard
Fawell

Investigations and Oversight

■ Phone: 225-4494   ■ Room: B374 RHOB

Roe — chairman

Glickman
Volkmer
Price
Brown
Traficant

Ritter
Sensenbrenner
Packard
Konnyu

Natural Resources, Agriculture Research and Environment

■ Phone: 226-6980   ■ Room: 388 HOB Annex #2

Scheuer — chairman

Valentine
McCurdy
Nowak
McMillen
Brown

Schneider
Smith (N.H.)
Henry
Hefley

Science, Research and Technology

■ Phone: 225-8844   ■ Room: 2319 RHOB

Walgren — chairman

MacKay
Hamilton
Nowak
Price
Brown
Mineta
Bruce
Perkins
Nagle
Hayes
Valentine
Chapman
Skaggs

Boehlert
Henry
Schneider
Ritter
Morrison
Slaughter
Smith (Texas)
Buechner

Space Science and Applications

■ Phone: 225-7858   ■ Room: 2324 RHOB

Nelson — chairman

Brown
Volkmer
Mineta
Torricelli
Traficant
Chapman
Perkins
McMillen
Nagle
Hayes
Scheuer
Hall
MacKay
Skaggs

Walker
Packard
Smith (N.H.)
Slaughter
Konnyu
Buechner
Hefley
Morella
Lewis

Transportation, Aviation and Materials

■ Phone: 225-9662   ■ Room: 2321 RHOB

McCurdy — chairman

Glickman	*Lewis*
Nelson	*Walker*
McMillen	*Sensenbrenner*
Hayes	

Select Aging

■ Phone: 226-3375   ■ Room: 712 HOB Annex #1

Problems of older Americans including income, housing, health, welfare, employment, education, recreation and participation in family and community life. Studies and reports findings to House, but cannot report legislation. Chairman and ranking minority member are members *ex officio* of all subcommittees of which they are not regular members.

Party Ratio: D 39 - R 25 †

Edward R. Roybal
Chairman

Matthew J. Rinaldo
Ranking Member

Edward R. Roybal, Calif.	*Matthew J. Rinaldo, N.J.*
Claude Pepper, Fla.	*John Paul Hammerschmidt,*
Mario Biaggi, N.Y.	*Ark.*
Don Bonker, Wash.	*Ralph Regula, Ohio*
Thomas J. Downey, N.Y.	*Norman D. Shumway, Calif.*
James J. Florio, N.J.	*Olympia J. Snowe, Maine*
Harold E. Ford, Tenn.	*James M. Jeffords, Vt.*
William J. Hughes, N.J.	*Tom Tauke, Iowa*
Marilyn Lloyd, Tenn.	*George C. Wortley, N.Y.*
Mary Rose Oakar, Ohio	*Jim Courter, N.J.*
Thomas A. Luken, Ohio	*Claudine Schneider, R.I.*
Beverly B. Byron, Md.	*Tom Ridge, Pa.*
Daniel A. Mica, Fla.	*Christopher H. Smith, N.J.*
Henry A. Waxman, Calif.	*Sherwood Boehlert, N.Y.*
Mike Synar, Okla.	*H. James Saxton, N.J.*
Butler Derrick, S.C.	*Helen Delich Bentley, Md.*
Bruce F. Vento, Minn.	*Jim Lightfoot, Iowa*

Barney Frank, Mass.	*Harris W. Fawell, Ill.*
Tom Lantos, Calif.	*Jan Meyers, Kan.*
Ron Wyden, Ore.	*Ben Blaz, Guam †*
George W. Crockett Jr., Mich.	*Pat Swindall, Ga.*
Bill Boner, Tenn.	*Paul B. Henry, Mich.*
Ike Skelton, Mo.	*Bill Schuette, Mich.*
Dennis M. Hertel, Mich.	*Floyd Spence, S.C.*
Robert A. Borski, Pa.	*William F. Clinger Jr., Pa.*
Rick Boucher, Va.	*Constance A. Morella, Md.*
Ben Erdreich, Ala.	*Patricia F. Saiki, Hawaii*
Buddy MacKay, Fla.	
Norman Sisisky, Va.	
Bob Wise, W.Va.	
Bill Richardson, N.M.	
Harold L. Volkmer, Mo.	
Bart Gordon, Tenn.	
Thomas J. Manton, N.Y.	
Tommy F. Robinson, Ark.	
Richard H. Stallings, Idaho	
James McClure Clarke, N.C.	
Joseph P. Kennedy II, Mass.	
Louise M. Slaughter, N.Y.	

† Party ratios do not include delegates or resident commissioner.

Majority Staff Director: Fernando Torres-Gill 226-3375 Rm 712 HOB Annex #1
Minority Staff Director: Paul Schlegel 226-3396 Rm 606 HOB Annex #1

Subcommittees

Health and Long-Term Care

■ Phone: 226-3381   ■ Room: 377 HOB Annex #2

Pepper — chairman

Florio	*Regula*
Ford	*Rinaldo*
Oakar	*Wortley*
Luken	*Courter*
Mica	*Schneider*
Waxman	*Ridge*
Synar	*Smith*
Derrick	*Boehlert*
Vento	*Saxton*
Frank	*Bentley*
Wyden	*Lightfoot*
Skelton	*Myers*
Hertel	*Blaz*
Borski	
Erdreich	
MacKay	
Sisisky	

Housing and Consumer Interests

■ Phone: 226-3344   ■ Room: 717 HOB Annex #1

Bonker — chairman

Lloyd	*Hammerschmidt*
Byron	*Wortley*
Lantos	*Ridge*
Boner	*Boehlert*
Boucher	*Schuette*
Richardson	*Clinger*
Volkmer	*Saiki*
Gordon	

Human Services

■ Phone: 226-3348   ■ Room: 716 HOB Annex #1

Downey — acting chairman †

Biaggi	*Snowe*
Florio	*Shumway*
Hughes	*Meyers*
Lantos	*Blaz*
Richardson	*Spence*
Robinson	*Clinger*
Clarke	*Morella*
Kennedy	*Saiki*
Slaughter	

† Rep. Downey was named acting chairman after Rep. Biaggi was forced to relinquish his chairmanship following his indictment on charges of bribery, fraud, conspiracy and obstruction of justice on March 16. House Democratic Caucus rules require that an indicted member step down from his chairmanship for the duration of the session or until charges are dismissed.

Retirement, Income and Employment

■ Phone: 226-3335   ■ Room: 714 HOB Annex #1

Roybal — chairman

Downey	*Tauke*
Lloyd	*Shumway*
Oakar	*Jeffords*
Synar	*Fawell*
Crockett	*Swindall*
Boucher	*Henry*
Wise	*Schuette*
Volkmer	*Spence*
Manton	
Stallings	

Select Children, Youth and Families

■ Phone: 226-7660   ■ Room: 385 HOB Annex #2

Problems of children, youth and families including income maintenance, health, nutrition, education, welfare, employment and recreation. Studies and reports findings to House, but cannot report legislation. Chairman and ranking minority member are members *ex officio* of all task forces.

Party Ratio: D 18 - R 12

George Miller
Chairman

Dan Coats
Ranking Member

George Miller, Calif.	*Dan Coats, Ind.*
William Lehman, Fla.	*Thomas J. Bliley Jr., Va.*
Patricia Schroeder, Colo.	*Frank R. Wolf, Va.*
Lindy (Mrs. Hale) Boggs, La.	*Nancy L. Johnson, Conn.*
Matthew F. McHugh, N.Y.	*Barbara F. Vucanovich, Nev.*
Ted Weiss, N.Y.	*Jack F. Kemp, N.Y.*
Beryl Anthony Jr., Ark.	*George C. Wortley, N.Y.*
Barbara Boxer, Calif.	*Ron Packard, Calif.*
Sander M. Levin, Mich.	*Beau Boulter, Texas*
Bruce A. Morrison, Conn.	*Dennis Hastert, Ill.*
J. Roy Rowland, Ga.	*Clyde C. Holloway, La.*
Gerry Sikorski, Minn.	*Fred Grandy, Iowa*
Alan Wheat, Mo.	
Matthew G. Martinez, Calif.	
Lane Evans, Ill.	
Richard J. Durbin, Ill.	
Thomas C. Sawyer, Ohio	
David E. Skaggs, Colo.	

Majority Staff Director: Ann Rosewater 226-7660 Rm 385 HOB Annex #2
Minority Staff Director: Mark Souder 226-7692 Rm 384 HOB Annex #2

Task Forces

Crisis Intervention

- Phone: 226-7660   - Room: 385 HOB Annex #2

Boggs — chairman

Anthony	Johnson
Levin	Vucanovich
Sikorski	Grandy
Weiss	Bliley
Rowland	
Wheat	

Economic Security

- Phone: 226-7660   - Room: 385 HOB Annex #2

Schroeder — chairman

Morrison	Wolf
Wheat	Kemp
Martinez	Boulter
Evans	Hastert
Sawyer	
McHugh	

Prevention Strategies

- Phone: 226-7660   - Room: 385 HOB Annex #2

Lehman — chairman

McHugh	Bliley
Weiss	Wortley
Boxer	Packard
Rowland	Holloway
Durbin	
Skaggs	

Select Committee to Investigate Covert Arms Transactions with Iran

- Phone: 225-7902   - Room: H-419 Capitol

Conduct an investigation and study regarding direct or indirect sale or transfer of arms, technology or intelligence information to Iran or Iraq involving U.S. government officers, employees, consultants, agents, or persons acting in concert with them, or occurring with their approval or knowledge; the relations of such sale or transfer to efforts to obtain the release of hostages and to U.S. policy regarding dealings with nations supporting terrorism; diversion or intended diversion of the funds realized in connection with such sale or transfer for financing assistance to anti-government forces in Nicaragua or any other disposition apart from deposit in the treasury; operational activities and the conduct of foreign and national security policy by the staff of the National Security Council or other White House personnel; authorization and supervision or lack thereof of these matters by the president and other entities outside the government, including foreign countries, entities and persons, in connection with these matters; inquiries regarding these matters, including actions based on those inquiries, by the attorney general, the departments of justice, state and defense, the intelligence community, the White House, and other governmental entities; actions of individuals in destroying, concealing, or failing to provide any evidence or information of possible value to those inquiries.

Party Ratio: D 9 - R 6

Lee H. Hamilton **Chairman**	**Dick Cheney** **Ranking Member**

Lee H. Hamilton, Ind.	*Dick Cheney, Wyo.*
Dante B. Fascell, Fla.	*William S. Broomfield, Mich.*
Thomas S. Foley, Wash.	*Henry J. Hyde, Ill.*
Peter W. Rodino Jr., N.J.	*Jim Courter, N.J.*
Jack Brooks, Texas	*Bill McCollum, Fla.*
Edward P. Boland, Mass.	*Michael DeWine, Ohio*
Louis Stokes, Ohio	
Les Aspin, Wis.	
Ed Jenkins, Ga.	

Staff Director: Casey Miller 225-7902 Rm H-419 Capitol

(No standing subcommittees.)

Select Hunger

■ Phone: 226-5470   ■ Room: 507 HOB Annex #2

Comprehensive study and review of hunger and malnutrition, including U.S. development and economic assistance programs; U.S. trade relations with less-developed nations; food production and distribution; agribusiness efforts to further international development; policies of development banks and international development institutions; and food assistance programs in the United States. Review of executive branch recommendations relating to programs affecting hunger and malnutrition, and to recommend legislation or other action with respect to such programs to the appropriate committees of the House. Studies and reports findings to House, but cannot report legislation. Chairman and ranking minority member are members *ex officio* of all task forces.

Party Ratio: D 16 - R 10

Mickey Leland
Chairman

Marge Roukema
Vice Chairman

Mickey Leland, Texas
Tony P. Hall, Ohio
Bob Traxler, Mich.
Leon E. Panetta, Calif.
Vic Fazio, Calif.
Sam Gejdenson, Conn.
Peter H. Kostmayer, Pa.
Byron L. Dorgan, N.D.
Bob Carr, Mich.
Timothy J. Penny, Minn.
Gary L. Ackerman, N.Y.
Mike Espy, Miss.
Floyd H. Flake, N.Y.
James Bilbray, Nev.
Kweisi Mfume, Md.
Liz J. Patterson, S.C.

Marge Roukema, N.J.
Bill Emerson, Mo.
Sid Morrison, Wash.
Benjamin A. Gilman, N.Y.
Robert F. Smith, Ore.
Doug Bereuter, Neb.
Fred Upton, Mich.
Hank Brown, Colo.
Guy V. Molinari, N.Y.
Vacancy

Majority Chief of Staff: Miranda G. Katsoyannis 226-5470 Rm 507 HOB Annex #2
Minority Staff Director: John D. Cuttell 226-5460 Rm 506 HOB Annex #2

Task Forces

Domestic

■ Phone: 226-5470   ■ Room: 507 HOB Annex #2

Panetta — chairman

Traxler	*Emerson*
Ackerman	*Morrison*
Espy	*Upton*
Flake	*Brown*
Bilbray	
Mfume	
Patterson	

International

■ Phone: 226-5470   ■ Room: 507 HOB Annex #2

Hall — chairman

Fazio	*Bereuter—vice chairman*
Gejdenson	*Morrison*
Kostmayer	*Gilman*
Dorgan	*Smith*
Carr	*Molinari*
Penny	

Select Intelligence

■ Phone: 225-4121   ■ Room: H-405 Capitol

Legislative and budgetary authority over the Central Intelligence Agency, the Defense Intelligence Agency, the National Security Agency, intelligence activities of the Federal Bureau of Investigation and other components of the federal intelligence community. House majority leader and minority leader are non-voting members *ex officio* of the full committee.

Party Ratio: D 11 - R 6

Louis Stokes, Ohio
Chairman

Henry J. Hyde, III.
Ranking Member

Louis Stokes, Ohio
Dave McCurdy, Okla.
Anthony C. Beilenson, Calif.
Robert W. Kastenmeier, Wis.
Dan Daniel, Va.
Robert A. Roe, N.J.
George E. Brown Jr., Calif.
Matthew F. McHugh, N.Y.
Bernard J. Dwyer, N.J.
Charles Wilson, Texas
Barbara B. Kennelly, Conn.

Henry J. Hyde, Ill.
Dick Cheney, Wyo.
Bob Livingston, La.
Bob McEwen, Ohio
Dan Lungren, Calif.
Bud Shuster, Pa.

Staff Director: Thomas K. Latimer 225-4121 Rm H-405 Capitol

Subcommittees

Legislation

■ Phone: 225-7310   ■ Room: H-405 Capitol

McHugh — chairman

Stokes
Kastenmeier
Dwyer
Wilson
Kennelly

Livingston
Shuster
Lungren

Oversight and Evaluation

■ Phone: 225-5657   ■ Room: H-405 Capitol

Beilenson — chairman

Dwyer
Wilson
Kennelly
McCurdy
Brown

McEwen
Shuster
Hyde

Program and Budget Authorization

■ Phone: 225-7690   ■ Room: H-405 Capitol

Stokes — chairman

McCurdy
Kastenmeier
Daniel
Roe
Brown

Cheney
Hyde
Lungren

Select Narcotics Abuse and Control

■ Phone: 226-3040   ■ Room: 234 HOB Annex #2

Problems of narcotics, drug and polydrug abuse and control including opium and its derivatives, other narcotic drugs, psychotropics and other controlled substances; trafficking, manufacturing and distribution; treatment, prevention and rehabilitation; narcotics-related violations of tax laws; international treaties and agreements relating to narcotics and drug abuse; role of organized crime in narcotics and drug abuse; abuse and control in the armed forces and in industry; criminal justice system and narcotics and drug law violations and crimes related to drug abuse. Studies and reports findings to House, but cannot report legislation.

*Party Ratio: D 15 - R 10 ***

Charles B. Rangel Chairman

Benjamin A. Gilman Ranking Member

Charles B. Rangel, N.Y.
Peter W. Rodino Jr., N.J.
Fortney H. "Pete" Stark, Calif.
James H. Scheuer, N.Y.
Cardiss Collins, Ill.
Daniel K. Akaka, Hawaii
Frank J. Guarini, N.J.
Robert T. Matsui, Calif.
Dante B. Fascell, Fla.
Walter E. Fauntroy, D.C.
William J. Hughes, N.J.
Mel Levine, Calif.
Solomon P. Ortiz, Texas
Lawrence J. Smith, Fla.
Edolphus Towns, N.Y.

Benjamin A. Gilman, N.Y.
Lawrence Coughlin, Pa.
E. Clay Shaw Jr., Fla.
Michael G. Oxley, Ohio
Stan Parris, Va.
Duncan Hunter, Calif.
Joseph J. DioGuardi, N.Y.
F. James Sensenbrenner Jr., Wis.
Bob Dornan, Calif.
Vacancy

* *Party ratio includes delegate.*

Majority Chief of Staff: Edward Jurith 226-3040 Rm 234 HOB Annex #2
Minority Staff Director: Elliott A. Brown 226-3040 Rm 234 HOB Annex #2

(No standing subcommittees.)

Small Business

- Phone: 225-5821   - Room: 2361 RHOB

Assistance to and protection of small business including financial aid; participation of small business enterprises in federal procurement and government contracts. Chairman and ranking minority member are members *ex officio* of all subcommittees of which they are not regular members.

Party Ratio: D 27 - R 17

John J. LaFalce
Chairman

Joseph M. McDade
Ranking Member

John J. LaFalce, N.Y.
Neal Smith, Iowa
Henry B. Gonzalez, Texas
Thomas A. Luken, Ohio
Ike Skelton, Mo.
Romano L. Mazzoli, Ky.
Nicholas Mavroules, Mass.
Charles Hatcher, Ga.
Ron Wyden, Ore.
Dennis E. Eckart, Ohio
Gus Savage, Ill.
Buddy Roemer, La.
Norman Sisisky, Va.
Esteban Edward Torres, Calif.
Jim Cooper, Tenn.
Jim Olin, Va.
Richard Ray, Ga.
Charles A. Hayes, Ill.
John Conyers Jr., Mich.
James Bilbray, Nev.
Kweisi Mfume, Md.
Floyd H. Flake, N.Y.
H. Martin Lancaster, N.C.
Ben Nighthorse Campbell, Colo.
Peter A. DeFazio, Ore.
David E. Price, N.C. *
Matthew G. Martinez, Calif. *

Joseph M. McDade, Pa.
Silvio O. Conte, Mass.
William S. Broomfield, Mich.
Andy Ireland, Fla.
John Hiler, Ind.
David Dreier, Calif.
D. French Slaughter Jr., Va.
Jan Meyers, Kan.
Dean A. Gallo, N.J.
J. Alex McMillan, N.C.
Larry Combest, Texas
Richard H. Baker, La.
John J. Rhodes III, Ariz.
Joel Hefley, Colo.
Fred Upton, Mich.
Elton Gallegly, Calif.
Vacancy

* *Member appointed temporarily for the 100th Congress only.*

Majority Staff Director: Don Terry 225-5821 Rm 2361 RHOB
Minority Staff Director: Drew Hiatt 225-4038 Rm B343-C RHOB

Subcommittees

Antitrust, Impact of Deregulation and Privatization

- Phone: 225-6026   - Room: B363 RHOB

Eckart — chairman

Gonzalez
Luken
Price
Martinez

Hiler
Slaughter
Rhodes

Energy and Agriculture

- Phone: 225-3171   - Room: H2-569 HOB Annex #2

Hatcher — chairman

Ray
Martinez
Bilbray
Vacancy

Dreier
Combest
Gallegly

Exports, Tourism and Special Problems

- Phone: 225-9368   - Room: B363 RHOB

Skelton — chairman

Bilbray
Lancaster
Campbell
Sisisky
Mfume

Ireland
Slaughter
Gallo
Upton

Procurement, Innovation and Minority Enterprise Development

- Phone: 225-8944   - Room: B363 RHOB

Mavroules — chairman

Hayes
Conyers
Mfume
Flake
Eckart
Savage
Torres
Lancaster

Conte
Rhodes
Gallo
Upton
Gallegly
Vacancy

Regulation and Business Opportunities

■ Phone: 225-7797   ■ Room: B363 RHOB

Wyden — chairman

DeFazio	*Broomfield*
Price	*Meyers*
Luken	*McMillan*
Mazzoli	*Combest*
Cooper	*Baker*
Olin	*Vacancy*
Flake	
Vacancy	

SBA and the General Economy

■ Phone: 225-5821   ■ Room: 2361 RHOB

LaFalce — chairman

Smith	*McDade*
Mazzoli	*Meyers*
Savage	*McMillan*
Roemer	*Baker*
Sisisky	*Hefley*
Torres	*Vacancy*
Cooper	
Olin	

Standards of Official Conduct

■ Phone: 225-7103   ■ Room: HT-2 Capitol

Measures relating to the Code of Official Conduct; conduct of House members and employees; Ethics in Government Act.

Party Ratio: D 6 - R 6

Julian C. Dixon
Chairman

Floyd Spence
Ranking Member

Julian C. Dixon, Calif.
Vic Fazio, Calif.
Bernard J. Dwyer, N.J.
Alan B. Mollohan, W.Va.
Joseph M. Gaydos, Pa.
Chester G. Atkins, Mass.

Floyd Spence, S.C.
John T. Myers, Ind.
James V. Hansen, Utah
Charles Pashayan Jr., Calif.
Thomas E. Petri, Wis.
Larry E. Craig, Idaho

Chief Counsel: Ralph L. Lotkin 225-7103 Rm HT-2 Capitol

(No standing subcommittees.)

Veterans' Affairs

■ Phone: 225-3527   ■ Room: 335 CHOB

Veterans' measures generally; compensation, vocational rehabilitation and education of veterans; armed forces life insurance; pensions; readjustment benefits; veterans' hospitals, medical care and treatment. Chairman and ranking minority member are members *ex officio* of all subcommittees of which they are not regular members.

Party Ratio: D 21 - R 13

G. V. "Sonny" Montgomery
Chairman

Gerald B.H. Solomon
Ranking Member

G. V. "Sonny" Montgomery, Miss.
Don Edwards, Calif.
Douglas Applegate, Ohio
Daniel A. Mica, Fla.
Wayne Dowdy, Miss.
Lane Evans, Ill.
Marcy Kaptur, Ohio
Timothy J. Penny, Minn.
Harley O. Staggers Jr., W.Va.
J. Roy Rowland, Ga.
John Bryant, Texas
James J. Florio, N.J.
Kenneth J. Gray, Ill.
Paul E. Kanjorski, Pa.
Tommy F. Robinson, Ark.

Gerald B. H. Solomon, N.Y.
John Paul Hammerschmidt, Ark.
Chalmers P. Wylie, Ohio
Bob Stump, Ariz.
Bob McEwen, Ohio
Christopher H. Smith, N.J.
Dan Burton, Ind.
Michael Bilirakis, Fla.
Tom Ridge, Pa.
John G. Rowland, Conn.
Bob Dornan, Calif.
Robert C. Smith, N.H.
Jack Davis, Ill.

Charles W. Stenholm, Texas
Claude Harris, Ala.
Joseph P. Kennedy II, Mass.
Liz J. Patterson, S.C.
Tim Johnson, S.D.
Jim Jontz, Ind.

*Majority Counsel and Staff Director: Mack G. Fleming 225-3527
Rm 335 CHOB*
*Minority Counsel and Staff Director: Rufus H. Wilson 225-3551
Rm 333 CHOB*

Subcommittees

Compensation, Pension and Insurance

■ Phone: 225-3569   ■ Room: 335 CHOB

Applegate — chairman

Penny	*McEwen*
Robinson	*Wylie*
Johnson	*Bilirakis*
Mica	*Smith (N.H.)*
Evans	

Education, Training and Employment

■ Phone: 225-9166   ■ Room: 335 CHOB

Dowdy — chairman

Patterson	*Smith (N.J.)*
Jontz	*Wylie*
Evans	*Ridge*
Kaptur	*Dornan*
Kennedy	

Hospitals and Health Care

■ Phone: 225-9154   ■ Room: 335 CHOB

Montgomery — chairman

Mica	*Hammerschmidt*
Penny	*Stump*
Staggers	*McEwen*
Rowland (Ga.)	*Smith (N.J.)*
Bryant	*Bilirakis*
Florio	*Ridge*
Gray	*Rowland (Conn.)*
Kanjorski	
Robinson	
Stenholm	
Harris	
Kennedy	

Housing and Memorial Affairs

■ Phone: 225-9164   ■ Room: 335 CHOB

Kaptur — chairman

Rowland (Ga.)	*Burton*
Harris	*Rowland (Conn.)*
Patterson	*Smith (N.H.)*
Florio	*Davis*

Oversight and Investigations

■ Phone: 225-3541   ■ Room: 335 CHOB

Evans — chairman

Edwards	*Stump*
Johnson	*Burton*
Applegate	*Dornan*
Mica	*Davis*
Dowdy	
Florio	

Ways and Means

■ Phone: 225-3625   ■ Room: 1102 LHOB

Revenue measures generally; reciprocal trade agreements; customs, collection districts and ports of entry and delivery; bonded debt of the United States; deposit of public moneys; transportation of dutiable goods; tax exempt foundations and charitable trusts; Social Security. Chairman and ranking minority member are members *ex officio* of all subcommittees of which they are not regular members.

Party Ratio: D 23 - R 13

Dan Rostenkowski
Chairman

John J. Duncan
Ranking Member

Dan Rostenkowski, Ill.
Sam Gibbons, Fla.
J. J. Pickle, Texas
Charles B. Rangel, N.Y.
Fortney H. "Pete" Stark, Calif.
Andrew Jacobs Jr., Ind.
Harold E. Ford, Tenn.
Ed Jenkins, Ga.
Richard A. Gephardt, Mo.
Thomas J. Downey, N.Y.
Frank J. Guarini, N.J.
Marty Russo, Ill.
Don J. Pease, Ohio
Robert T. Matsui, Calif.
Beryl Anthony Jr., Ark.
Ronnie G. Flippo, Ala.
Byron L. Dorgan, N.D.
Barbara B. Kennelly, Conn.
Brian J. Donnelly, Mass.
William J. Coyne, Pa.
Michael A. Andrews, Texas
Sander M. Levin, Mich.
Jim Moody, Wis.

John J. Duncan, Tenn.
Bill Archer, Texas
Guy Vander Jagt, Mich.
Philip M. Crane, Ill.
Bill Frenzel, Minn.
Richard T. Schulze, Pa.
Bill Gradison, Ohio
William M. Thomas, Calif.
Raymond J. McGrath, N.Y.
Hal Daub, Neb.
Judd Gregg, N.H.
Hank Brown, Colo.
Rod Chandler, Wash.

Majority Chief Counsel: Joseph K. Dowley 225-3625 Rm 1102 LHOB
Minority Chief of Staff: A. L. Singleton 225-4021 Rm 1106 LHOB

Subcommittees

Health

■ Phone: 225-7785   ■ Room: 1114 LHOB

Stark — chairman

Donnelly	*Gradison*
Coyne	*Daub*
Pickle	*Gregg*
Anthony	*Chandler*
Levin	
Moody	

Oversight

■ Phone: 225-2743   ■ Room: 1105 LHOB

Pickle — chairman

Anthony	*Schulze*
Flippo	*Frenzel*
Dorgan	*Thomas*
Ford	*McGrath*
Rangel	
Jacobs	

Public Assistance and Unemployment Compensation

■ Phone: 225-1025   ■ Room: B317 RHOB

Downey — acting chairman †

Ford	*Brown*
Pease	*Frenzel*
Matsui	*Gradison*
Kennelly	*Chandler*
Donnelly	
Andrews	

† Rep. Ford, the subcommittee chairman, was indicted on charges of bank, mail and tax fraud on April 24. House Democratic Caucus rules require that an indicted member step down from his chairmanship for the duration of the session or until charges are dismissed.

Select Revenue Measures

■ Phone: 225-9710   ■ Room: 1111 LHOB

Rangel — chairman

Flippo	*Vander Jagt*
Dorgan	*McGrath*
Kennelly	*Gregg*
Andrews	*Brown*
Stark	
Coyne	

Social Security

■ Phone: 225-9263   ■ Room: B316 RHOB

Jacobs — chairman

Gephardt	*Archer*
Gibbons	*Crane*
Levin	*Daub*
Moody	

Trade

■ Phone: 225-3943   ■ Room: 1136 LHOB

Gibbons — chairman

Rostenkowski	*Crane*
Jenkins	*Archer*
Downey	*Vander Jagt*
Pease	*Frenzel*
Russo	*Schulze*
Gephardt	
Guarini	
Matsui	

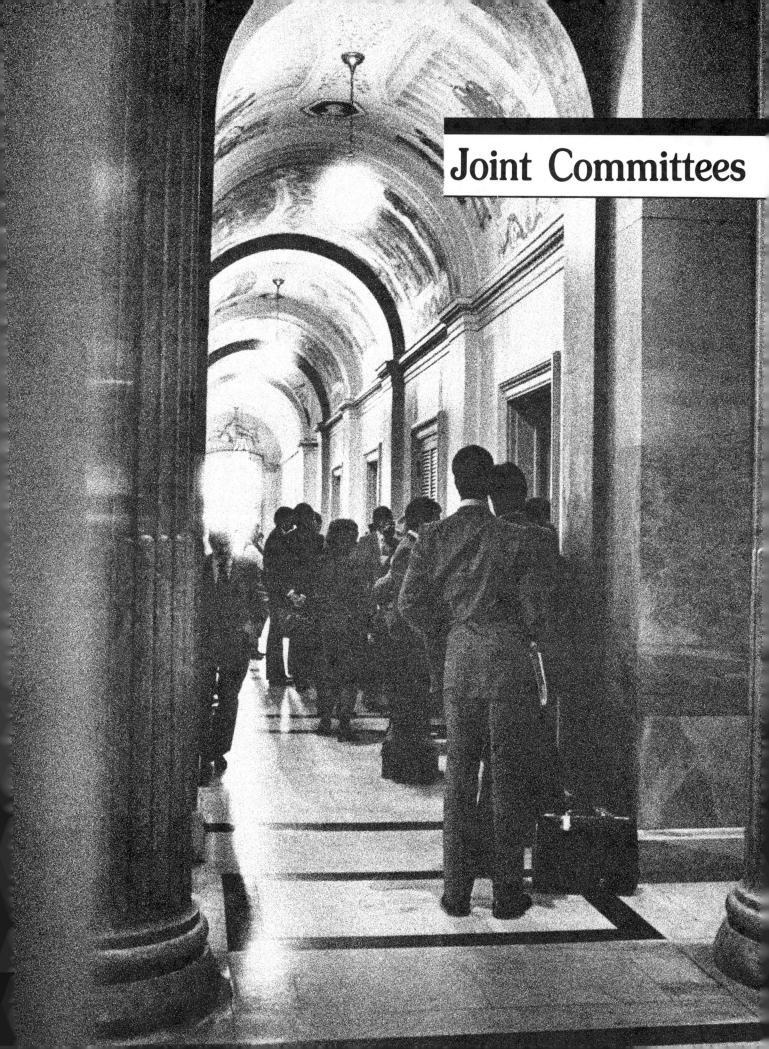

Joint Committees

Joint Committee Assignments, 100th Congress

Joint committees are set up to examine specific questions and are established by public law. Membership is drawn from both chambers and both parties. When a senator serves as chairman, the vice chairman is usually a representative, and vice versa. The chairmanship usually rotates from one chamber to the other at the beginning of each Congress. Democrats are listed on the left in roman type; Republicans are listed on the right *in italics*.

Economic

■ Phone: 224-5171   ■ Room: SD-G01

Studies and investigates all recommendations in the president's annual Economic Report to Congress. Reports findings and recommendations to the House and Senate.

Sen. Paul S. Sarbanes
Chairman

Rep. Lee H. Hamilton
Vice Chairman

Senate Members

Paul S. Sarbanes, Md.	*William V. Roth Jr., Del.*
William Proxmire, Wis.	*Steve Symms, Idaho*
Lloyd Bentsen, Texas	*Alfonse M. D'Amato, N.Y.*
Edward M. Kennedy, Mass.	*Pete Wilson, Calif.*
John Melcher, Mont.	
Jeff Bingaman, N.M.	

House Members

Lee H. Hamilton, Ind.	*Chalmers P. Wylie, Ohio*
Augustus F. Hawkins, Calif.	*Olympia J. Snowe, Maine*
David R. Obey, Wis.	*Hamilton Fish Jr., N.Y.*
James H. Scheuer, N.Y.	*J. Alex McMillan, N.C.*
Fortney H. "Pete" Stark, Calif.	
Stephen J. Solarz, N.Y.	

Executive Director: Judith Davison 224-5171 Rm SD-G01
Minority Assistant Director: Robert J. Tosterud 224-5171 Rm SD-G01

Subcommittees

Economic Goals and Intergovernmental Policy

■ Phone: 224-5171   ■ Room: SD-G01

Rep. Hamilton — chairman

Senate Members

Melcher	*Roth*
Bentsen	*Wilson*

House Members

Hawkins	*Snowe*

Economic Growth, Trade and Taxes

■ Phone: 224-5171   ■ Room: SD-G01

Sen. Bentsen — chairman

Senate Members

Melcher	*D'Amato*
	Roth

House Members

Hamilton	*Fish*
Obey	
Stark	

Economic Resources and Competitiveness

■ Phone: 224-5171   ■ Room: SD-G01

Rep. Obey — chairman

Senate Members

Melcher	*Symms*
Bingaman	

House Members

Scheuer	*Wylie*
	McMillan

Education and Health

■ Phone: 224-5171   ■ Room: SD-G01

Rep. Scheuer — chairman

Senate Members

Bingaman	*Wilson*
Bentsen	*D'Amato*

House Members

Hawkins	*Snowe*
Stark	

Fiscal and Monetary Policy

■ Phone: 224-5171   ■ Room: SD-G01

Sen. Kennedy — chairman

Senate Members

Proxmire	*Symms*

House Members

Stark	*Wylie*
Solarz	*McMillan*

International Economic Policy

■ Phone: 224-5171   ■ Room: SD-G01

Sen. Sarbanes — chairman

Senate Members

Proxmire	*Roth*
Kennedy	

House Members

Hamilton	*Snowe*
Solarz	*Wylie*

Investment, Jobs and Prices

■ Phone: 224-5171   ■ Room: SD-G01

Rep. Hawkins — chairman

Senate Members

Kennedy	*D'Amato*
Sarbanes	*Symms*

House Members

Solarz	*Fish*

National Security Economics

■ Phone: 224-5171   ■ Room: SD-G01

Sen. Proxmire — chairman

Senate Members

Bingaman	*Wilson*
Sarbanes	

House Members

Obey	*McMillan*
Scheuer	*Fish*

Library

■ Phone: 224-6352   ■ Room: SR-305

Management and expansion of the Library of Congress; receipt of gifts for the benefit of the library; development and maintenance of the Botanic Garden; placement of statues and other works of art in the Capitol.

Sen. Claiborne Pell	**Rep. Frank Annunzio**
Chairman	**Vice Chairman**

Senate Members

Claiborne Pell, R.I.	*Mark O. Hatfield, Ore.*
Dennis DeConcini, Ariz.	*Ted Stevens, Alaska*
Daniel Patrick Moynihan, N.Y.	

House Members

Frank Annunzio, Ill.	*Newt Gingrich, Ga.*
Mary Rose Oakar, Ohio	*Pat Roberts, Kan.*
Ed Jones, Tenn.	

Staff Director: James O. King 224-6352 Rm SR-305

(No standing subcommittees.)

Printing

■ Phone: 224-5241   ■ Room: SH-818

Probes inefficiency and waste in the printing, binding and distribution of federal government publications. Oversees arrangement and style of the *Congressional Record*.

Rep. Frank Annunzio
Chairman

Sen. Wendell H. Ford
Vice Chairman

Senate Members

Wendell H. Ford, Ky.
Dennis DeConcini, Ariz.
Albert Gore Jr., Tenn.

Ted Stevens, Alaska
Mark O. Hatfield, Ore.

House Members

Frank Annunzio, Ill.
Joseph M. Gaydos, Pa.
Leon E. Panetta, Calif.

Robert E. Badham, Calif.
Pat Roberts, Kan.

Staff Director: Richard Oleszewski 224-5241 Rm SH-818

(No standing subcommittees.)

Taxation

■ Phone: 225-3621   ■ Room: 1015 LHOB

Operation, effects and administration of the federal system of internal revenue taxes; measures and methods for simplification of taxes.

Rep. Dan Rostenkowski
Chairman

Sen. Lloyd Bentsen
Vice Chairman

Senate Members

Lloyd Bentsen, Texas
Spark M. Matsunaga, Hawaii
Daniel Patrick Moynihan, N.Y.

Bob Packwood, Ore.
Robert Dole, Kan.

House Members

Dan Rostenkowski, Ill.
Sam Gibbons, Fla.
J. J. Pickle, Texas

John J. Duncan, Tenn.
Bill Archer, Texas

Chief of Staff: David H. Brockway 225-3621 Rm 1015 LHOB
Deputy Chief of Staff: Randall Weiss 225-6801 Rm 1015 LHOB

(No standing subcommittees.)

Index of Senators' Committee Assignments

Adams: Commerce, Science and Transportation; Foreign Relations; Labor and Human Resources; Rules and Administration

Armstrong: Banking, Housing and Urban Affairs; Budget; Finance

Baucus: Environment and Public Works; Finance; Small Business

Bentsen: Commerce, Science and Transportation; Finance (chairman); Select Intelligence; Joint Economic; Joint Taxation

Biden: Foreign Relations; Judiciary (chairman)

Bingaman: Armed Services; Energy and Natural Resources; Governmental Affairs; Joint Economic

Bond: Agriculture, Nutrition and Forestry; Banking, Housing and Urban Affairs; Small Business

Boren: Agriculture, Nutrition and Forestry; Finance; Select Committee on Secret Military Assistance to Iran and the Nicaraguan Opposition; Select Intelligence (chairman); Small Business

Boschwitz: Agriculture, Nutrition and Forestry; Budget; Foreign Relations; Small Business

Bradley: Energy and Natural Resources; Finance; Select Intelligence; Special Aging

Breaux: Agriculture, Nutrition and Forestry; Commerce, Science and Transportation; Environment and Public Works; Special Aging

Bumpers: Appropriations; Energy and Natural Resources; Small Business (chairman)

Burdick: Appropriations; Environment and Public Works (chairman); Select Indian Affairs; Special Aging

Byrd: Majority Leader; Appropriations; Judiciary; Rules and Administration

Chafee: Banking, Housing and Urban Affairs; Environment and Public Works; Finance; Special Aging

Chiles: Appropriations; Budget (chairman); Governmental Affairs; Special Aging

Cochran: Agriculture, Nutrition and Forestry; Appropriations; Labor and Human Resources

Cohen: Armed Services; Governmental Affairs; Select Committee on Secret Military Assistance to Iran and the Nicaraguan Opposition; Select Intelligence; Special Aging

Conrad: Agriculture, Nutrition and Forestry; Budget; Energy and Natural Resources

Cranston: Banking, Housing and Urban Affairs; Foreign Relations; Select Intelligence; Veterans' Affairs (chairman)

D'Amato: Appropriations; Banking, Housing and Urban Affairs; Small Business; Joint Economic

Danforth: Budget; Commerce, Science and Transportation; Finance

Daschle: Agriculture, Nutrition and Forestry; Finance; Select Indian Affairs

DeConcini: Appropriations; Judiciary; Rules and Administration; Select Indian Affairs; Select Intelligence; Veterans' Affairs; Joint Library; Joint Printing

Dixon: Armed Services; Banking, Housing and Urban Affairs; Small Business

Dodd: Banking, Housing and Urban Affairs; Budget; Foreign Relations; Labor and Human Resources; Rules and Administration

Dole: Minority Leader; Agriculture, Nutrition and Forestry; Finance; Rules and Administration; Joint Taxation

Domenici: Appropriations; Budget; Energy and Natural Resources; Special Aging

Durenberger: Environment and Public Works; Finance; Special Aging

Evans: Energy and Natural Resources; Foreign Relations; Select Indian Affairs

Exon: Armed Services; Budget; Commerce, Science and Transportation

Ford: Commerce, Science and Transportation; Energy and Natural Resources; Rules and Administration (chairman); Joint Printing

Fowler: Agriculture, Nutrition and Forestry; Budget; Energy and Natural Resources

Garn: Appropriations; Banking, Housing and Urban Affairs; Rules and Administration

Glenn: Armed Services; Governmental Affairs (chairman); Special Aging

Gore: Armed Services; Commerce, Science and Transportation; Rules and Administration; Joint Printing

Graham: Banking, Housing and Urban Affairs; Environment and Public Works; Veterans' Affairs

Gramm: Armed Services; Banking, Housing and Urban Affairs

Grassley: Appropriations; Budget; Judiciary; Special Aging

Harkin: Agriculture, Nutrition and Forestry; Appropriations; Labor and Human Resources; Small Business

Hatch: Judiciary; Labor and Human Resources; Select Committee on Secret Military Assistance to Iran and the Nicagraguan Opposition; Select Intelligence

Hatfield: Appropriations; Energy and Natural Resources; Rules and Administration; Joint Library; Joint Printing

Hecht: Banking, Housing and Urban Affairs; Energy and Natural Resources; Select Intelligence

Heflin: Agriculture, Nutrition and Forestry; Judiciary; Select Committee on Secret Military Assistance to Iran and the Nicaraguan Opposition; Select Ethics (chairman)

Heinz: Banking, Housing and Urban Affairs; Finance; Governmental Affairs; Special Aging

Helms: Agriculture, Nutrition and Forestry; Foreign Relations; Rules and Administration; Select Ethics

Hollings: Appropriations; Budget; Commerce, Science and Transportation (chairman); Select Intelligence

Humphrey: Armed Services; Judiciary; Labor and Human Resources

Inouye: Appropriations; Commerce, Science and Transportation; Rules and Administration; Select Committee on Secret Military Assistance to Iran and the Nicaraguan Opposition (chairman); Select Indian Affairs (chairman)

Johnston: Appropriations; Budget; Energy and Natural Resources (chairman); Special Aging

Karnes: Agriculture, Nutrition and Forestry; Banking, Housing and Urban Affairs; Small Business

Kassebaum: Budget; Commerce, Science and Transportation; Foreign Relations; Select Ethics

Kasten: Appropriations; Budget; Commerce, Science and Transportation; Small Business

Kennedy: Armed Services; Judiciary; Labor and Human Resources (chairman); Joint Economic

Kerry: Commerce, Science and Transportation; Foreign Relations; Small Business

Lautenberg: Appropriations; Budget; Environment and Public Works

Leahy: Agriculture, Nutrition and Forestry (chairman); Appropriations; Judiciary

Levin: Armed Services; Governmental Affairs; Small Business

Lugar: Agriculture, Nutrition and Forestry; Foreign Relations

Matsunaga: Finance; Labor and Human Resources; Veterans' Affairs; Joint Taxation

McCain: Armed Services; Commerce, Science and Transportation; Select Indian Affairs

McClure: Appropriations; Energy and Natural Resources; Rules and Administration; Select Committee on Secret Military Assistance to Iran and the Nicaraguan Opposition

McConnell: Agriculture, Nutrition and Forestry; Foreign Relations

Melcher: Agriculture, Nutrition and Forestry; Energy and Natural Resources; Select Indian Affairs; Special Aging (chairman); Joint Economic

Metzenbaum: Energy and Natural Resources; Judiciary; Labor and Human Resources; Select Intelligence

Mikulski: Appropriations; Environment and Public Works; Labor and Human Resources; Small Business

Mitchell: Environment and Public Works; Finance; Governmental Affairs; Select Committee on Secret Military Assistance to Iran and the Nicaraguan Opposition; Veterans' Affairs

Moynihan: Environment and Public Works; Finance; Foreign Relations; Rules and Administration; Joint Library; Joint Taxtation

Murkowski: Energy and Natural Resources; Foreign Relations; Select Indian Affairs; Select Intelligence; Veterans' Affairs

Nickles: Appropriations; Budget; Energy and Natural Resources

Nunn: Armed Services (chairman); Governmental Affairs; Select Intelligence; Select Committee on Secret Military Assistance to Iran and the Nicaraguan Opposition; Small Business

Packwood: Commerce, Science and Transportation; Finance; Joint Taxation

Pell: Foreign Relations (chairman); Labor and Human Resources; Rules and Administration; Joint Library (chairman)

Pressler: Commerce, Science and Transportation; Environment and Public Works; Foreign Relations; Small Business; Special Aging

Proxmire: Appropriations; Banking, Housing and Urban Affairs (chairman); Joint Economic

Pryor: Agriculture, Nutrition and Forestry; Finance; Governmental Affairs; Select Ethics; Special Aging

Quayle: Armed Services; Budget; Labor and Human Resources

Reid: Appropriations; Environment and Public Works; Special Aging

Riegle: Banking, Housing and Urban Affairs; Budget; Commerce, Science and Transportation; Finance

Rockefeller: Commerce, Science and Transportation; Finance; Veterans' Affairs

Roth: Finance; Governmental Affairs; Select Intelligence; Joint Economic

Rudman: Appropriations; Budget; Governmental Affairs; Select Committee on Secret Military Assistance to Iran and the Nicaraguan Opposition; Select Ethics; Small Business

Sanford: Banking, Housing and Urban Affairs; Budget; Foreign Relations; Select Ethics

Sarbanes: Banking, Housing and Urban Affairs; Foreign Relations; Select Committee on Secret Military Assistance to Iran and the Nicaraguan Opposition; Joint Economic (chairman)

Sasser: Appropriations; Banking, Housing and Urban Affairs; Budget; Governmental Affairs; Small Business

Shelby: Armed Services; Banking, Housing and Urban Affairs; Special Aging

Simon: Budget; Foreign Relations; Judiciary; Labor and Human Resources

Simpson: Environment and Public Works; Judiciary; Special Aging; Veterans' Affairs

Specter: Appropriations; Judiciary; Select Intelligence; Veterans' Affairs

Stafford: Environment and Public Works; Labor and Human Resources; Veterans' Affairs

Stennis: Appropriations (chairman); Armed Services

Stevens: Appropriations; Commerce, Science and Transportation; Governmental Affairs; Rules and Administration; Joint Library; Joint Printing

Symms: Armed Services; Budget; Environment and Public Works; Joint Economic

Thurmond: Armed Services; Judiciary; Labor and Human Resources; Veterans' Affairs

Trible: Commerce, Science and Transportation; Foreign Relations; Governmental Affairs; Select Committee to Investigate Secret Military Assistance to Iran and the Nicaraguan Opposition

Wallop: Energy and Natural Resources; Finance; Small Business

Warner: Armed Services; Environment and Public Works; Rules and Administration; Select Intelligence

Weicker: Appropriations; Energy and Natural Resources; Labor and Human Resources; Small Business

Wilson: Agriculture, Nutrition and Forestry; Armed Services; Commerce, Science and Transportation; Joint Economic; Special Aging

Wirth: Armed Services; Banking, Housing and Urban Affairs; Budget; Energy and Natural Resources

Index of Representatives' Committee Assignments

Ackerman: Foreign Affairs; Post Office and Civil Service; Select Hunger

Akaka: Appropriations; Select Narcotics Abuse and Control

Alexander: Appropriations

Anderson: Merchant Marine and Fisheries; Public Works and Transportation

Andrews: Ways and Means

Annunzio: Banking, Finance and Urban Affairs; House Administration (chairman); Joint Library; Joint Printing (chairman)

Anthony: Select Children, Youth and Families; Ways and Means

Applegate: Public Works and Transportation; Veterans' Affairs

Archer: Ways and Means; Joint Taxation

Armey: Budget; Education and Labor

Aspin: Armed Services (chairman); Select Committee to Investigate Covert Arms Transactions with Iran

Atkins: Budget; Education and Labor; Foreign Affairs; Standards of Official Conduct

AuCoin: Appropriations

Badham: Armed Services; House Administration; Joint Printing

Baker: Interior and Insular Affairs; Small Business

Ballenger: Education and Labor; Public Works and Transportation

Barnard: Banking, Finance and Urban Affairs; Government Operations

Bartlett: Banking, Finance and Urban Affairs; Education and Labor

Barton: Energy and Commerce

Bateman: Armed Services; Merchant Marine and Fisheries

Bates: Energy and Commerce; House Administration

Beilenson: Rules; Select Intelligence

Bennett: Armed Services; Merchant Marine and Fisheries

Bentley: Merchant Marine and Fisheries; Public Works and Transportation; Select Aging

Bereuter: Banking, Finance and Urban Affairs; Foreign Affairs; Select Hunger

Berman: Foreign Affairs; Judiciary

Bevill: Appropriations

Biaggi: Education and Labor; Merchant Marine and Fisheries; Select Aging

Bilbray: Foreign Affairs; Small Business; Select Hunger

Bilirakis: Energy and Commerce; Veterans' Affairs

Blaz: Foreign Affairs; Interior and Insular Affairs; Select Aging

Bliley: District of Columbia; Energy and Commerce; Select Children, Youth and Families

Boehlert: Public Works and Transportation; Science, Space and Technology; Select Aging

Boggs: Appropriations; Select Children, Youth and Families

Boland: Appropriations; Select Committee to Investigate Covert Arms Transactions with Iran

Boner: Appropriations; Select Aging

Bonior: Rules

Bonker: Foreign Affairs; Merchant Marine and Fisheries; Select Aging

Borski: Merchant Marine and Fisheries; Public Works and Transportation; Select Aging

Bosco: Merchant Marine and Fisheries; Public Works and Transportation

Boucher: Energy and Commerce; Judiciary; Science, Space and Technology; Select Aging

Boulter: Budget; Government Operations; Select Children, Youth and Families

Boxer: Armed Services; Budget; Select Children, Youth and Families

Brennan: Armed Services; Merchant Marine and Fisheries

Brooks: Government Operations (chairman); Judiciary; Select Committee to Investigate Covert Arms Transactions with Iran

Broomfield: Foreign Affairs; Select Committee to Investigate Covert Arms Transactions with Iran; Small Business

Brown (Calif.): Agriculture; Science, Space and Technology; Select Intelligence

Brown (Colo.): Select Hunger; Ways and Means

Bruce: Energy and Commerce; Science, Space and Technology

Bryant: Energy and Commerce; Judiciary; Veterans' Affairs

Buechner: Budget; Science, Space and Technology

Bunning: Banking, Finance and Urban Affairs; Merchant Marine and Fisheries

Burton: Foreign Affairs; Post Office and Civil Service; Veterans' Affairs

Bustamante: Armed Services; Government Operations

Byron: Armed Services; Interior and Insular Affairs; Select Aging

Callahan: Energy and Commerce

Campbell: Agriculture; Interior and Insular Affairs; Small Business

Cardin: Judiciary; Public Works and Transportation

Carper: Banking, Finance and Urban Affairs; Merchant Marine and Fisheries

Carr: Appropriations; Select Hunger

Chandler: Ways and Means

Chapman: Public Works and Transportation; Science, Space and Technology

Chappell: Appropriations

Cheney: Interior and Insular Affairs; Select Committee to Investigate Covert Arms Transactions with Iran; Select Intelligence

Clarke: Foreign Affairs; Interior and Insular Affairs; Select Aging

Clay: Education and Labor; House Administration; Post Office and Civil Service

Clinger: Government Operations; Public Works and Transportation; Select Aging

Coats: Energy and Commerce; Select Children, Youth and Families

Coble: Judiciary; Merchant Marine and Fisheries

Coelho: Agriculture; House Administration; Interior and Insular Affairs

Coleman (Mo.): Agriculture; Education and Labor

Coleman (Texas): Appropriations

Collins: Energy and Commerce; Government Operations; Select Narcotics Abuse and Control

Combest: Agriculture; District of Columbia; Small Business

Conte: Appropriations; Small Business

Conyers: Government Operations; Judiciary; Small Business

Cooper: Energy and Commerce; Small Business

Coughlin: Appropriations; Select Narcotics Abuse and Control

Courter: Armed Services; Select Aging; Select Committee to Investigate Covert Arms Transactions with Iran

Coyne: Ways and Means

Craig: Government Operations; Interior and Insular Affairs; Standards of Official Conduct

Crane: Ways and Means

Crockett: Foreign Affairs; Judiciary; Select Aging

Daniel: Armed Services; Select Intelligence

Dannemeyer: Energy and Commerce; Judiciary

Darden: Armed Services; Interior and Insular Affairs
Daub: Ways and Means
Davis (Ill.): Armed Services; Veterans' Affairs
Davis (Mich.): Armed Services; Merchant Marine and Fisheries
de la Garza: Agriculture (chairman)
DeFazio: Interior and Insular Affairs; Public Works and Transportation; Small Business
DeLay: Appropriations
Dellums: Armed Services; District of Columbia (chairman)
de Lugo: Interior and Insular Affairs; Post Office and Civil Service; Public Works and Transportation
Derrick: Budget; Rules; Select Aging
DeWine: Foreign Affairs; Judiciary; Select Committee to Investigate Covert Arms Transaction with Iran
Dickinson: Armed Services; House Administration
Dicks: Appropriations
Dingell: Energy and Commerce (chairman)
DioGuardi: Government Operations; Merchant Marine and Fisheries; Select Narcotics Abuse and Control
Dixon: Appropriations; Standards of Official Conduct (chairman)
Donnelly: Ways and Means
Dorgan: Select Hunger; Ways and Means
Dornan: Foreign Affairs; Select Narcotics Abuse and Control; Veterans' Affairs
Dowdy: Energy and Commerce; Veterans' Affairs
Downey: Select Aging; Ways and Means
Dreier: Banking, Finance and Urban Affairs; Small Business
Duncan: Ways and Means; Joint Taxation
Durbin: Appropriations; Budget; Select Children, Youth and Families
Dwyer: Appropriations; Select Intelligence; Standards of Official Conduct
Dymally: District of Columbia; Foreign Affairs; Post Office and Civil Service
Dyson: Armed Services; Merchant Marine and Fisheries
Early: Appropriations
Eckart: Energy and Commerce; Small Business
Edwards (Calif.): Judiciary; Veterans' Affairs
Edwards (Okla.): Appropriations; Budget
Emerson: Agriculture; Interior and Insular Affairs; Select Hunger
English: Agriculture; Government Operations
Erdreich: Banking, Finance and Urban Affairs; Government Operations; Select Aging
Espy: Agriculture; Budget; Select Hunger
Evans: Agriculture; Select Children, Youth and Families; Veterans' Affairs
Fascell: Foreign Affairs (chairman); Select Committee to Investigate Covert Arms Transactions with Iran; Select Narcotics Abuse and Control
Fauntroy: Banking, Finance and Urban Affairs; District of Columbia; Select Narcotics Abuse and Control
Fawell: Education and Labor; Science, Space and Technology; Select Aging
Fazio: Appropriations; Budget; Select Hunger; Standards of Official Conduct
Feighan: Foreign Affairs; Judiciary
Fields: Energy and Commerce; Merchant Marine and Fisheries
Fish: Judiciary; Joint Economic
Flake: Banking, Finance and Urban Affairs; Select Hunger; Small Business
Flippo: Ways and Means
Florio: Energy and Commerce; Select Aging; Veterans' Affairs
Foglietta: Armed Services; Merchant Marine and Fisheries
Foley: Budget; Select Committee to Investigate Covert Arms Transactions with Iran
Ford (Tenn.): Select Aging; Ways and Means

Ford (Mich.): Education and Labor; Post Office and Civil Service (chairman)
Frank: Banking, Finance and Urban Affairs; Government Operations; Judiciary; Select Aging
Frenzel: House Administration; Ways and Means
Frost: Budget; Rules
Fuster: Foreign Affairs; Interior and Insular Affairs
Gallegly: Interior and Insular Affairs; Small Business
Gallo: Public Works and Transportation; Small Business
Garcia: Banking, Finance and Urban Affairs; Post Office and Civil Service
Gaydos: Education and Labor; House Administration; Standards of Official Conduct; Joint Printing
Gejdenson: Foreign Affairs; House Administration; Interior and Insular Affairs; Select Hunger
Gekas: Judiciary
Gephardt: Ways and Means
Gibbons: Ways and Means; Joint Taxation
Gilman: Foreign Affairs; Post Office and Civil Service; Select Hunger; Select Narcotics Abuse and Control
Gingrich: House Administration; Public Works and Transportation; Joint Library
Glickman: Agriculture; Judiciary; Science, Space and Technology
Gonzalez: Banking, Finance and Urban Affairs; Small Business
Goodling: Budget; Education and Labor
Gordon: Rules; Select Aging
Gradison: Budget; Ways and Means
Grandy: Agriculture; Education and Labor; Select Children, Youth and Families
Grant: Government Operations; Public Works and Transportation
Gray (Ill.): Public Works and Transportation; Veterans' Affairs
Gray (Pa.): Appropriations; Budget (chairman); District of Columbia
Green: Appropriations
Gregg: Ways and Means
Guarini: Budget; Select Narcotics Abuse and Control; Ways and Means
Gunderson: Agriculture; Education and Labor
Hall (Texas): Energy and Commerce; Science, Space and Technology
Hall (Ohio): Rules; Select Hunger
Hamilton: Foreign Affairs; Science, Space and Technology; Select Committee to Investigate Covert Arms Transactions with Iran (chairman); Joint Economic
Hammerschmidt: Public Works and Transportation; Select Aging; Veterans' Affairs
Hansen: Armed Services; Interior and Insular Affairs; Standards of Official Conduct
Harris: Agriculture; Veterans' Affairs
Hastert: Government Operations; Public Works and Transportation; Select Children, Youth and Families
Hatcher: Agriculture; Small Business
Hawkins: Education and Labor (chairman); Joint Economic
Hayes (Ill.): Education and Labor; Small Business
Hayes (La.): Public Works and Transportation; Science, Space and Technology
Hefley: Science, Space and Technology; Small Business
Hefner: Appropriations
Henry: Education and Labor; Science, Space and Technology; Select Aging
Herger: Agriculture; Merchant Marine and Fisheries
Hertel: Armed Services; Merchant Marine and Fisheries; Select Aging
Hiler: Banking, Finance and Urban Affairs; Small Business
Hochbrueckner: Armed Services; Merchant Marine and Fisheries

Holloway: Agriculture; Select Children, Youth and Families
Hopkins: Agriculture; Armed Services
Horton: Government Operations; Post Office and Civil Service
Houghton: Budget; Government Operations
Howard: Public Works and Transportation (chairman)
Hoyer: Appropriations
Hubbard: Banking, Finance and Urban Affairs; Merchant Marine and Fisheries
Huckaby: Agriculture; Interior and Insular Affairs
Hughes: Judiciary; Merchant Marine and Fisheries; Select Aging; Select Narcotics Abuse and Control
Hunter: Armed Services; Select Narcotics Abuse and Control
Hutto: Armed Services; Merchant Marine and Fisheries
Hyde: Foreign Affairs; Judiciary; Select Committee to Investigate Covert Arms Transactions with Iran; Select Intelligence
Inhofe: Government Operations; Public Works and Transportation
Ireland: Armed Services; Small Business
Jacobs: Ways and Means
Jeffords: Agriculture; Education and Labor; Select Aging
Jenkins: Budget; Select Committee to Investigate Covert Arms Transactions with Iran; Ways and Means
Johnson (Conn.): Budget; Public Works and Transportation; Select Children, Youth and Families
Johnson (S.D.): Agriculture; Veterans' Affairs
Jones (Tenn.): Agriculture; House Administration; Joint Library
Jones (N.C.): Agriculture; Merchant Marine and Fisheries (chairman)
Jontz: Agriculture; Education and Labor; Veterans' Affairs
Kanjorski: Banking, Finance and Urban Affairs; Veterans' Affairs
Kaptur: Banking, Finance and Urban Affairs; Veterans' Affairs
Kasich: Armed Services
Kastenmeier: Judiciary; Select Intelligence
Kemp: Appropriations; Select Children, Youth and Families
Kennedy: Banking, Finance and Urban Affairs; Veterans' Affairs; Select Aging
Kennelly: Select Intelligence; Ways and Means
Kildee: Education and Labor; Interior and Insular Affairs
Kleczka: Banking, Finance and Urban Affairs; Government Operations
Kolbe: Appropriations
Kolter: Government Operations; Public Works and Transportation
Konnyu: Government Operations; Science, Space and Technology
Kostmayer: Foreign Affairs; Interior and Insular Affairs; Select Hunger
Kyl: Armed Services; Government Operations
LaFalce: Banking, Finance and Urban Affairs; Small Business (chairman)
Lagomarsino: Foreign Affairs; Interior and Insular Affairs
Lancaster: Public Works and Transportation; Small Business
Lantos: Foreign Affairs; Government Operations; Select Aging
Latta: Budget; Rules
Leach: Banking, Finance and Urban Affairs; Foreign Affairs
Leath: Armed Services; Budget
Lehman (Calif.): Banking, Finance and Urban Affairs; Interior and Insular Affairs
Lehman (Fla.): Appropriations; Select Children, Youth and Families
Leland: Energy and Commerce; Post Office and Civil Service; Select Hunger (chairman)
Lent: Energy and Commerce; Merchant Marine and Fisheries
Levin: Select Children, Youth and Families; Ways and Means
Levine: Foreign Affairs; Interior and Insular Affairs; Select Narcotics Abuse and Control

Lewis (Calif.): Appropriations
Lewis (Ga.): Interior and Insular Affairs; Public Works and Transportation
Lewis (Fla.): Agriculture; Science, Space and Technology
Lightfoot: Government Operations; Public Works and Transportation; Select Aging
Lipinski: Merchant Marine and Fisheries; Public Works and Transportation
Livingston: Appropriations; Select Intelligence
Lloyd: Armed Services; Science, Space and Technology; Select Aging
Lott: Rules
Lowery: Appropriations
Lowry: Budget; Merchant Marine and Fisheries
Lujan: Interior and Insular Affairs; Science, Space and Technology
Luken: Energy and Commerce; Select Aging; Small Business
Lukens: Foreign Affairs; Government Operations
Lungren: Judiciary; Select Intelligence
Mack: Budget; Foreign Affairs
MacKay: Budget; Science, Space and Technology; Select Aging
Madigan: Agriculture; Energy and Commerce
Manton: Banking, Finance and Urban Affairs; Merchant Marine and Fisheries; Select Aging
Markey: Energy and Commerce; Interior and Insular Affairs
Marlenee: Agriculture; Interior and Insular Affairs
Martin (N.Y.): Armed Services
Martin (Ill.): Armed Services; District of Columbia
Martinez: Education and Labor; Government Operations; Select Children, Youth and Families; Small Business
Matsui: Select Narcotics Abuse and Control; Ways and Means
Mavroules: Armed Services; Small Business
Mazzoli: District of Columbia; Judiciary; Small Business
McCandless: Banking, Finance and Urban Affairs; Government Operations
McCloskey: Armed Services; Post Office and Civil Service
McCollum: Banking, Finance and Urban Affairs; Judiciary; Select Committee to Investigate Covert Arms Transactions with Iran
McCurdy: Armed Services; Science, Space and Technology; Select Intelligence
McDade: Appropriations; Small Business
McEwen: Public Works and Transportation; Select Intelligence; Veterans' Affairs
McGrath: Ways and Means
McHugh: Appropriations; Select Children, Youth and Families; Select Intelligence
McMillan: Banking, Finance and Urban Affairs; Small Business; Joint Economic
McMillen: Banking, Finance and Urban Affairs; Science, Space and Technology
Meyers: Foreign Affairs; Select Aging; Small Business
Mfume: Banking, Finance and Urban Affairs; Small Business; Select Hunger
Mica: Foreign Affairs; Select Aging; Veterans' Affairs
Michel: Minortiy Leader
Miller (Ohio): Appropriations
Miller (Calif.): Budget; Interior and Insular Affairs; Select Children, Youth and Families (chairman)
Miller (Wash.): Foreign Affairs; Merchant Marine and Fisheries
Mineta: Public Works and Transportation; Science, Space and Technology
Moakley: Rules
Molinari: Public Works and Transportation; Select Hunger
Mollohan: Appropriations; Standards of Official Conduct
Montgomery: Armed Services; Veterans' Affairs (chairman)
Moody: Ways and Means
Moorhead: Energy and Commerce; Judiciary

Morella: Post Office and Civil Service; Science, Space and Technology; Select Aging

Morrison (Conn.): Banking, Finance and Urban Affairs; Judiciary; Select Children, Youth and Families

Morrison (Wash.): Agriculture; Science, Space and Technology; Select Hunger

Mrazek: Appropriations

Murphy: Education and Labor; Interior and Insular Affairs

Murtha: Appropriations

Myers: Appropriations; Post Office and Civil Service; Standards of Official Conduct;

Nagle: Agriculture; Science, Space and Technology

Natcher: Appropriations

Neal: Banking, Finance and Urban Affairs; Government Operations

Nelson: Banking, Finance and Urban Affairs; Science, Space and Technology

Nichols: Armed Services

Nielson: Energy and Commerce; Government Operations

Nowak: Public Works and Transportation; Science, Space and Technology

Oakar: Banking, Finance and Urban Affairs; House Administration; Post Office and Civil Service; Select Aging; Joint Library

Oberstar: Budget; Public Works and Transportation

Obey: Appropriations; Joint Economic

Olin: Agriculture; Small Business

Ortiz: Armed Services; Merchant Marine and Fisheries; Select Narcotics Abuse and Control

Owens (N.Y.): Education and Labor; Government Operations

Owens (Utah): Foreign Affairs; Interior and Insular Affairs

Oxley: Energy and Commerce; Select Narcotics Abuse and Control

Packard: Public Works and Transportation; Science, Space and Technology; Select Children, Youth and Families

Panetta: Agriculture; House Administration; Select Hunger; Joint Printing

Parris: Banking, Finance and Urban Affairs; District of Columbia; Select Narcotics Abuse and Control

Pashayan: Interior and Insular Affairs; Post Office and Civil Service; Standards of Official Conduct

Patterson: Banking, Finance and Urban Affairs; Select Hunger; Veterans' Affairs

Pease: Ways and Means

Pelosi: Banking, Finance and Urban Affairs; Government Operations

Penny: Agriculture; Education and Labor; Select Hunger; Veterans' Affairs

Pepper: Rules (chairman); Select Aging

Perkins: Education and Labor; Public Works and Transportation; Science, Space and Technology

Petri: Education and Labor; Public Works and Transportation; Standards of Official Conduct

Pickett: Armed Services; Merchant Marine and Fisheries

Pickle: Ways and Means; Joint Taxation

Porter: Appropriations

Price (N.C.): Banking, Finance and Urban Affairs; Science, Space and Technology; Small Business

Price (Ill.): Armed Services

Pursell: Appropriations

Quillen: Rules

Rahall: Interior and Insular Affairs; Public Works and Transportation

Rangel: Select Narcotics Abuse and Control (chairman); Ways and Means

Ravenel: Armed Services

Ray: Armed Services; Small Business

Regula: Appropriations; Select Aging

Rhodes: Interior and Insular Affairs; Small Business

Richardson: Education and Labor; Energy and Commerce; Interior and Insular Affairs; Select Aging

Ridge: Banking, Finance and Urban Affairs; Select Aging; Veterans' Affairs

Rinaldo: Energy and Commerce; Select Aging

Ritter: Energy and Commerce; Science, Space and Technology

Roberts: Agriculture; House Administration; Joint Library; Joint Printing

Robinson: Armed Services; Education and Labor; Select Aging; Veterans' Affairs

Rodino: Judiciary (chairman); Select Committee to Investigate Covert Arms Transactions with Iran; Select Narcotics Abuse and Control

Roe: Public Works and Transportation; Science, Space and Technology (chairman); Select Intelligence

Roemer: Banking, Finance and Urban Affairs; Small Business

Rogers: Appropriations; Budget

Rose: Agriculture; House Administration

Rostenkowski: Ways and Means (chairman); Joint Taxation (chairman)

Roth: Banking, Finance and Urban Affairs; Foreign Affairs

Roukema: Banking, Finance and Urban Affairs; Education and Labor; Select Hunger

Rowland (Ga.): Public Works and Transportation; Select Children, Youth and Families; Veterans' Affairs

Rowland (Conn.): Armed Services; Veterans' Affairs

Roybal: Appropriations; Select Aging (chairman)

Russo: Budget; Ways and Means

Sabo: Appropriations

Saiki: Banking, Finance and Urban Affairs; Merchant Marine and Fisheries; Select Aging

St Germain: Banking, Finance and Urban Affairs (chairman)

Savage: Public Works and Transportation; Small Business

Sawyer: Education and Labor; Government Operations; Select Children, Youth and Families

Saxton: Banking, Finance and Urban Affairs; Merchant Marine and Fisheries; Select Aging

Schaefer: Energy and Commerce

Scheuer: Energy and Commerce; Science, Space and Technology; Select Narcotics Abuse and Control; Joint Economic

Schneider: Merchant Marine and Fisheries; Science, Space and Technology; Select Aging

Schroeder: Armed Services; Judiciary; Post Office and Civil Service; Select Children, Youth and Families

Schuette: Agriculture; Select Aging

Schulze: Ways and Means

Schumer: Banking, Finance and Urban Affairs; Budget; Judiciary

Sensenbrenner: Judiciary; Science, Space and Technology; Select Narcotics Abuse and Control

Sharp: Energy and Commerce; Interior and Insular Affairs

Shaw: Judiciary; Public Works and Transportation; Select Narcotics Abuse and Control

Shumway: Banking, Finance and Urban Affairs; Merchant Marine and Fisheries; Select Aging

Shuster: Public Works and Transportation; Select Intelligence

Sikorski: Energy and Commerce; Post Office and Civil Service; Select Children, Youth and Families

Sisisky: Armed Services; Select Aging; Small Business

Skaggs: Public Works and Transportation; Science, Space and Technology; Select Children, Youth and Families

Skeen: Appropriations

Skelton: Armed Services; Select Aging; Small Business

Slattery: Budget; Energy and Commerce

Slaughter (Va.): Judiciary; Science, Space and Technology; Small Business

Slaughter (N.Y.): Government Operations; Public Works and Transportation; Select Aging

Smith (N.J.): Foreign Affairs; Select Aging; Veterans' Affairs

Smith, Denny (Ore.): Budget; Interior and Insular Affairs

Smith (Texas): Judiciary; Science, Space and Technology

Smith (Fla.): Foreign Affairs; Judiciary; Select Narcotics Abuse and Control

Smith (Iowa): Appropriations; Small Business

Smith (N.H.): Science, Space and Technology; Veterans' Affairs

Smith, Robert F. (Ore.): Agriculture; Select Hunger

Smith (Neb.): Appropriations

Snowe: Foreign Affairs; Select Aging; Joint Economic

Solarz: Education and Labor; Foreign Affairs; Post Office and Civil Service; Joint Economic

Solomon: Foreign Affairs; Veterans' Affairs

Spence: Armed Services; Select Aging; Standards of Official Conduct

Spratt: Armed Services; Government Operations

Staggers: Agriculture; Judiciary; Veterans' Affairs

Stallings: Agriculture; Science, Space and Technology; Select Aging

Stangeland: Agriculture; Public Works and Transportation

Stark: District of Columbia; Select Narcotics Abuse and Control; Ways and Means; Joint Economic

Stenholm: Agriculture; Veterans' Affairs

Stokes: Appropriations; Select Committee to Investigate Covert Arms Transactions with Iran; Select Intelligence (chairman)

Stratton: Armed Services

Studds: Foreign Affairs; Merchant Marine and Fisheries

Stump: Armed Services; Veterans' Affairs

Sundquist: Budget; Public Works and Transportation

Sunia: Foreign Affairs; Interior and Insular Affairs; Public Works and Transportation

Sweeney: Armed Services; Merchant Marine and Fisheries

Swift: Energy and Commerce; House Administration

Swindall: Banking, Finance and Urban Affairs; Judiciary; Select Aging

Synar: Energy and Commerce; Government Operations; Judiciary; Select Aging

Tallon: Agriculture; Merchant Marine and Fisheries

Tauke: Education and Labor; Energy and Commerce; Select Aging

Tauzin: Energy and Commerce; Merchant Marine and Fisheries

Taylor: Post Office and Civil Service; Rules

Thomas (Ga.): Agriculture; Merchant Marine and Fisheries

Thomas (Calif.): Budget; House Administration; Ways and Means

Torres: Banking, Finance and Urban Affairs; Small Business

Torricelli: Foreign Affairs; Science, Space and Technology

Towns: Government Operations; Public Works and Transportation; Select Narcotics Abuse and Control

Traficant: Public Works and Transportation; Science, Space and Technology

Traxler: Appropriations; Select Hunger

Udall: Foreign Affairs; Interior and Insular Affairs (chairman); Post Office and Civil Service

Upton: Public Works and Transportation; Select Hunger; Small Business

Valentine: Public Works and Transportation; Science, Space and Technology

Vander Jagt: Ways and Means

Vento: Banking, Finance and Urban Affairs; Interior and Insular Affairs; Select Aging

Visclosky: Education and Labor; Interior and Insular Affairs; Public Works and Transportation

Volkmer: Agriculture; Science, Space and Technology; Select Aging

Vucanovich: House Administration; Interior and Insular Affairs; Select Children, Youth and Families

Walgren: Energy and Commerce; Science, Space and Technology

Walker: Government Operations; Science, Space and Technology

Watkins: Appropriations

Waxman: Energy and Commerce; Government Operations; Select Aging

Weber: Appropriations

Weiss: Foreign Affairs; Government Operations; Select Children, Youth and Families

Weldon: Armed Services; Merchant Marine and Fisheries

Wheat: District of Columbia; Rules; Select Children, Youth and Families

Whittaker: Energy and Commerce

Whitten: Appropriations (chairman)

Williams: Budget; Education and Labor

Wilson: Appropriations; Select Intelligence

Wise: Education and Labor; Government Operations; Public Works and Transportation; Select Aging

Wolf: Appropriations; Select Children, Youth and Families

Wolpe: Budget; Foreign Affairs

Wortley: Banking, Finance and Urban Affairs; Select Aging; Select Children, Youth and Families

Wright: Speaker of the House

Wyden: Energy and Commerce; Select Aging; Small Business

Wylie: Banking, Finance and Urban Affairs; Veterans' Affairs; Joint Economic

Yates: Appropriations

Yatron: Foreign Affairs; Post Office and Civil Service

Young (Fla.): Appropriations

Young (Alaska): Interior and Insular Affairs; Merchant Marine and Fisheries; Post Office and Civil Service

Officers and Committees of the 100th Congress

Officers of the Senate

	Phone	Room
President — George Bush	224-8391	S-212 Capitol
President Pro Tempore — John C. Stennis, D-Miss.	224-6253	SR-205
Secretary — Walter J. Stewart	224-2115	S-208 Capitol
Parliamentarian —Alan Frumin	224-6128	S-132 Capitol
Sergeant-at-Arms — Henry K. Giugni	224-2341	S-321 Capitol
Secretary for the Majority — C. Abbott Saffold	224-3735	S-309 Capitol
Secretary for the Minority — Howard O. Greene Jr.	224-3835	S-337 Capitol
Bill Status	224-2971	
Document Room	224-7860	SH-B04
Legal Counsel — Michael Davidson	224-4435	SH-642
Legislative Counsel — Douglas B. Hester	224-6461	SD-668
Press Gallery Superintendent — Robert E. Peterson	224-0241	S-316 Capitol
Republican Cloakroom	224-6191	S-226 Capitol
Recorded Announcements	224-8601	
Democratic Cloakroom	224-4691	S-225 Capitol
Recorded Announcements	224-8541	
Chaplain — Rev. Richard C. Halverson	224-2510	SH-204

Senate Committees

	Majority Phone	Majority Room	Minority Phone	Minority Room
Agriculture, Nutrition and Forestry	224-2035	SR-328A	224-6901	SR-328
Appropriations	224-3471	SD-118	224-7335	SD-119
Armed Services	224-3871	SR-222	224-8626	SR-232A
Banking, Housing and Urban Affairs	224-7391	SD-534	224-1577	SD-545
Budget	224-0642	SD-621	224-0769	SD-634A
Commerce, Science and Transportation	224-5115	SD-508	224-1251	SD-554
Energy and Natural Resources	224-4971	SD-364	224-1017	SD-310
Environment and Public Works	224-6176	SD-458	224-8832	SD-410
Finance	224-4515	SD-205	224-5315	SD-G08
Foreign Relations	224-4651	SD-446	224-3941	SD-447
Governmental Affairs	224-4751	SD-340	224-2627	SD-346
Judiciary	224-5225	SD-224	224-2891	SD-145
Labor and Human Resources	224-5375	SD-428	224-1283	SH-833
Rules and Administration	224-6352	SR-305	224-8923	SR-479
Select Secret Military Assistance to Iran	224-9960	SH-901	224-9960	SH-901
Select Ethics	224-2981	SH-220	224-2981	SH-220
Select Indian Affairs	224-2251	SH-838	224-2251	SH-838
Select Intelligence	224-1700	SH-211	224-1700	SH-211
Small Business	224-5175	SR-428A	224-7884	SH-622
Special Aging	224-5364	SH-628	224-1467	SD-G41
Veterans' Affairs	224-9126	SR-414	224-2074	SH-202

Senate Party Committees

	Phone	Room
Democratic Policy Committee	224-5551	S-118 Capitol
Democratic Legislative Review Committee	224-3735	S-118 Capitol
Democratic Steering Committee	224-3735	S-309 Capitol
Democratic Senatorial Campaign Committee	224-2447	430 South Capitol St. S.E. 20003
Republican Policy Committee	224-2946	SR-347
Republican Committee on Committees	224-4024	SH-517
National Republican Senatorial Committee	224-2351	440 First St. N.W. 20001

Officers of the House

	Phone	Room
Speaker — Jim Wright, D-Texas	225-8040	H-204 Capitol
Clerk — Donnald K. Anderson	225-7000	H-105 Capitol
Sergeant-at-Arms — Jack Russ	225-2459	H-125 Capitol
Parliamentarian — William H. Brown	225-7373	H-209 Capitol
Doorkeeper — James T. Molloy	225-3505	H-154 Capitol
Postmaster — Robert V. Rota	225-3856	B225 LHOB
Bill Status	225-1772	
Document Room (members only)	225-3456	H-226 Capitol
General Counsel to the Clerk — Steven R. Ross	225-7000	H-105 Capitol
Legislative Counsel — Ward M. Hussey	225-6060	136 CHOB

Press Gallery Superintendent — Thayer Illsley .... 225-3945 .... H-315 Capitol
Democratic Cloakroom .... 225-7330 .... H-222 Capitol
   Recorded Floor Schedule 225-1600
   Recorded Floor Action 225-7400
Republican Cloakroom .... 225-7350 .... H-223 Capitol
   Recorded Floor Schedule 225-2020
   Recorded Floor Action 225-7430
Chaplain — Rev. James David Ford., D.D. .... 225-2509 .... HB-25 Capitol

House Committees

	Majority Phone	Majority Room	Minority Phone	Minority Room
Agriculture	225-2171	1301 LHOB	225-0025	1304 LHOB
Appropriations	225-2771	H-218 Capitol	225-3481	1016 LHOB
Armed Services	225-4151	2120 RHOB	225-4151	2120 RHOB
Banking, Finance and Urban Affairs	225-4247	2129 RHOB	225-7502	B301-C RHOB
Budget	226-7200	214 HOB Annex #1	226-7270	278 HOB Annex #2
District of Columbia	225-4457	1310 LHOB	225-7158	1307 LHOB
Education and Labor	225-4527	2181 RHOB	225-3725	2101 RHOB
Energy and Commerce	225-2927	2125 RHOB	225-3641	2322 RHOB
Foreign Affairs	225-5021	2170 RHOB	225-6735	B360 RHOB
Government Operations	225-5051	2157 RHOB	225-5074	2153 RHOB
House Administration	225-2061	H-326 Capitol	225-8281	H-330 Capitol
Interior and Insular Affairs	225-2761	1324 LHOB	225-6065	1329 LHOB
Judiciary	225-3951	2137 RHOB	225-6906	B351-C RHOB
Merchant Marine and Fisheries	225-4047	1334 LHOB	225-2650	1337 LHOB
Post Office and Civil Service	225-4054	309 CHOB	225-0073	304-A CHOB
Public Works and Transportation	225-4472	2165 RHOB	225-9446	2165 RHOB
Rules	225-9486	H-312 Capitol	225-9191	H-305 Capitol
Science, Space and Technology	225-6371	2321 RHOB	225-8772	2320 RHOB
Select Aging	226-3375	712 HOB Annex #1	226-3393	606 HOB Annex #1
Select Children, Youth and Families	226-7660	385 HOB Annex #2	226-7692	384 HOB Annex #2
Select Covert Arms Transactions with Iran	225-7902	H-419 Capitol	225-7902	H419 Capitol
Select Hunger	226-5470	507 HOB Annex #2	226-5460	506 HOB Annex #2
Select Intelligence	225-4121	H-405 Capitol	225-4121	H-405 Capitol
Select Narcotics Abuse and Control	226-3040	234 HOB Annex #2	226-3040	234 HOB Annex #2
Small Business	225-5821	2361 RHOB	225-4038	B343-C RHOB
Standards of Official Conduct	225-7103	HT-2 Capitol	225-7103	HT-2 Capitol
Veterans' Affairs	225-3527	335 CHOB	225-3551	333 CHOB
Ways and Means	225-3625	1102 LHOB	225-4021	1106 LHOB

House Party Committees

	Phone	Room
Democratic Steering and Policy Committee	225-8550	H-324 Capitol
Democratic Congressional Campaign Committee	863-1500	430 South Capitol St. S.E. 20003
Democratic Personnel Committee	225-4068	B343-D RHOB
Republican Committee on Committees	225-0600	H-230 Capitol
Republican Policy Committee	225-6168	1620 LHOB
Republican Research Committee	225-0871	1616 LHOB
National Republican Congressional Committee	479-7000	320 First St. S.E. 20003

Joint Committees

	Phone	Room
Economic	224-5171	SD-G01
Library	224-6352	SR-305
Printing	224-5241	SH-818
Taxation	225-3621	1015 LHOB

Senate Office Buildings, Washington, D.C. 20510

SD — Dirksen Senate Office Building, First St. and Constitution Ave. N.E.
SH — Hart Senate Office Building, Second St. and Constitution Ave. N.E.
SR — Russell Senate Office Building, Delaware and Constitution Aves. N.E.

House Office Buildings, Washington, D.C. 20515

HOB Annex #1 — House Office Building Annex #1, 300 New Jersey Ave. S.E.
HOB Annex #2 — House Office Building Annex #2, 300 D St. S.W.
CHOB — Cannon House Office Building, First St. and Independence Ave. S.E.
LHOB — Longworth House Office Building, Independence and New Jersey Aves. S.E.
RHOB — Rayburn House Office Building, Independence Ave. and South Capitol St. S.W.

Senators' Phone and Room Directory

Capitol Switchboard: (202) 224-3121
Senate ZIP Code: 20510

SD — Dirksen Building   **SH** — Hart Building   **SR** — Russell Building

Name, Party, State	Phone	Room
Adams, Brock, D-Wash.	224-2621	SH-513
Armstrong, William L., R-Colo.	224-5941	SH-528
Baucus, Max, D-Mont.	224-2651	SH-706
Bentsen, Lloyd, D-Texas	224-5922	SH-703
Biden, Joseph R. Jr., D-Del.	224-5042	SR-489
Bingaman, Jeff, D-N.M.	224-5521	SH-502
Bond, Christopher S. "Kit," R-Mo.	224-5721	SR-293
Boren, David L., D-Okla.	224-4721	SR-453
Boschwitz, Rudy, R-Minn.	224-5641	SH-506
Bradley, Bill, D-N.J.	224-3224	SH-731
Breaux, John B., D-La.	224-4623	SH-516
Bumpers, Dale, D-Ark.	224-4843	SD-229
Burdick, Quentin N., D-N.D.	224-2551	SH-511
Byrd, Robert C., D-W.Va.	224-3954	SH-311
Chafee, John H., R-R.I.	224-2921	SD-567
Chiles, Lawton, D-Fla.	224-5274	SR-250
Cochran, Thad, R-Miss.	224-5054	SR-326
Cohen, William S., R-Maine	224-2523	SH-322
Conrad, Kent, D-N.D.	224-2043	SD-361
Cranston, Alan, D-Calif.	224-3553	SH-112
D'Amato, Alfonse M., R-N.Y.	224-6542	SH-520
Danforth, John C., R-Mo.	224-6154	SR-497
Daschle, Thomas A., D-S.D.	224-2321	SH-317
DeConcini, Dennis, D-Ariz.	224-4521	SH-328
Dixon, Alan J., D-Ill.	224-2854	SH-331
Dodd, Christopher J., D-Conn.	224-2823	SR-444
Dole, Robert, R-Kan.	224-6521	SH-141
Domenici, Pete V., R-N.M.	224-6621	SD-434
Durenberger, Dave, R-Minn.	224-3244	SR-154
Evans, Daniel J. R-Wash.	224-3441	SH-324
Exon, J. James, D-Neb.	224-4224	SH-330
Ford, Wendelll H., D-Ky.	224-4343	SR-173A
Fowler, Wyche Jr., D-Ga.	224-3643	SR-204
Garn, Jake, R-Utah	224-5444	SD-505
Glenn, John, D-Ohio.	224-3353	SH-503
Gore, Albert J., D-Tenn.	224-4944	SR-393
Graham, Bob, D-Fla.	224-3041	SD-241
Gramm, Phil, R-Texas	224-2934	SR-370
Grassley, Charles E., R-Iowa	224-3744	SH-135
Harkin, Tom, D-Iowa	224-3254	SH-316
Hatch, Orrin G., R-Utah	224-5251	SR-135
Hatfield, Mark O., R-Ore.	224-3753	SH-711
Hecht, Chic, R-Nev.	224-6244	SH-302
Heflin, Howell, D-Ala.	224-4124	SH-728
Heinz, John, R-Pa.	224-6324	SR-277
Helms, Jesse, R-N.C.	224-6342	SD-403
Hollings, Ernest F., D-S.C.	224-6121	SR-125
Humphrey, Gordon J., R-N.H.	224-2841	SH-531
Inouye, Daniel K., D-Hawaii	224-3934	SH-722
Johnston, J. Bennett, D-La.	224-5824	SH-136

Name, Party, State	Phone	Room
Karnes, David, R-Neb.	224-6551	SD-104
Kassebaum, Nancy Landon, R-Kan.	224-4774	SR-302
Kasten, Bob, R-Wis.	224-5323	SH-110
Kennedy, Edward M., D-Mass.	224-4543	SR-315
Kerry, John, D-Mass.	224-2742	SR-362
Lautenberg, Frank R., D-N.J.	224-4744	SH-717
Leahy, Patrick J., D-Vt.	224-4242	SR-433
Levin, Carl, D-Mich.	224-6221	SR-459
Lugar, Richard G., R-Ind.	224-4814	SH-306
Matsunaga, Spark M., D-Hawaii	224-6361	SH-109
McCain, John, R-Ariz.	224-2235	SR-111
McClure, James A., R-Idaho	224-2752	SH-309
McConnell, Mitch, R-Ky.	224-2541	SR-120
Melcher, John, D-Mont.	224-2644	SH-730
Metzenbaum, Howard M., D-Ohio	224-2315	SR-140
Mikulski, Barbara A., D-Md.	224-4654	SH-320
Mitchell, George J., D-Maine	224-5344	SR-176
Moynihan, Daniel Patrick, D-N.Y.	224-4451	SR-464
Murkowski, Frank H., R-Alaska	224-6665	SH-709
Nickles, Don, R-Okla.	224-5754	SH-713
Nunn, Sam, D-Ga.	224-3521	SD-303
Packwood, Bob, R-Ore.	224-5244	SR-259
Pell, Claiborne, D-R.I.	224-4642	SR-355
Pressler, Larry, R-S.D.	224-5842	SR-411
Proxmire, William, D-Wis.	224-5653	SD-530
Pryor, David, D-Ark.	224-2353	SR-264
Quayle, Dan, R-Ind.	224-5623	SH-524
Reid, Harry, D-Nev.	224-3542	SH-702
Riegle, Donald W. Jr., D-Mich.	224-4822	SD-105
Rockefeller, John D. IV, D-W.Va.	224-6472	SD-241
Roth, William V. Jr., R-Del.	224-2441	SH-104
Rudman, Warren B., R-N.H.	224-3324	SH-530
Sanford, Terry, D-N.C.	224-3154	SH-716
Sarbanes, Paul S., D-Md.	224-4524	SD-332
Sasser, Jim, D-Tenn.	224-3344	SR-363
Shelby, Richard C., D-Ala.	224-5744	SH-313
Simon, Paul, D-Ill.	224-2152	SD-462
Simpson, Alan K., R-Wyo.	224-3424	SD-261
Specter, Arlen, R-Pa.	224-4254	SH-303
Stafford, Robert T., R-Vt.	224-5141	SH-133
Stennis, John C., D-Miss.	224-6253	SR-205
Stevens, Ted, R-Alaska	224-3004	SH-522
Symms, Steve, R-Idaho	224-6142	SH-509
Thurmond, Strom, R-S.C.	224-5972	SR-218
Trible, Paul S. Jr., R-Va.	224-4024	SH-517
Wallop, Malcolm, R-Wyo.	224-6441	SR-237
Warner, John W. R-Va.	224-2023	SR-421
Weicker, Lowell P. Jr., R-Conn.	224-4041	SR-225
Wilson, Pete, R-Calif.	224-3841	SH-720
Wirth, Timothy E., D-Colo.	224-5852	SR-380

Representatives' Phone and Room Directory

Capitol Switchboard: (202) 224-3121
House ZIP Code: 20515

Three-digit room numbers are in the Cannon Building; four-digit numbers beginning with 1 are in the Longworth Building; four-digit numbers beginning with 2 are in the Rayburn Building.

Name, Party, State	Phone	Room
Ackerman, Gary L., D-N.Y. (7)	225-2601	1725
Akaka, Daniel K., D-Hawaii (2)	225-4906	2301
Alexander, Bill, D-Ark. (1)	225-4076	233
Anderson, Glenn M., D-Calif. (32)	225-6676	2329
Andrews, Michael A., D-Texas (25)	225-7508	322
Annunzio, Frank, D-Ill. (11)	225-6661	2303
Anthony, Beryl Jr., D-Ark. (4)	225-3772	1117
Applegate, Douglas, D-Ohio (18)	225-6265	2183
Archer, Bill, R-Texas (7)	225-2571	1135
Armey, Dick, R-Texas (26)	225-7772	514
Aspin, Les, D-Wis. (1)	225-3031	2336
Atkins, Chester G., D-Mass. (5)	225-3411	504
AuCoin, Les, D-Ore. (1)	225-0855	2159
Badham, Robert E., R-Calif. (40)	225-5611	2427
Baker, Richard H., R-La. (6)	225-3901	506
Ballenger, Cass, R-N.C. (10)	225-2576	116
Barnard, Doug Jr., D-Ga. (10)	225-4101	2227
Bartlett, Steve, R-Texas (3)	225-4201	1709
Barton, Joe L., R-Texas (6)	225-2002	1225
Bateman, Herbert H., R-Va. (1)	225-4261	1527
Bates, Jim, D-Calif. (44)	225-5452	1404
Beilenson, Anthony C., D-Calif. (23)	225-5911	1025
Bennett, Charles E., D-Fla. (3)	225-2501	2107
Bentley, Helen Delich, R-Md. (2)	225-3061	1610
Bereuter, Doug, R-Neb. (1)	225-4806	2446
Berman, Howard L., D-Calif. (26)	225-4695	137
Bevill, Tom, D-Ala. (4)	225-4876	2302
Biaggi, Mario, D-N.Y. (19)	225-2464	2428
Bilbray, James, D-Nev. (1)	225-5965	1431
Bilirakis, Michael, R-Fla. (9)	225-5755	1530
Blaz, Ben, R-Guam	225-1188	1130
Bliley, Thomas J. Jr., R-Va. (3)	225-2815	213
Boehlert, Sherwood, R-N.Y. (25)	225-3665	1641
Boggs, Lindy (Mrs. Hale), D-La. (2)	225-6636	2353
Boland, Edward P., D-Mass. (2)	225-5601	2426
Boner, Bill, D-Tenn. (5)	225-4311	107
Bonior, David E., D-Mich. (12)	225-2106	2242
Bonker, Don, D-Wash. (3)	225-3536	434
Borski, Robert A., D-Pa. (3)	225-8251	314
Bosco, Douglas H., D-Calif. (1)	225-3311	408
Boucher, Rick, D-Va. (9)	225-3861	428
Boulter, Beau, R-Texas (13)	225-3706	124
Boxer, Barbara, D-Calif. (6)	225-5161	307
Brennan, Joseph E., D-Maine (1)	225-6116	1428
Brooks, Jack, D-Texas (9)	225-6565	2449
Broomfield, William S., R-Mich. (18)	225-6135	2306
Brown, George E. Jr., D-Calif. (36)	225-6161	2256
Brown, Hank, R-Colo. (4)	225-4676	1424
Bruce, Terry L., D-Ill. (19)	225-5001	419
Bryant, John, D-Texas (5)	225-2231	412
Buechner, Jack, R-Mo. (2)	225-2561	502
Bunning, Jim, R-Ky. (4)	225-3465	1123
Burton, Dan, R-Ind. (6)	225-2276	120
Bustamante, Albert G., D-Texas (23)	225-4511	1116
Byron, Beverly B., D-Md. (6)	225-2721	2430
Callahan, Sonny, R-Ala. (1)	225-4931	1232
Campbell, Ben Nighthorse, D-Colo. (3)	225-4761	1724
Cardin, Benjamin L., D-Md. (3)	225-4016	507
Carper, Thomas R., D-Del. (AL)	225-4165	131
Carr, Bob, D-Mich. (6)	225-4872	2439
Chandler, Rod, R-Wash. (8)	225-7761	223
Chapman, Jim, D-Texas (1)	225-3035	429
Chappell, Bill Jr., D-Fla. (4)	225-4035	2468
Cheney, Dick, R-Wyo. (AL)	225-2311	104
Clarke, James McClure, D-N.C. (11)	225-6401	217
Clay, William L., D-Mo. (1)	225-2406	2470
Clinger, William F. Jr., R-Pa. (23)	225-5121	1122
Coats, Dan, R-Ind. (4)	225-4436	1417
Coble, Howard, R-N.C. (6)	225-3065	430
Coelho, Tony, D-Calif. (15)	225-6131	403
Coleman, E. Thomas, R-Mo. (6)	225-7041	2344
Coleman, Ronald D., D-Texas (16)	225-4831	416
Collins, Cardiss, D-Ill. (7)	225-5006	2264
Combest, Larry, R-Texas (19)	225-4005	1529
Conte, Silvio O., R-Mass. (1)	225-5335	2300
Conyers, John Jr., D-Mich. (1)	225-5126	2313
Cooper, Jim, D-Tenn. (4)	225-6831	125
Coughlin, Lawrence, R-Pa. (13)	225-6111	2467
Courter, Jim, R-N.J. (12)	225-5801	2422
Coyne, William J., D-Pa. (14)	225-2301	424
Craig, Larry E., R-Idaho (1)	225-6611	1034
Crane, Philip M., R-Ill. (12)	225-3711	1035
Crockett, George W. Jr., D-Mich. (13)	225-2261	1531
Daniel, Dan, D-Va. (5)	225-4711	2308
Dannemeyer, William E., R-Calif. (39)	225-4111	1214
Darden, George "Buddy," D-Ga. (7)	225-2931	1330
Daub, Hal, R-Neb. (2)	225-4155	1019
Davis, Jack, R-Ill. (4)	225-3635	1234
Davis, Robert W., R-Mich. (11)	225-4735	2417
DeFazio, Peter A., D-Ore. (4)	225-6416	1729
de la Garza, E. "Kika," D-Texas (15)	225-2531	1401
DeLay, Thomas D., R-Texas (22)	225-5951	1039
Dellums, Ronald V., D-Calif. (8)	225-2661	2136
de Lugo, Ron, D-Virgin Islands	225-1790	2238
Derrick, Butler, D-S.C. (3)	225-5301	201
DeWine, Michael, R-Ohio (7)	225-4324	1705
Dickinson, William L., R-Ala. (2)	225-2901	2406

Name, Party, State	Phone	Room
Dicks, Norman D., D-Wash. (6)	225-5916	2429
Dingell, John D., D-Mich. (16)	225-4071	2221
DioGuardi, Joseph J., R-N.Y. (20)	225-6506	325
Dixon, Julian C., D-Calif. (28)	225-7084	2400
Donnelly, Brian J., D-Mass. (11)	225-3215	438
Dorgan, Byron L., D-N.D. (AL)	225-2611	238
Dornan, Bob, R-Calif. (38)	225-2965	301
Dowdy, Wayne, D-Miss. (4)	225-5865	240
Downey, Thomas J., D-N.Y. (2)	225-3335	2232
Dreier, David, R-Calif. (33)	225-2305	410
Duncan, John J., R-Tenn. (2)	225-5435	2206
Durbin, Richard J., D-Ill. (20)	225-5271	417
Dwyer, Bernard J., D-N.J. (6)	225-6301	404
Dymally, Mervyn M., D-Calif. (31)	225-5425	1717
Dyson, Roy, D-Md. (1)	225-5311	224
Early, Joseph D., D-Mass. (3)	225-6101	2349
Eckart, Dennis E., D-Ohio (11)	225-6331	1210
Edwards, Don, D-Calif. (10)	225-3072	2307
Edwards, Mickey, R-Okla. (5)	225-2132	2434
Emerson, Bill, R-Mo. (8)	225-4404	418
English, Glenn, D-Okla. (6)	225-5565	2235
Erdreich, Ben, D-Ala. (6)	225-4921	439
Espy, Mike, D-Miss. (2)	225-5876	216
Evans, Lane, D-Ill. (17)	225-5905	328
Fascell, Dante B., D-Fla. (19)	225-4506	2354
Fauntroy, Walter E., D-D.C.	225-8050	2135
Fawell, Harris W., R-Ill. (13)	225-3515	318
Fazio, Vic, D-Calif. (4)	225-5716	2433
Feighan, Edward F., D-Ohio (19)	225-5731	1124
Fields, Jack, R-Texas (8)	225-4901	413
Fish, Hamilton Jr., R-N.Y. (21)	225-5441	2269
Flake, Floyd H., D-N.Y. (6)	225-3461	1427
Flippo, Ronnie G., D-Ala. (5)	225-4801	2334
Florio, James J., D-N.J. (1)	225-6501	2162
Foglietta, Thomas M., D-Pa. (1)	225-4731	231
Foley, Thomas S., D-Wash. (5)	225-2006	1201
Ford, Harold E., D-Tenn. (9)	225-3265	2305
Ford, William D., D-Mich. (15)	225-6261	239
Frank, Barney, D-Mass. (4)	225-5931	1030
Frenzel, Bill, R-Minn. (3)	225-2871	1026
Frost, Martin, D-Texas (24)	225-3605	2459
Fuster, Jaime B., Pop. Dem.-Puerto Rico	225-2615	427
Gallegly, Elton, R-Calif. (21)	225-5811	1020
Gallo, Dean A., R-N.J. (11)	225-5034	1318
Garcia, Robert, D-N.Y. (18)	225-4361	2338
Gaydos, Joseph M., D-Pa. (20)	225-4631	2186
Gejdenson, Sam, D-Conn. (2)	225-2076	1410
Gekas, George W., R-Pa. (17)	225-4315	1519
Gephardt, Richard A., D-Mo. (3)	225-2671	1432
Gibbons, Sam, D-Fla. (7)	225-3376	2204
Gilman, Benjamin A., R-N.Y. (22)	225-3776	2160
Gingrich, Newt, R-Ga. (6)	225-4501	2438
Glickman, Dan, D-Kan. (4)	225-6216	1212
Gonzalez, Henry B., D-Texas (20)	225-3236	2413
Goodling, Bill, R-Pa. (19)	225-5836	2263
Gordon, Bart, D-Tenn. (6)	225-4231	1517
Gradison, Bill, R-Ohio (2)	225-3164	2311
Grandy, Fred, R-Iowa (6)	225-5476	1711
Grant, Bill, D-Fla. (2)	225-5235	1331
Gray, Kenneth J., D-Ill. (22)	225-5201	2109
Gray, William H. III, D-Pa. (2)	225-4001	204
Green, Bill, R-N.Y. (15)	225-2436	1110
Gregg, Judd, R-N.H. (2)	225-5206	308
Guarini, Frank J., D-N.J. (14)	225-2765	2458
Gunderson, Steve, R-Wis. (3)	225-5506	227
Hall, Ralph M., D-Texas (4)	225-6673	236
Hall, Tony P., D-Ohio (3)	225-6465	2448
Hamilton, Lee H., D-Ind. (9)	225-5315	2187
Hammerschmidt, John Paul, R-Ark. (3)	225-4301	2207
Hansen, James V., R-Utah (1)	225-0453	1113
Harris, Claude, D-Ala. (7)	225-2665	1009
Hastert, Dennis, R-Ill. (14)	225-2976	515
Hatcher, Charles, D-Ga. (2)	225-3631	405
Hawkins, Augustus F., D-Calif. (29)	225-2201	2371
Hayes, Charles A., D-Ill. (1)	225-4372	1028
Hayes, Jimmy, D-La. (7)	225-2031	503
Hefley, Joel, R-Colo. (5)	225-4422	508
Hefner, W. G. "Bill," D-N.C. (8)	225-3715	2161
Henry, Paul B., R-Mich. (5)	225-3831	215
Herger, Wally, R-Calif. (2)	225-3076	1630
Hertel, Dennis M., D-Mich. (14)	225-6276	218
Hiler, John, R-Ind. (3)	225-3915	407
Hochbrueckner, George J., D-N.Y. (1)	225-3826	1008
Holloway, Clyde C., R-La. (8)	225-4926	1207
Hopkins, Larry J., R-Ky. (6)	225-4706	2437
Horton, Frank, R-N.Y. (29)	225-4916	2229
Houghton, Amo, R-N.Y. (34)	225-3161	1217
Howard, James J., D-N.J. (3)	225-4671	2188
Hoyer, Steny H., D-Md. (5)	225-4131	1513
Hubbard, Carroll Jr., D-Ky. (1)	225-3115	2182
Huckaby, Jerry, D-La. (5)	225-2376	2421
Hughes, William J., D-N.J. (2)	225-6572	341
Hunter, Duncan, R-Calif. (45)	225-5672	133
Hutto, Earl, D-Fla. (1)	225-4136	2435
Hyde, Henry J., R-Ill. (6)	225-4561	2104
Inhofe, James M., R-Okla. (1)	225-2211	1017
Ireland, Andy, D-Fla. (10)	225-5015	2416
Jacobs, Andrew Jr., D-Ind. (10)	225-4011	1533
Jeffords, James M., R-Vt. (AL)	225-4115	2431
Jenkins, Ed, D-Ga. (9)	225-5211	203
Johnson, Nancy L., R-Conn. (6)	225-4476	119
Johnson, Tim, D-S.D. (AL)	225-2801	513
Jones, Ed, D-Tenn. (8)	225-4714	108
Jones, Walter B., D-N.C. (1)	225-3101	241
Jontz, Jim, D-Ind. (5)	225-5037	1005
Kanjorski, Paul E., D-Pa. (11)	225-6511	1518
Kaptur, Marcy, D-Ohio (9)	225-4146	1228
Kasich, John R., R-Ohio (12)	225-5355	1133
Kastenmeier, Robert W., D-Wis. (2)	225-2906	2328
Kemp, Jack F., R-N.Y. (31)	225-5265	2252
Kennedy, Joseph P. II, D-Mass. (8)	225-5111	1631
Kennelly, Barbara B., D-Conn. (1)	225-2265	1230
Kildee, Dale E., D-Mich. (7)	225-3611	2262
Kleczka, Gerald D., D-Wis. (4)	225-4572	226
Kolbe, Jim, R-Ariz. (5)	225-2542	1222
Kolter, Joe, D-Pa. (4)	225-2565	212
Konnyu, Ernest L., R-Calif. (12)	225-5411	511
Kostmayer, Peter H., D-Pa. (8)	225-4276	123
Kyl, Jon, R-Ariz. (4)	225-3361	313
LaFalce, John J., D-N.Y. (32)	225-3231	2367
Lagomarsino, Robert J., R-Calif. (19)	225-3601	2332
Lancaster, H. Martin, D-N.C. (3)	225-3415	1408
Lantos, Tom, D-Calif. (11)	225-3531	1707
Latta, Delbert L., R-Ohio (5)	225-6405	2309
Leach, Jim, R-Iowa (1)	225-6576	1514
Leath, Marvin, D-Texas (11)	225-6105	336
Lehman, Richard H., D-Calif. (18)	225-4540	1319
Lehman, William, D-Fla. (17)	225-4211	2347

Name, Party, State	Phone	Room
Leland, Mickey, D-Texas (18)	225-3816	2236
Lent, Norman F., R-N.Y. (4)	225-7896	2408
Levin, Sander M., D-Mich. (17)	225-4961	323
Levine, Mel, D-Calif. (27)	225-6451	132
Lewis, Jerry, R-Calif. (35)	225-5861	326
Lewis, John, D-Ga. (5)	225-3801	501
Lewis, Tom, R-Fla. (12)	225-5792	1216
Lightfoot, Jim, R-Iowa (5)	225-3806	1609
Lipinski, William O., D-Ill. (5)	225-5701	1032
Livingston, Bob, R-La. (1)	225-3015	2412
Lloyd, Marilyn, D-Tenn. (3)	225-3271	2266
Lott, Trent, R-Miss. (5)	225-5772	2185
Lowery, Bill, R-Calif. (41)	225-3201	225
Lowry, Mike, D-Wash. (7)	225-3106	2454
Lujan, Manuel Jr., R-N.M. (1)	225-6316	1323
Luken, Thomas A., D-Ohio (1)	225-2216	2368
Lukens, Donald E. "Buz," R-Ohio (8)	225-6205	117
Lungren, Dan, R-Calif. (42)	225-2415	2440
Mack, Connie, R-Fla. (13)	225-2536	228
MacKay, Buddy, D-Fla. (6)	225-5744	330
Madigan, Edward R., R-Ill. (15)	225-2371	2312
Manton, Thomas J., D-N.Y. (9)	225-3965	327
Markey, Edward J., D-Mass. (7)	225-2836	2133
Marlenee, Ron, R-Mont. (2)	225-1555	2465
Martin, David O'B., R-N.Y. (26)	225-4611	442
Martin, Lynn, R-Ill. (16)	225-5676	1208
Martinez, Matthew G., D-Calif. (30)	225-5464	109
Matsui, Robert T., D-Calif. (3)	225-7163	2419
Mavroules, Nicholas, D-Mass. (6)	225-8020	2432
Mazzoli, Romano L., D-Ky. (3)	225-5401	2246
McCandless, Al, R-Calif. (37)	225-5330	435
McCloskey, Frank, D-Ind. (8)	225-4636	127
McCollum, Bill, R-Fla. (5)	225-2176	1507
McCurdy, Dave, D-Okla. (4)	225-6165	409
McDade, Joseph M., R-Pa. (10)	225-3731	2370
McEwen, Bob, R-Ohio (6)	225-5705	329
McGrath, Raymond J., R-N.Y. (5)	225-5516	205
McHugh, Matthew F., D-N.Y. (28)	225-6335	2335
McMillan, J. Alex, R-N.C. (9)	225-1976	401
McMillen, Tom, D-Md. (4)	225-8090	1508
Meyers, Jan, R-Kan. (3)	225-2865	315
Mfume, Kweisi, D-Md. (7)	225-4741	1107
Mica, Daniel A., D-Fla. (14)	225-3001	2455
Michel, Robert H., R-Ill. (18)	225-6201	2112
Miller, Clarence E., R-Ohio (10)	225-5131	2208
Miller, George, D-Calif. (7)	225-2095	2228
Miller, John R., R-Wash. (1)	225-6311	1224
Mineta, Norman Y., D-Calif. (13)	225-2631	2350
Moakley, Joe, D-Mass. (9)	225-8273	221
Molinari, Guy V., R-N.Y. (14)	225-3371	208
Mollohan, Alan B., D-W.Va. (1)	225-4172	516
Montgomery, G.V. "Sonny," D-Miss. (3)	225-5031	2184
Moody, Jim, D-Wis. (5)	225-3571	1721
Moorhead, Carlos J., R-Calif. (22)	225-4176	2346
Morella, Constance A., R-Md. (8)	225-5341	1024
Morrison, Bruce A., D-Conn. (3)	225-3661	437
Morrison, Sid, R-Wash. (4)	225-5816	1434
Mrazek, Robert J., D-N.Y. (3)	225-5956	306
Murphy, Austin J., D-Pa. (22)	225-4665	2210
Murtha, John P., D-Pa. (12)	225-2065	2423
Myers, John T., R-Ind. (7)	225-5805	2372
Nagle, David R., D-Iowa (3)	225-3301	214
Natcher, William H., D-Ky. (2)	225-3501	2333
Neal, Stephen L., D-N.C. (5)	225-2071	2463
Nelson, Bill, D-Fla. (11)	225-3671	2404
Nichols, Bill, D-Ala. (3)	225-3261	2405
Nielson, Howard C., R-Utah (3)	225-7751	1229
Nowak, Henry J., D-N.Y. (33)	225-3306	2240
Oakar, Mary Rose, D-Ohio (20)	225-5871	2231
Oberstar, James L., D-Minn. (8)	225-6211	2351
Obey, David R., D-Wis. (7)	225-3365	2217
Olin, Jim, D-Va. (6)	225-5431	1238
Ortiz, Solomon P., D-Texas (27)	225-7742	1524
Owens, Major R., D-N.Y. (12)	225-6231	114
Owens, Wayne, D-Utah (2)	225-3011	1728
Oxley, Michael G., R-Ohio (4)	225-2676	1108
Packard, Ron, R-Calif. (43)	225-3906	316
Panetta, Leon E., D-Calif. (16)	225-2861	339
Parris, Stan, R-Va. (8)	225-4376	1526
Pashayan, Charles Jr., R-Calif. (17)	225-3341	129
Patterson, Liz, D-S.C. (4)	225-6030	1022
Pease, Don J., D-Ohio (13)	225-3401	1127
Pelosi, Nancy, D-Calif. (5)	225-4965	1632
Penny, Timothy J., D-Minn. (1)	225-2472	436
Pepper, Claude, D-Fla. (18)	225-3931	2239
Perkins, Carl C., D-Ky. (7)	225-4935	1004
Petri, Thomas E., R-Wis. (6)	225-2476	2443
Pickett, Owen B., D-Va. (2)	225-4215	1429
Pickle, J. J., D-Texas (10)	225-4865	242
Porter, John Edward, R-Ill. (10)	225-4835	1131
Price, David E., D-N.C. (4)	225-1784	1223
Price, Melvin, D-Ill. (21)	225-5661	2110
Pursell, Carl D., R-Mich. (2)	225-4401	1414
Quillen, James H., R-Tenn. (1)	225-6356	102
Rahall, Nick J. II, D-W.Va. (4)	225-3452	343
Rangel, Charles B., D-N.Y. (16)	225-4365	2330
Ravenel, Arthur Jr., R-S.C. (1)	225-3176	1730
Ray, Richard, D-Ga. (3)	225-5901	425
Regula, Ralph, R-Ohio (16)	225-3876	2209
Rhodes, John J. III, R-Ariz. (1)	225-2635	510
Richardson, Bill, D-N.M. (3)	225-6190	332
Ridge, Tom, R-Pa. (21)	225-5406	1714
Rinaldo, Matthew J., R-N.J. (7)	225-5361	2469
Ritter, Don, R-Pa. (15)	225-6411	2447
Roberts, Pat, R-Kan. (1)	225-2715	1314
Robinson, Tommy F., D-Ark. (2)	225-2506	1541
Rodino, Peter W. Jr., D-N.J. (10)	225-3436	2462
Roe, Robert A., D-N.J. (8)	225-5751	2243
Roemer, Buddy, D-La. (4)	225-2777	103
Rogers, Harold, R-Ky. (5)	225-4601	206
Rose, Charlie, D-N.C. (7)	225-2731	2230
Rostenkowski, Dan, D-Ill. (8)	225-4061	2111
Roth, Toby, R-Wis. (8)	225-5665	2352
Roukema, Marge, R-N.J. (5)	225-4465	303
Rowland, J. Roy, D-Ga. (8)	225-6531	423
Rowland, John G., R-Conn. (5)	225-3822	512
Roybal, Edward R., D-Calif. (25)	225-6235	2211
Russo, Marty, D-Ill. (3)	225-5736	2233
Sabo, Martin Olav, D-Minn. (5)	225-4755	2201
Saiki, Patricia F., R-Hawaii (1)	225-2726	1407
St Germain, Fernand J., D-R.I. (1)	225-4911	2108
Savage, Gus, D-Ill. (2)	225-0773	1121
Sawyer, Thomas C., D-Ohio (14)	225-5231	1338
Saxton, H. James, R-N.J. (13)	225-4765	324
Schaefer, Dan L., R-Colo. (6)	225-7882	1317
Scheuer, James H., D-N.Y. (8)	225-5471	2466
Schneider, Claudine, R-R.I. (2)	225-2735	1512
Schroeder, Patricia, D-Colo. (1)	225-4431	2410

Name, Party, State	Phone	Room
Schuette, Bill, R-Mich. (10)	225-3561	415
Schulze, Richard T., R-Pa. (5)	225-5761	2369
Schumer, Charles E., D-N.Y. (10)	225-6616	126
Sensenbrenner, F. James Jr., R-Wis. (9)	225-5101	2444
Sharp, Philip R., D-Ind. (2)	225-3021	2452
Shaw, E. Clay Jr., R-Fla. (15)	225-3026	440
Shumway, Norman D., R-Calif. (14)	225-2511	1203
Shuster, Bud, R-Pa. (9)	225-2431	2268
Sikorski, Gerry, D-Minn. (6)	225-2271	414
Sisisky, Norman, D-Va. (4)	225-6365	426
Skaggs, David E., D-Colo. (2)	225-2161	1723
Skeen, Joe, R-N.M. (2)	225-2365	1007
Skelton, Ike, D-Mo. (4)	225-2876	2453
Slattery, Jim, D-Kan. (2)	225-6601	1440
Slaughter, D. French Jr., R-Va. (7)	225-6561	319
Slaughter, Louise M., D-N.Y. (30)	225-3615	1313
Smith, Christopher H., R-N.J. (4)	225-3765	422
Smith, Denny, R-Ore. (5)	225-5711	1213
Smith, Lamar, R-Texas (21)	225-4236	509
Smith, Lawrence J., D-Fla. (16)	225-7931	113
Smith, Neal, D-Iowa (4)	225-4426	2373
Smith, Robert C., R-N.H. (1)	225-5456	115
Smith, Robert F., R-Ore. (2)	225-6730	118
Smith, Virginia, R-Neb. (3)	225-6435	2202
Snowe, Olympia J., R-Maine (2)	225-6306	2464
Solarz, Stephen J., D-N.Y. (13)	225-2361	1536
Solomon, Gerald B. H., R-N.Y. (24)	225-5614	2342
Spence, Floyd, R-S.C. (2)	225-2452	2113
Spratt, John M. Jr., D-S.C. (5)	225-5501	1118
Staggers, Harley O. Jr., D-W.Va. (2)	225-4331	1504
Stallings, Richard H., D-Idaho (2)	225-5531	1221
Stangeland, Arlan, R-Minn. (7)	225-2165	2245
Stark, Fortney H. "Pete," D-Calif. (9)	225-5065	1125
Stenholm, Charles W., D-Texas (17)	225-6605	1226
Stokes, Louis, D-Ohio (21)	225-7032	2365
Stratton, Samuel S., D-N.Y. (23)	225-5076	2205
Studds, Gerry E., D-Mass. (10)	225-3111	1501
Stump, Bob, R-Ariz. (3)	225-4576	211
Sundquist, Don, R-Tenn. (7)	225-2811	230
Sunia, Fofō I. F., D-American Samoa	225-8577	1206
Sweeney, Mac, R-Texas (14)	225-2831	1713
Swift, Al, D-Wash. (2)	225-2605	1502
Swindall, Pat, R-Ga. (4)	225-4272	331
Synar, Mike, D-Okla. (2)	225-2701	2441
Tallon, Robin, D-S.C. (6)	225-3315	432
Tauke, Tom, R-Iowa (2)	225-2911	2244
Tauzin, W. J. "Billy," D-La. (3)	225-4031	222
Taylor, Gene, R-Mo. (7)	225-6536	2134
Thomas, Robert Lindsay, D-Ga. (1)	225-5831	431
Thomas, William M., R-Calif. (20)	225-2915	2402
Torres, Esteban Edward, D-Calif. (34)	225-5256	1740
Torricelli, Robert G., D-N.J. (9)	225-5061	317
Towns, Edolphus, D-N.Y. (11)	225-5936	1726
Traficant, James A. Jr., D-Ohio (17)	225-5261	128
Traxler, Bob, D-Mich. (8)	225-2806	2366
Udall, Morris K., D-Ariz. (2)	225-4065	235
Upton, Fred, R-Mich (4)	225-3761	1607
Valentine, Tim, D-N.C. (2)	225-4531	1510
Vander Jagt, Guy, R-Mich. (9)	225-3511	2409
Vento, Bruce F., D-Minn. (4)	225-6631	2304
Visclosky, Peter J., D-Ind. (1)	225-2461	420
Volkmer, Harold L., D-Mo. (9)	225-2956	2411
Vucanovich, Barbara F., R-Nev. (2)	225-6155	312
Walgren, Doug, D-Pa. (18)	225-2135	2241
Walker, Robert S., R-Pa. (16)	225-2411	2445
Watkins, Wes, D-Okla. (3)	225-4565	2348
Waxman, Henry A., D-Calif. (24)	225-3976	2418
Weber, Vin, R-Minn. (2)	225-2331	106
Weiss, Ted, D-N.Y. (17)	225-5635	2442
Weldon, Curt, R-Pa. (7)	225-2011	1233
Wheat, Alan, D-Mo. (5)	225-4535	1204
Whittaker, Bob, R-Kan. (5)	225-3911	2436
Whitten, Jamie L., D-Miss. (1)	225-4306	2314
Williams, Pat, D-Mont. (1)	225-3211	2457
Wilson, Charles, D-Texas (2)	225-2401	2265
Wise, Bob, D-W.Va. (3)	225-2711	1421
Wolf, Frank R., R-Va. (10)	225-5136	130
Wolpe, Howard, D-Mich. (3)	225-5011	1535
Wortley, George C., R-N.Y. (27)	225-3701	229
Wright, Jim, D-Texas (12)	225-5071	1236
Wyden, Ron, D-Ore. (3)	225-4811	1406
Wylie, Chalmers P., R-Ohio (15)	225-2015	2310
Yates, Sidney R., D-Ill. (9)	225-2111	2234
Yatron, Gus, D-Pa. (6)	225-5546	2267
Young, C. W. Bill, R-Fla. (8)	225-5961	2407
Young, Don, R-Alaska (AL)	225-5765	2331

Pronunciation Guide

The following is a list of the correct pronunciations of often mispronounced names
of members of Congress.

SENATE

John B. Breaux, D-La. (BRO)
Alfonse M. D'Amato, R-N.Y. (dah MAH toe)
Thomas A. Daschle, D-S.D. (DASH el)
Dennis DeConcini, D-Ariz. (dee con SEE nee)
Pete V. Domenici, R-N.M. (da MEN ah chee)
Wyche Fowler Jr., D-Ga. (WHY-CH)
Daniel K. Inouye, D-Hawaii (in NO ay)

HOUSE

Les AuCoin, D-Ore. (oh COIN)
Anthony C. Beilenson, D-Calif. (BEE lin son)
Doug Bereuter, R-Neb. (BEE right er)
Michael Bilirakis, R-Fla. (bill a RACK us)
Sherwood Boehlert, R-N.Y. (BO lert)
David E. Bonior, D-Mich. (BON yer)
Rick Boucher, D-Va. (BOUGH cher)
Jack Buechner, R-Mo. (BEEK ner)
Tony Coelho, D-Calif. (KWELL oh)
Lawrence Coughlin, R-Pa. (COFF lin)
Joseph J. DioGuardi, R-N.Y. (dee oh GWAR dee)
Mervyn M. Dymally, D-Calif. (DIE mal ee)
Ben Erdreich, D-Ala. (ER dritch)
Dante B. Fascell, D-Fla. (fuh SELL)
Edward F. Feighan, D-Ohio (FEE an)
Thomas M. Foglietta, D-Pa. (fo lee ET ah)
Jaime B. Fuster, Pop. Dem.-Puerto Rico
  (HI may FOO ster)
Elton Gallegly, R-Calif. (GAL uh glee)
Joseph M. Gaydos, D-Pa. (GAY dis)

Sam Gejdenson, D-Conn. (GAY den son)
Frank J. Guarini, D-N.J. (gwar EE nee)
George J. Hochbrueckner, D-N.Y. (HOCK brewk ner)
Amo Houghton, R-N.Y. (HO tun)
John R. Kasich, R-Ohio (KAY sick)
Gerald D. Kleczka, D-Wis. (KLETCH ka)
Jim Kolbe, R-Ariz. (COLE bee)
Ernest L. Konnyu, R-Calif. (CON you)
Mel Levine, D-Calif. (la VINE)
Manuel Lujan Jr., R-N.M. (LOO han)
Ron Marlenee, R-Mont. (MAR la nay)
Bob McEwen, R-Ohio (mac YOU in)
Kweisi Mfume, D-Md. (kwy E say mm FU may)
Robert J. Mrazek, D-N.Y. (ma RAH zik)
Charles Pashayan Jr., R-Calif. (Pah SHAY an)
Thomas E. Petri, R-Wis. (PEE try)
Arthur Ravenel Jr., R-S.C. (RAV nel)
Ralph Regula, R-Ohio (REG you la)
Buddy Roemer, D-La. (RO mer)
Marge Roukema, R-N.J. (ROCK ah ma)
Patricia F. Saiki, R-Hawaii (CY kee)
Bill Schuette, R-Mich. (SHOO tee)
Richard T. Schulze, R-Pa. (SHOOLS)
Arlan Stangeland, R-Minn. (STANG land)
Fofō I. F. Sunia, D-American Samoa
  (soo NEE ah)
Tom Tauke, R-Iowa (TAW kee)
W. J. "Billy" Tauzin, D-La. (TOE zan)
Robert G. Torricelli, D-N.J. (tor ah SELL ee)
Guy Vander Jagt, R-Mich. (VAN der jack)
Barbara F. Vucanovich, R-Nev. (voo CAN oh vitch)
Gus Yatron, D-Pa. (YAT ron)

Map of Capitol Hill

(Dotted line indicates the city's quadrants, which are noted in the corners of the map)

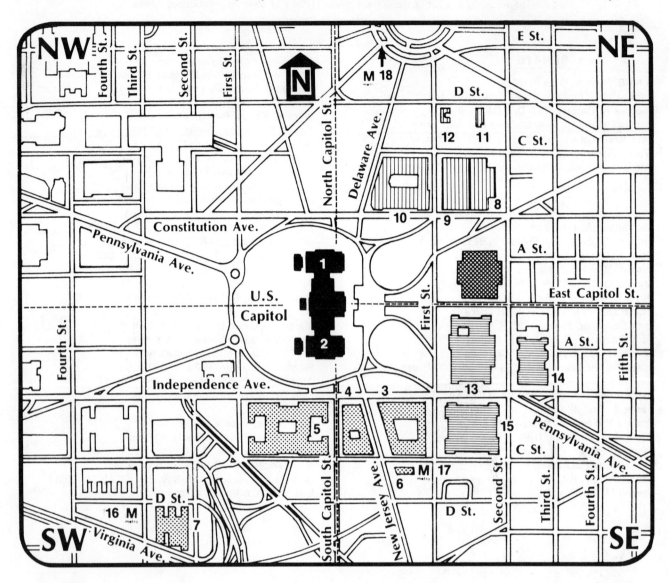

■ U.S. Capitol,
Washington, D.C. 20510, 20515*

    1 Senate Wing
    2 House Wing

▨ House Office Buildings
Washington, D.C. 20515

    3 Cannon
    4 Longworth
    5 Rayburn
    6 House Annex No. 1
    7 House Annex No. 2

▥ Senate Office Buildings,
Washington, D.C. 20510

    8 Hart
    9 Dirksen
    10 Russell
    11 Immigration Building
    12 Plaza Hotel (Capitol Police)

▨ Supreme Court
Washington, D.C. 20543

▤ Library of Congress,
Washington, D.C. 20540

    13 Jefferson
    14 Adams
    15 Madison

M Subway System
metro

    16 Federal Center SW Station
    17 Capitol South Station
    18 Union Station Station

* Mail sent to the U.S. Capitol should bear the ZIP code of the chamber to which it is addressed.
The House code is 20515; the Senate code is 20510.